The American Soul Rush

QUALITATIVE STUDIES IN RELIGION
General Editor: Janet Jacobs

The Qualitative Studies in Religion series was founded to make a place for careful, sustained, engaged reflection on the link between the kinds of qualitative methods being used and the resulting shape, tone, and substance of our empirical work on religion. We seek to showcase a wide range of qualitative methodologies including ethnography; analysis of religious texts, discourses, rituals, and daily practices; in-depth interviews and life histories; and narrative analyses. We present empirical studies from diverse disciplines that address a particular problem or argument in the study of religion. We welcome a variety of approaches, including those drawing on multiple qualitative methods or combining qualitative and quantitative methods. We believe that excellent empirical studies can best further a critical discussion of the link between methods, epistemology, and social scientific theory and thereby help to reconceptualize core problems and advance our understanding of religion and society.

Evangelical Christian Women: War Stories in the Gender Battles
Julie Ingersoll

Every Time I Feel the Spirit: Religious Experience and Ritual in an African American Church
Timothy J. Nelson

The Virgin of El Barrio: Marian Apparitions, Catholic Evangelizing, and Mexican American Activism
Kristy Nabhan-Warren

Words upon the Word: An Ethnography of Evangelical Group Bible Study
James S. Bielo

The American Soul Rush: Esalen and the Rise of Spiritual Privilege
Marion Goldman

The American Soul Rush

Esalen and the Rise of Spiritual Privilege

Marion Goldman

NEW YORK UNIVERSITY PRESS
New York and London

NEW YORK UNIVERSITY PRESS
New York and London
www.nyupress.org

© 2012 by New York University

References to Internet websites (URLs) were accurate at the time of writing.
Neither the author nor New York University Press is responsible for URLs
that may have expired or changed since the manuscript was prepared.

Library of Congress Cataloging-in-Publication Data

Goldman, Marion S.
The American soul rush : Esalen and the rise of spiritual privilege /
Marion Goldman.
p. cm. — (Qualitative studies in religion)
Includes bibliographical references (p.   ) and index.
ISBN 978-0-8147-3287-8 (cl)
ISBN 978-0-8147-3290-8 (ebook)
ISBN 978-0-8147-3338-7 (ebook)
1. Esalen Institute—History. 2. United States—Religion—1960–
3. Religion and sociology—United States—History—20th century.
4. Religion and sociology—United States—History—21st century.
I. Title.
BL2525.G65   2011 2012
204'.350979476—dc23   2011031463

New York University Press books are printed on acid-free paper,
and their binding materials are chosen for strength and durability.
We strive to use environmentally responsible suppliers and materials
to the greatest extent possible in publishing our books.

Manufactured in the United States of America
10 9 8 7 6 5 4 3 2 1

For my family

Contents

List of Illustrations   ix

Acknowledgments   xi

Introduction: Esalen, the Soul Rush, and Spiritual Privilege   1

1   Esalen's Wellspring: Foundational Doctrines   25

2   Esalen's Reach: A Brief History   48

3   Spiritual Privilege and Personal Transformation   72

4   Living Privilege: Four Esalen Men   92

5   Gender at Esalen   120

6. Esalen's Legacies   139

Conclusion: New Beginnings   161

Appendix 1: Experiential Exercises: When Words Fail   173

Appendix 2: The Walter Truett Anderson Collection   181

References   185

Index   197

About the Author   207

List of Illustrations

1   A View from Esalen   3

2   An Early Esalen Workshop   15

3   Charlotte Selver and the Bode Gymnastik   16

4   Michael Murphy and Richard Price   54

5   The Hot Springs and Massage Area   62

6   Buddha on the Esalen Grounds   69

7   Aldous Huxley   75

8   Babatunde's Friends with Aleksander Price   111

9   Fritz Perls   127

10 Joan Baez and David Price   142

11 The InnerLight Bookstore at the California Institute   151
    of Integral Studies

12 Signs Everywhere at CIIS Support Spiritual Privilege   151

13 Pet Massage   179

Acknowledgments

It is impossible to fully acknowledge everyone who helped me learn and write about spiritual privilege. Individuals associated with Esalen contributed to my understanding throughout this project, and my colleagues and friends sustained me in every way.

Research funding from the Donald C. Davidson Library at the University of California at Santa Barbara and from the Summer Research Program at the University of Oregon made it possible for me to spend time in Big Sur, Palo Alto, San Francisco, and Santa Barbara. When I could not be there, Donna Lowe provided essential research assistance in California.

In the University of Oregon Department of Sociology, Jennifer Maarefi-Memar transcribed tapes and Shelley Carlson continually offered good ideas and unflagging encouragement. From start to finish, Christopher Blum solved the mysteries of Macs and made me smile.

Linda Long's knowledge about manuscript collections on alternative religions made a world of difference to this project. Gordon Melton helped me discover key themes and guided me to critical sources in the American Religion and Humanistic Psychology Collections in Special Collections at the Davidson Library at UCSB. David Gartrell, Manuscripts Curator for the Humanistic Psychology Archives and the American Religion Collection at UCSB, went out of his way to find hidden treasures that I would have missed otherwise.

Nicole Sheikh portrayed the California Institute of Integral Studies through a few extraordinary images. And Lori Lewis's pictures of Esalen reflect her deep connection to the Institute, as well as her talent and insight.

Amy Jo Woodruff was not only a copy editor but also a source of good cheer and great ideas. Jennifer Hammer, my editor at NYU Press, was right about almost everything! She understood the idea of spiritual privilege long before I fully articulated it, and she called my attention to the differences between things like a wooly llama and a wise lama.

Despina Papazoglou Gimbel shepherded the manuscript through publication with understanding and generosity. Thanks also to the graduate students and faculty in the Religion Working Group at the University of Washington, especially to Steve Pfaff and Jim Wellman. And thanks to former Ducks, Vikas Gumbhir, and Wonderwoman Kate Ristau.

A number of other sociologists, historians, and social psychologists critiqued parts of this book and advised me to make it a jargon-free zone. Mary Romero's great sense of humor quelled my occasional desires to drown my laptop. Steve Warner's personal understanding of Esalen made him a great resource. Glenn W. Shuck added to my knowledge about the Institute and the historical roots of new religions in America. Rod Stark listened to my ideas, provided guidance, and never once asked: "Why aren't you done yet?"

Janet Jacobs was a perceptive, generous academic editor with broad knowledge about American religion. Her empathic suggestions nourished this research from the beginning. Mary Jo Neitz offered careful critiques that reflected her extraordinary grasp of ethnography and social theory. She was never too busy to talk about Esalen, despite her many commitments.

Members of Esalen's founding generation, including Sukie Miller and the late George Leonard, presented their personal perspectives about the Institute's history and how it changed people's lives. Brita Ostrom, Peggy Horan, and Ellen Watson taught me about the lasting impact of Esalen massage, dance, and bodywork.

The four men who are profiled in chapter 4 made this book possible. I am so grateful for their willingness to help me understand Esalen's contributions and contradictions. Thank you, Michael Murphy, Gordon Wheeler, David Price, and Albert Wong!

And thanks to my terrific family. My sons, Michael and Henry, left for college well before I finished writing, but they were always with me. My husband, Paul, endured years of living with someone who seemed to be studying for perpetual prelim exams and he rarely complained! There is no way to fully acknowledge or described his fantastic support over the years.

Introduction

Esalen, the Soul Rush, and Spiritual Privilege

Millions of contemporary Americans search for personal and spiritual fulfillment through meditation, yoga, and other practices that engage simultaneously their bodies, minds, emotions, and spirits. Today, these activities are commonplace, unremarkable. Yet, before the early 1960s, they were rare options for most people outside the upper class or small groups of educated spiritual seekers. The contemporary soul rush for self-transformation and individualized spirituality began on the central California coast at Esalen Institute. Its founding generation made myriad options for spiritual experiences and personal growth available to ordinary Americans who were disenchanted with mainstream religions.

Esalen encouraged widespread enthusiasm for an enormous range of spiritual paths that offered possibilities for individuals to live joyfully and discover fresh truths about themselves and the cosmos. The Institute democratized spiritual privilege by popularizing options that had once been available to relatively few Americans and made the religious marketplace more diverse and open. Esalen played a critical role in introducing and promoting esoteric spirituality so that it flowed into mainstream culture. Millions of contemporary Americans identify themselves as spiritual, not religious, because the Institute paved the way for them to explore spirituality without affiliating with established denominations (Roof 1999).

The Institute's founding generation started lasting organizations and social networks that continue to facilitate the development and spread of alternative spirituality and humanistic psychology in the twenty-first century. This book is about spiritual privilege at Esalen, its sweeping impact on American religion, and some of the people who have organized their lives around the Institute's imperatives to achieve their full human potentials.

Innovative approaches to spiritual growth and personal transformation did not spring up suddenly like magic mushrooms in the cultural forests of the 1960s. Instead, they were cultivated on Esalen's 120 acres in Big Sur, California, and introduced to middle-class Americans through media and by word of mouth. People who learned about Esalen at a distance, individuals who passed through briefly, and even those who lived on the property viewed the Institute in different ways because of their own priorities and experiences. They might characterize it as an esoteric think tank, a sacred retreat, a spa, a center for humanistic group psychology, a place for psychedelic trips, a massage school, or an intentional community (Back 1972; Bart 1971). The Institute continues to be all of those things and more.

Esalen's many identities and its eclectic workshops and programs reflected its founders' inclusive approach to spirituality. The first generation modified, combined, and popularized varied spiritual doctrines and practices for self-actualization that had been developed elsewhere.

Little of Esalen's basic spiritual doctrine was new, but the Institute presented original combinations and applications of arcane philosophies and religious perspectives. Esalen's founders, Michael Murphy and Dick Price, sought out cultural innovators and opinion leaders who enthused about new kinds of psychotherapy, physical practices such as massage, and fresh approaches to spirituality. The Institute's menu of varied workshops and small-group experiences quickly became known at university campuses, churches and synagogues, therapists' offices, health spas, and other emerging growth centers.

Esalen's Major Contributions

Esalen is interesting in itself, but its unique historical significance rests on the ways that it made the prerogatives of spiritual privilege widely known, meaningful, and accessible throughout the United States. *Spiritual privilege is an individual's ability to devote time and resources to select, combine, and revise his or her personal religious beliefs and practices over the course of a lifetime.*

The growth and rapid spread of spiritual privilege reflects two long-term influences that are embedded in America's social structure: widespread economic comfort and numerous religious alternatives. Religious pluralism and the vibrant post–World War II economy allowed many middle-class Americans to pursue alternative religions and personal growth psychology. As established liberal faiths waned, there was a mounting demand for new, more meaningful religion, and Esalen rose up to meet it (Brooks 2001).

The Institute transformed spiritual privilege into a human right that could be available to any American dedicated to maximizing her or his potential in

Esalen overlooks the Pacific, and this is one of many vistas. © Lori A. Lewis

mind, body, spirit, and emotion. Different kinds of people have access to different degrees of spiritual privilege, but Esalen's founders emphasized the fact that *all* could benefit in some ways from the doctrines and practices available there.

Individual spiritual privilege rests on a dynamic mixture of four attributes—affinities for supernatural meanings, experiences, and explanations; religious and cultural knowledge; participation in supportive social networks; and economic resources. The Institute's leaders assumed, somewhat erroneously, that almost every American possessed enough of all four elements to select and benefit from the varied practices that emerged in Big Sur.

Esalen promoted the growth and spread of spiritual privilege because its foundational doctrine held that everyone had sparks of divinity that could be connected to a benevolent, distant cosmic force. This essential belief linked apparently disparate approaches to spirituality and defined them as complementary to one another.

The faith that everyone could cultivate a personal divine spark seemed to make the rewards of spiritual privilege somewhat independent of social class, gender, or ethnicity. Because of the divinity within each person, everyone was entitled to become spiritually and emotionally fulfilled in some ways. In reality, however, spiritual privilege has not influenced working-class or poor Americans to the same degree as it has touched members of the middle and upper classes, who hungered for more meaningful lives because they did not worry much about their material survival (Brooks 2001).

The Institute's other three important, but somewhat less significant, contributions linked alternative spirituality to other avenues for personal and social change: the human potential movement in humanistic psychology, progressive political groups that connected social and personal issues, and the men's movement. Each of these three additional innovations connected the Institute to late-twentieth-century social movements and made the rewards of spiritual privilege more accessible and attractive to ever wider audiences.

When they defined the pursuit of full human potential as a new national goal, the Institute's founding generation combined alternative approaches to spirituality and the psychology of personal growth (Anderson 1983:115–116). Esalen's varied workshops about personal fulfillment encouraged participants to redefine arcane spiritual experiences like trances and past life connections as reasonable routes to greater happiness and self-actualization (Litwak 1967). The fusion of spiritual expansion and humanistic psychology made Big Sur a crucible for the emerging human potential movement that refuted traditional dichotomies of mental health and illness and focused on helping individuals create more vital and meaningful lives (Wood 2008).

In the mid-1960s, Esalen became the flagship venue for new approaches dedicated to self-transformation through more honest and emotionally intimate interpersonal relationships. The human potential movement brought innovative individual and group psychotherapies together, with a focus on enhancing present and future relationships, rather than on mending old psychic wounds. Human potential psychology attracted thousands of Americans because it fundamentally redefined psychotherapy as a context for personal growth rather than recovery from mental illness, and it provided group experiences that were not as time or money consuming as traditional therapies.

The Institute's founding generation also affirmed humanistic psychology's ideal of self-actualization, an enhanced capacity to lead a meaningful and socially useful life. Esalen connected humanistic psychology and alternative spirituality and normalized spiritual practices like vision quests and yoga as pathways to better mental and physical health.

Public service and support for liberal social reform constituted another area of interest at Esalen, and the Institute's political stance bridged spiritual privilege and worldly activities beyond Big Sur. The founding generation believed that true self-actualization had to include the pursuit of social justice and peace. Actualized humans were compassionate toward those who were less fortunate and were obligated to help others lead better lives by means of both personal assistance and collective activities (Leonard and Murphy 1995:41). Esalen became even more visible when its founding generation developed informal ties to social movements for peace, racial equality, psychiatric patients' rights, and educational reform in an historical period when progressive politics were part of public discourse (Rakstis 1971).

Because of its early links to the human potential movement and campaigns for social justice, the Institute became a crucible for the loosely configured men's movements that unfolded during the 1980s and 1990s. People at Esalen advocated spirituality, emotional disclosure, and men's connection to other men as pathways to a new, better kind of masculinity. And, in the late 1980s and early 1990s, the Institute once again linked spirituality to affluent Americans' personal and political concerns.

The full exercise of spiritual privilege requires a large supply of religious options that can be joined to established faiths, practiced individually, or cobbled together in different combinations. The Institute's most important contribution to the soul rush involved opening up a vast range of complementary religious choices to middle-class Americans and alerting them to their right to maximize their spiritual and emotional satisfaction. Esalen popularized established practices and brought together alternative spirituality, psychotherapy, and social reform in order to democratize spiritual exploration and personal growth.

Early Achievements and Lasting Effects

By 1971, Esalen was the model for more than ninety similar centers, known informally as "Little Esalens." They were large and small, rural and urban, with the majority located in California or in or near major cities like Chicago, Boston, and New York (Rakstis 1971:311). Most of these "Little Esalens," like Kairos, in San Diego, or the Center for the Whole Person, in Philadelphia, survived for less than a decade. However, two of the early retreats that were modeled on Esalen reorganized in the late 1970s and early 1980s and still thrive: Hollyhock, in British Columbia, and Oasis, in New York State

During the 1960s, Americans who had never before heard of spiritual retreats or growth centers considered visiting Big Sur after detailed descriptions of Esalen appeared in mainstream media. Whether favorable or critical, pieces in *Holiday*, *Life*, *Newsweek*, *Ramparts*, *Look*, and *Time* contributed to the Institute's reputation as a catalyst for individual psychological trans-formation, improved intimate relationships, and new social arrangements (Carter 1997:34). Will Schutz, the Institute's best-known encounter group leader, reached deep into mainstream culture when he appeared for three consecutive nights on the popular *The Tonight Show starring Johnny Carson* soon after the release of his best-seller *Joy* (1967), a book that went through nine printings by Grove Press in the late 1960s.

Seventeen books by authors directly associated with the Institute came out between 1969 and 1975 as part of the short-lived Esalen/Viking series (Kripal 2007a:527–528). College and university faculty assigned Esalen books to their classes and encouraged students to sample practices that involved alternative spirituality and humanistic psychology.

The Institute's call to explore and expand human potential resonated with the historical moment when undergraduates at elite universities believed that they could transform themselves and build a better society (Keniston 1968). People talked about Esalen at schools like Stanford, Harvard, and Brandeis and also at high-status public universities like the University of California at Berkeley and the University of California at Los Angeles (Anderson 1983:59; Gagarin 1969).

I first heard about Esalen in a Berkeley social psychology class in the late 1960s. The professor enthused about the Institute's fresh approaches to self-actualization, and he required one hundred undergraduates to participate in weekly sensitivity-training groups that were milder versions of Esalen's encounters where participants focused on their immediate interpersonal reactions to one another, scrutinized the actions of other members and examined the process of the group as a whole (Back 1972).

Many of the theories and practices developed in Big Sur challenged both conventional middle-class social relationships and established American institutions. Esalen's critiques resonated with campus activists, although the Institute's leading theorists and practitioners wanted to revitalize religion, education, and psychology, rather than destroy society so that it could be completely rebuilt (Leonard 1988). Because Esalen promoted personal and social reform rather than revolution, radicals disparaged the Institute at the same time that conservatives attacked it as a hotbed of radical experimen-tation (Bart 1971; Kopkind 1973). Liberal reformers in education and psy-chology, however, appreciated the Institute's goals and incorporated some of Esalen's approaches to maximizing human potential when they organized the American Association for Humanistic Psychology and the Confluent

Education Program at the University of California at Santa Barbara (Anderson 1983:183–184, 190–191).

In the late 1960s, Esalen's cofounder Michael Murphy and some members of his inner circle reached out to clergy through the National Council of Churches' Division of Education and Ministry. The NCC sent ministers to Big Sur for workshops on Gestalt therapy, which focused on emotions and events in the immediate therapeutic setting; sensory awareness, which involved exercises in breathing, touching, and balancing; and interpersonal encounter groups (Kripal 2007a:187; Murphy 2005:309). Popular contemporary marriage and peace encounters that are now associated with mainline Protestant denominations have their roots in some of Esalen's early programs for religious leaders.

Before the NCC sponsored its members' visits to Big Sur, the Institute's informal relationships with established liberal faiths had already generated surprise and humor among Esalen residents and regular visitors. As early as 1964, participants in workshops and seminars, no matter how sexually experimental or otherwise outrageous, laughingly called themselves seminarians, because of Esalen's reputation as a cloistered space dedicated to transforming spiritual and emotional life. People at Esalen still use the term "seminarian," although the Institute's formal ties to liberal faiths and the NCC faded away long ago.

Along with liberal clergy, another influential group, teachers from grades kindergarten through twelve, came to Big Sur in the 1960s because of a Ford Foundation grant to bring creativity, emotions, and physical expression into classrooms (Kripal 2007a :213).

Esalen's collaboration with clergy and educators illustrates how it directly influenced two major American Institutions: schools and churches. Participants took what they had learned in Big Sur back to their colleagues and to the people that they served, who then passed it on. Like many other religious innovations, Esalen's first traveled through informal interpersonal networks of influential advocates (Stark 1996a:19–23).

The Institute affected American psychology because therapists and social workers interested in psychology, psychedelics, and spirituality visited Big Sur individually and in small groups (Anderson 1983:184–188). Between 1962 and 1967, almost seven hundred psychotherapists sampled new clinical techniques in Esalen workshops and seminars (Litwak 1967:120). When they returned home, many urged their clients and colleagues to try out some of the Institute's approaches to personal and spiritual growth. Their spreading the Big Sur blend of spirituality and humanistic psychology was another example of the person-to-person transmission of the Institute's innovations.

By the mid-1970s, external competition and internal disorganization had diminished the Institute's cultural visibility and its direct influence on educators, clergy, and psychotherapists. People in Big Sur turned inward to examine their own lives and reconsider their mission. Esalen's message of individual divinity and human potential, however, continued to influence many Americans.

In the late 1990s, the Institute developed new programs for professionals, a growing presence on the Web, and connections to alternative institutions and emerging social networks that linked spirituality, personal growth, and social change in a global perspective. Esalen also began to define itself once more as a center for Gestalt and humanistic psychology, reemphasizing themes from its first two decades. Although it no longer has a dramatic public presence, the Institute continues to be important to the thriving shadow culture where individuals pursue alternative spirituality and emotional expansion.

Religious Diversity and Spiritual Privilege

Esalen's inclusive approach encouraged people to mix and match diverse sacred traditions from all parts of the world (Kripal 2007a). The Institute transformed American spirituality by introducing varied sacred practices that people could pursue without blending them together. Spiritual seekers responded to this religious inclusivity by becoming *bricoleurs*, people who create their own mosaics of separate meanings and practices (Levi-Strauss 1962; McGuire 2008:195–199). They join together various spiritual doctrines and practices, but they remain separate and distinct from one another. For example, a regular Esalen visitor's recent practice includes Zen meditation, tai chi, African drumming, and Gregorian chanting. *Bricolage* is always unfinished, so it generates virtually limitless demand for new spiritual innovations. People can sample different choices throughout their lifetimes and revise their spiritual paths from adolescence through very old age. If their material wealth and health diminish over time, they can use the spiritual privilege that they have already accumulated to make their lives less difficult.

Throughout the history of the United States and in the present, advantaged individuals have dominated alternative religious movements that posit an amorphous, divine cosmic spark linked to individuals' personal sparks of divinity. These faiths have ranged from nineteenth-century Transcendentalism to contemporary Scientology (Goldman 1999; Menand 2001). Economic security or its viable possibility has enabled people to seek new practices that affirm their personal divinity. Spiritually privileged Americans resemble the chanters of the morning Buddhist Sutras who began their worship listening to these words: "O sons and daughters of good family. You people who can afford to be listening to me, who aren't starving to death" (Downing 2001:108).

Esalen's founders enjoyed extraordinary spiritual privilege that went far beyond simple material security, and their uncommon resources made it possible for them to create the Institute. Each man possessed a personal affinity for supernatural meanings and explanations, financial flexibility because of his family's wealth, religious and cultural knowledge, and access to established social networks of elite seekers. Other people at Esalen have benefited from various aspects of their own privilege to different degrees.

Americans are well off compared to citizens of most other nations, and the fact that the majority of people in the United States have few problems meeting their basic needs for food and shelter has opened them to the potential rewards of spiritual privilege. Millions of Americans who are economically marginal or poor, however, also search for self-actualization because spiritual privilege is embedded in many areas of contemporary social life. Esalen's early influence on public education, psychotherapy, and liberal religions has not disappeared, and it reaches far beyond the middle class.

Other affluent nations, such as Denmark and Sweden, without strong mainstream or alternative religions, have not experienced the dramatic growth and spread of spiritual privilege, although there are pockets of interest in alternative religions and personal growth in Scandinavia (Zuckerman 2008). Opportunities to enact and accumulate spiritual privilege multiply in societies like that in the United States, where most people believe in some supernatural power, there are many religious options, and switching religious loyalties or affiliations is acceptable to most (Finke and Iannaccone 1993).

Religious pluralism is central to the growth of widespread spiritual privilege, and constitutional safeguards for the free exercise of religion facilitated the Institute's cultural impact (Stark 1996a). The open, competitive religious marketplace made Esalen and its diffusion of alternative spirituality possible.

An important historical coincidence also enriched the Institute's early offerings and further diversified the spiritual choices that it provided. More religious possibilities became readily available to Americans when the 1965 Immigration Act opened the United States to hundreds of Asian teachers and their devotees (Melton 1993). Through its seminars, workshops, and public celebrations of specific individuals and approaches, Esalen introduced global spiritualities to ordinary Americans (Roof 1993, 1999). The extensive demand for new kinds of spirituality increased as the supply of religious choices grew (Finke and Iannaccone 1993; Roof 1999; Warner 1993).

The American Soul Rush

During the 1960s, in the midst of widespread affluence and the growth of social movements for equality, baby boomers and some members of the Depression generation cut loose from liberal Protestant denominations and Roman Catholic congregations and embarked on searches for personalized religious meaning (Bellah, Masden, Sullivan, Swidler, and Tipton 1985; Roof 1999). Some found homes in charismatic evangelical congregations and participated in the extraordinary growth of those faiths (Wellman 2008). Others engaged in searches for religious meanings and personal authenticity among alternative doctrines and practices, which they tried out sequentially or pieced together by means of *bricolage* (Roof 1993).

Over the past six decades, millions of spiritually privileged Americans have sampled alternative practices that stand apart from mainstream religious denominations (Bader and BSIR Study Group 2006). Some have limited their interest to listening to Oprah Winfrey exhort women and men to get in touch with their inner sparks of godliness. For many years on the *Oprah Show*, she described her "aha" moments and offered interviews with popular alternative spirituality icons like Eckhart Tolle and Elizabeth Gilbert.

Oprah's endorsements made best sellers of Tolle's *A New Earth* (2005), Gilbert's *Eat, Pray, Love* (2006), and other books that explain how people can transform their lives. Barnes and Noble, for example, stocks more than eight thousand titles in the broad category of alternative spirituality, where the works of a number of Esalen-connected authors can be found.

Others move beyond relatively passive consumption through television and books and spend time and money actively seeking spiritual well-being and personal growth. Americans cultivate their connection to the supernatural when they try out products like healing oils, meditation classes, or structured groups focusing on a single spiritual practice like Hatha Yoga.

Some journey to contemporary holistic retreat centers that incorporate many of Esalen's contributions. They may spend weekends meditating at Kripalu in Stockbridge, Massachusetts, or exercising and doing yoga at the Canyon Ranch Spa in Tucson, Arizona, or Lenox, Massachusetts (Newman 2008). More adventurous pilgrims tour sacred sites in New Mexico or embark on treks in the Himalayas.

Individualized approaches to spirituality and expanded emotional and physical powers are the lifeblood of the rising numbers of twenty-first century retreats and self-enhancement programs that promise "Lifestyles of Health and Sustainability" (LOHAS) (Newman 2008). While Esalen is no longer the vortex of alternative spirituality and personal growth in the United States, it continues to occupy a special place in the field because of its pioneering role in offering workshops and seminars that promise to integrate mind, body, spirit, and psyche. Moreover, Esalen is the only retreat that still sustains an explicit commitment to research, theory, and writing that explore the intersections of spirituality, psychology, physical experience, and social change.

Americans who pursue alternative spirituality and personal growth in varied contexts tend to share a basic assumption about the hidden sparks of divinity that are located deep within all humans and link them to one another and to the cosmos (Stark 2001:9–30). Close to a quarter of adults in the United States view God as a distant, benign cosmic force, similar to the supernatural power in Esalen's doctrine. Many of these people, whether they are affiliated or separated from established religions, eagerly participate in the market for alternative spiritualities (Bader and BSIR Study Group 2006:27).

Baby boomers, Americans born between 1946 and 1964, are those who are most likely to sample alternative spiritual practices, although most of them casually retain their formal affiliations to established religious faiths as well (Roof 1999). These aging seekers are relatively affluent, and people living in households with yearly incomes over $100,000 are more than twice as likely to be theologically liberal as people in households earning less than $35,000 annually. Moreover, only 6.1 percent of Americans with high school or less education define themselves as religiously liberal, whereas more than a fifth of the individuals who have attended college or graduate or professional schools do so (Bader and BSIR Study Group 2006:16–17).

Secretary of State Hillary Clinton exemplifies the affluent, religiously liberal cohort of boomers who embrace inclusive spirituality that combines mainstream and alternative religious perspectives. Clinton grew up attending a suburban Methodist church, and, during her eight years in the White House, she went to Sunday services at various liberal Protestant churches in the D.C. area. However, she was looking for something more, so she invited Jean Houston, a psychologist, psychic, and seminar leader long associated with Esalen, to visit her in the White House.

Houston writes about personal growth and spirituality in books like *Mystical Dogs: Animals as Guides to Our Inner Life* (2004). At the White House, she led the First Lady in imaginary conversations with Mahatma Gandhi and Eleanor Roosevelt. These exchanges helped Clinton cultivate her own spiritual sparks and pursue emotional growth in the same directions that Esalen first charted in the 1960s (Brown 1997:9).

Like Clinton, Esalen's two founders grew up in liberal congregations, and they believed in a distant, benevolent God that was compatible with the Gods of other faiths. Dick, whose father had renounced Judaism to become an Episcopalian, was confirmed in his suburban Chicago church. Michael served as an altar boy in Salinas, and he once considered becoming an Episcopal priest (Anderson 1983:24–25). By the time they reached college, however, both young men sought spiritual rewards beyond what was offered by established denominations. They desired mystical moments, not just old doctrine and dry ritual.

Esalen's conceptions of divine personal essence are vague, and that makes them attractive to a range of people. The phrase "My life will be better" can cover many different meanings. Even individuals with strong ties to the Institute describe their own divine sparks in very different ways. An attorney in her late forties who is a regular Esalen visitor summed up her sacred experience and personal beliefs in a casual conversation. She sighed: "I sat and watched the ocean at Esalen and suddenly I knew, I felt that I was God!" The basic assumption that God is part of all beings and that we are gods is Esalen's cornerstone.

Esalen's Invitation

The Institute's creation narrative describes how it took shape during a long summer road trip from Big Sur south past the Mexican border and back again in 1961. Two handsome young Californians, Michael and Dick, had vague plans to create a retreat center on Michael's family property in Big Sur, when they headed their battered red Jeep pickup down Highway 1 toward Tecate, in Baja California, drinking beer and debating arcane philosophy (Anderson 1983:9–10; Price 1982). By the end of their trip, they had mulled over advice from elders in Southern California and Baja and had made specific plans to open a modest center for intellectual debate about spirituality and psychology. Over the next few years, Esalen grew into something quite different and became a mecca for prosperous seekers of meaningful religious experiences, emotional catharsis, and sexual adventures.

During the Institute's dynamic first decade, streams of Hollywood insiders visited and increased Esalen's public visibility. Two major celebrities,

Dyan Cannon and her husband, the iconic actor Cary Grant, often drove up Highway 1 to Big Sur. Cannon joined Natalie Wood, another Esalen habitué, to star in *Bob & Carol & Ted & Alice*, a hit 1969 movie that both satirized and publicized the Institute. Another major star, Jane Fonda, learned about Zen and human potential psychology during her brief romance with Dick at Esalen.

Most celebrities who helped make Esalen fashionable during its first decade soon discovered other paths to self-actualization and largely forgot about the Institute. Big Sur is no longer au courant with Hollywood's A-list. Monty Python's John Cleese and the Clinton administration's labor secretary Robert Reich are the most famous popular figures publicly connected with Esalen in recent years.

Men who were part of the founding circle still refer to their old associations with movie stars from the 1960s in order to underscore the Institute's cultural significance and also to recall the distant times when they were all young, beautiful, and wild. Esalen's brief impact on Hollywood augmented its early cultural status and amplified its initial public visibility and broad appeal during an era when relatively few Americans seemed to be interested in alternative spirituality (Verter 2003:165; Wuthnow 1976).

When it began, in 1962, Esalen provided weekend accommodations so that guests could attend talks and workshops about Asian religions and human creativity. However, a growing stream of twenty- and thirty-something visitors who had heard about the Institute by word of mouth and in local media sought sudden insights and active participation, and, in response to this demand, Esalen expanded to embrace activities that addressed every aspect of human potential: spirit, emotion, mind, and body. Esalen's many paths to self-discovery and personal transformation quickly became more intense and included marathon encounter groups where people displayed extreme emotions and sometimes attacked one another physically, as well as nude massage, group sex, and psychedelic trips.

Twenty-first-century media still rehash some of the controversies from the 1960s and describe the Institute's most embarrassing moments. In December 2007, an influential international magazine, *The Economist*, portrayed Esalen as the place where all of the strange and wonderful lifestyle innovations associated with California in the 1960s "bubbled up" (*The Economist* 2007). Another recent article in a different British periodical characterized the contemporary Institute less sympathetically, describing it as a place where people hugged each other relentlessly and justified material indulgences like new Porsches as balm for their past emotional wounds (Marsh 2008:45).

Today, new guests, often aging boomers, join returning seminarians in workshops about massage, health, yoga, and personal relationships. Almost ten thousand people stay at the Institute yearly, although only about fifteen hundred of them are under thirty-five years old (Watanabe 2004). Despite attempts to reach out to new constituencies, almost everyone at Esalen is white and well over forty, reflecting the composition of its first generation. Nevertheless, even with the limitations of age and ethnicity, the Institute attracts enough visitors and committed seekers in their twenties and early thirties to spread its doctrine and practices to younger generations and different ethnic groups, who enjoy their own versions of spiritual privilege.

The sacred pathways and possibilities for personal growth that unfolded in Big Sur engaged men and women in different ways. Privileged men developed and spread Esalen's unique approaches to essence spirituality, and they continue to elaborate its doctrine and quietly control the Institute through its Center for Theory and Research.

The CTR was formally named and differentiated from the rest of Esalen in 1998, but Michael and his inner circle have lived out, written about, and publicized Esalen's doctrines of expanding human potential since the Institute was founded (Kripal 2007a:439). Michael drew other men into his orbit who supported his intellectual and spiritual priorities, and they joined him in reaching out to the general public. Dick never fully participated in Michael's circle, but he shared the unspoken assumptions about the innate differences between men and women that led to persistent, almost accidental inequality between the sexes at Esalen.

Others at Esalen

Men associated with the inner circle that became the CTR represented the Institute's public face in the high-profile networks for personal and spiritual growth that developed in the 1960s and continue in the twenty-first century. They defined Esalen's central spiritual agenda and embodied spiritual privilege at the Institute, in spite of the handful of women who participated in their circle over the decades. While women at Esalen and in the society as a whole have far more economic and cultural resources than they did during the early 1960s, the initial gender differentiation that marked Esalen remains a fact of life in Big Sur.

Two other major overlapping groups of people that stand apart from the CTR have also built their lives at the Institute: bodyworkers and operations

This is an early workshop on the lawn near the Esalen Lodge. (Charlotte Selver Collection in the Humanistic Psychology Archives at the University of California at Santa Barbara Davidson Library)

staff. Women have collaborated with men at Esalen to create practices that bring together care of the body and care for the soul in massage, tai chi, and dance (Johnson 1994). Since an informal group first came together around the hot springs in the late 1960s, women have been central to the bodyworkers' network. Both women and men created and later copyrighted Esalen Massage, the Institute's signature bodywork practice.

Their unique approach to massage reflects their own activities in Big Sur and also guidance from an earlier generation of well-known women who taught and practiced at Esalen for a time (Rolf 1978; Roth 1998; Selver 1979). Charlotte Selver (1979), who emigrated from Germany in the late 1930s and taught sensory awareness at the New School for Social Research in New York City, communicated the European Gymnastik movement's vision of the body as a site for spirituality, emotional expression, and healing (Johnson 1994:16–17, 176–188).

Massage, bodywork, holistic health, and ecstatic dance unfolded at the Institute long before the bodyworkers assumed an official group identity as the Esalen Massage and Bodywork Association in the late 1990s. The name EMBA emphasized the primacy of massage in the group's varied practices.

Charlotte Selver participated in the European Gymnastics Movement in the late 1920s and 1930s. She taught physical culture classes that emphasized acceptance, appreciation, and spirituality associated with the human body. (Charlotte Selver Collection in the Humanistic Psychology Archives at the University of California at Santa Barbara Davidson Library)

Research about these bodyworkers would prioritize questions about women and men's interdependence and the relationships between healing and spirituality, rather than the issue of spiritual privilege, which is our focus in this book.

The third major subgroup whose lives revolve around the Institute are the Big Sur residents and long-term work-study students who take care of daily operations in Esalen's gardens, kitchens, and guest quarters. A closer look at them would foreground questions about intentional community and the survival of 1960s countercultures.

Each of the three interdependent groups can illuminate different aspects of Esalen and alternative spirituality in America. It is the group that became the CTR, however, that founded the Institute and remains at its doctrinal center. Their activities at the Institute and beyond Big Sur reveal the full impact of spiritual privilege and Esalen's enduring influence on American spirituality.

Slouching Toward Esalen

The research for this book began when Michael first talked with me at length over lunch at a casual bistro in San Rafael, across the Golden Gate Bridge from San Francisco. He displayed his sense of humor and his legendary charm as he talked about the Institute and its foundational spiritual doctrine (Schwartz 1995; Tompkins 1976). When Michael described Esalen's emergence during the tumultuous 1960s, he effortlessly quoted William Butler Yeats, "And what rough beast, its hour come at last, slouches toward Bethlehem to be born?" He mentioned Yeats's poem "Second Coming" and also noted Joan Didion's chronicles of desire and despair in California during the 1960s, *Slouching Toward Bethlehem* ([1968] 1990). Slouching became an apt metaphor for this project, as I wove between collecting data and making sense of all of the information that I collected.

Thousands of pages of interview transcripts, archival materials, legal records, published sources, field notes, and ephemera helped me slouch toward the emerging framework of spiritual privilege. Multiple qualitative research methods were essential to uncover the Institute's many layers and its extensive influence on contemporary spirituality. Each cycle of questions brought new information and sociological surprises that generated further questions (Becker 1998). This process—analytic induction—involves moving back and forth between specific information and general themes (Becker 1998:146–214). My primary focus slowly shifted to people close to the contemporary CTR, because Michael and his comrades had shaped Esalen and defined it to a wide audience.

Michael and I met for three hours during lunch and later at his home office in winter of 1999. He provided the names of Esalen insiders, whom I interviewed over the next six months and he also recommended dozens of readings, generously loading my arms with books, manuscripts, notes, and lists. For the next four months, I followed Michael's suggestions for interviewing and reading, also talking on the phone with him six times and adding names and references to the earlier lists. These sources supported his views about Esalen's contemporary influence and the CTR's importance.

People on Michael's lists led me to more respondents and other written resources. Some of his friends provided names of dissidents who had left Esalen or were vocal inside critics of its leadership and current directions. They also suggested that I contact people born after the baby boom ended in

1964, which Michael did not. This is snowball sampling, where one respondent identifies others, who then in turn suggest yet other people; the ball of information grows larger and larger (Chambliss and Schutt 2010:124–125).

During this second stage of interviews, I talked with another twenty people for one to two hours each. After these relatively short interviews, extensive documentary research, and preliminary fieldwork, I contacted people from the three major groups within Esalen: the CTR, the EMBA, and the operations staff. Twenty-three people, sixteen men and seven women who had lived or worked at the Institute for three years or more, participated in long, unstructured interviews for at least two hours. They also provided additional information in short follow-up conversations. Although few specific questions were common to all of these interviews, I asked each respondent: "Can you name three or four people who somehow symbolize Esalen to you?" All of them talked about Michael, but at least two different people from each of the three subgroups also mentioned three younger men who were at Esalen during the late 1990s: Gordon Wheeler, David Price, and Albert Wong.

These four men personify Esalen's doctrines of essence spirituality and self-actualization. Their lives illuminate the intersection of spiritual privilege and religious affinities in ways that more general descriptions cannot (McGuire 2008; Orsi 2005). They also reveal how Esalen's different generations have developed and reworked the founding circle's priorities and perspectives about spirituality through their collective histories and their different mixtures of individual spiritual privilege. The men not only talked with me during a number of long interviews but also discussed themselves and their ideas in books and other publications. Anonymity is not an issue because each one is easily identified by his relatively well-known life history.

Documentary Sources

Published documents, unpublished manuscripts, and other materials provided additional information. The Humanistic Psychology Archives at the University of California at Santa Barbara's Davidson Library contains more than two hundred collections that include personal papers, institutional records, correspondence, photographs, audiotapes, videotapes, and printed materials such as Esalen catalogues. Thousands of unpublished manuscripts and published materials chart the Institute's extraordinary first decade and also record the diffusion of its doctrines and practices.

Private letters and diaries in different collections were particularly useful for understanding daily life at Esalen and learning about social networks in alternative spirituality and humanistic psychology. Documents that were personal and relatively private enriched and sometimes contradicted my interviews, published materials, and formal organizational records in ways that often affect historical research (Bloch 1953).

For example, an internationally acclaimed family therapist briefly directed Esalen's first residential fellows' program in 1966. Less than two months after the program began, she suddenly decamped without notifying anyone. She later explained openly that she had never really wanted to assume leadership at Esalen (Anderson 1983:125–127.) Her personal papers, however, revealed her hope to establish a competitive personal growth center, and the manuscript collection contained copies of obsequious letters to Esalen donors like the toy manufacturing heiress Barbara Marx Hubbard. These private documents illuminated not only the therapist's goals but also the more general issue of outreach and competition for funding (Satir 1916–1993).

The single most important Esalen collection in the Humanistic Psychology Archives includes forty-eight audiocassettes of interviews, now digitally reformatted, that Walter Truett Anderson recorded for his 1983 book, *The Upstart Spring*. Appendix 2 lists them (Anderson Collection 1976–1986). Anderson talked with people who had built Esalen and remained affiliated with the Institute over many decades and also with individuals who left Big Sur quickly because of personal or ideological differences.

The tapes also provided useful unintentional information. For example, cofounder Dick Price died in a 1985 accident, but he came alive to me through his quirky inflections and humorous asides in the interviews. Even background noises, like a waitress whispering to Michael in the Esalen dining room, revealed nuanced interactions that were missing from written accounts.

On the Anderson tapes, people told stories that had changed years later and mentioned events that they failed to recall when they talked with me. There were also interviews with others who were no longer alive, whose personal narratives and interpretations had been erased from Esalen's in-house histories (Kripal 2007a).

The Anderson collection also contains clues about legal documents like David Gold's 1970 wrongful-death lawsuit, which implicated the Institute in his wife's suicide (Anderson 1983:138). Michael settled with Gold out of court, and the depositions and documents from the case are no longer available. However, the Gold lawsuit led me to county records in Salinas and to useful documents such as Esalen's articles of incorporation as a nonprofit in 1963, various property assessments and maps, Murphy Family Trust records, and Dick's will. The legal documents provide explicit details of the ways that Michael and Dick's economic privilege made Esalen viable.

The documentary materials were particularly useful because many respondents were wary and sometimes hostile about discussing sensitive issues like financial arrangements, suicides at Esalen, or conflicts within the Institute. As we talked, people who lived and worked at Esalen often tried to find out where I stood in relation to their friends and to people that they perceived as their opponents. These kinds of questions about loyalties are common to field research, and problems surface because sociologists inevitably walk a fine line between participating and standing aside, usually traveling between both paths (Neitz 2002).

In most public situations at Esalen, I observed and participated without emphasizing or even mentioning my role as a researcher. I ate in the community dining room, soaked in the hot springs, and painted in the Art Barn alongside other visitors. I sweated and danced at informal morning sessions open to everyone at the Institute, welcoming the day with other participants. After class, however, I introduced myself to the stylish session leader, who had been at the Institute for almost twenty years, and we arranged an interview.

No matter how or where I introduced my research goals, once I had been around for a day or so, people at the Institute seemed to overlook my role as a sociologist at work. In the midst of a dining-room crunch, staff asked me to set out food. Another time, I helped clean kitchen counters. A young man whom I had already interviewed at length joined me at lunch in order to charm my attractive roommate. A member of the EMBA crew offered to arrange a date for me when we sat together at the small bar near the dining room.

Like most people who were there, I was passing through Esalen, and almost everyone forgot that I kept a private journal and took extensive field notes. During most long personal conversations or informal interviews, I mentioned my project briefly, but then I was quiet.

Once people provide invitations into to their social spaces, they tend to see the sociologist as a person, not a professional. Passing as a "civilian" is surprisingly easy (Becker 1998; Didion [1968] 1990). In public settings, my primary concerns were my own experience and general interactions. However, the roles of participant and observer became muddled in two contexts: a CTR-sponsored conference in the spring of 2003 and two psychodrama workshops in Southern California. During both situations, I silently slipped from being a full participant to a critical observer, as issues of spiritual privilege came to the foreground.

Other Approaches to Esalen

This is the first book to explore Esalen and its enduring influence that has not been written by an Institute insider. Individuals closely associated with Esalen and the CTR have written primarily as advocates, rather than as distanced observers. They rarely looked to sources outside Big Sur or examined the ways that Esalen contributed to the growth and spread of spiritual privilege.

In the 1970s, a number of well-known public intellectuals contributed to seminars and workshops and later used their academic credentials to validate the Institute (Cox 1977; Glock and Bellah 1976; Maslow 1971; Watts 1973). They believed that Americans were careening into a spiritual chasm of amoral individualism, and they hoped that Esalen's spiritual innovations would generate a fresh consciousness and widespread dedication to collective well-being. They ignored issues such as some workshop leaders' systematic misuse of power or their pervasive sexism, and they were unaware of the ways that their own spiritual privilege shaped their apparently unbiased perceptions.

Recently, Jeffery Kripal, a university professor and an active CTR member, described the Institute as a harbinger of a better, more humane society with a conviction reminiscent of intellectuals' endorsements in the 1960s and 1970s. He characterized the Institute as a crucial middle ground between arid atheism and unreasonable fundamentalism. Kripal's book (2007a) praised its many contributions to philosophy and religion, linking Esalen to various spiritual and philosophical traditions. And he specifically targeted an audience of other academics in *The Chronicle of Higher Education* (2007b), when he praised the Institute's foundational doctrine of personal divinity linked to benevolent higher powers.

Kripal's focus on Esalen's contributions to philosophy and American religion bewildered reviewers and readers who had steeped in the hot springs, sunned on Esalen's lawns, and casually dropped into a few workshops over the years (Johnson 2007). They had simply visited Big Sur to enjoy the seductive setting, meet interesting people, and possibly take away some insights about themselves. However, the amused critics who dissected Kripal's work resembled him and the earlier scholars and advocates, because they never looked beyond Big Sur to examine the importance of Esalen's central contributions to the religious marketplace.

Spiritual Experience

The myriad sacred practices and innovative approaches to psychology that Esalen has offered over the years incorporate direct spiritual experience. Feelings of transcendence can unfold in praying, meditating, doing yoga, exploring Gestalt psychology, or participating in other activities at the Institute. In the course of their practice, individuals often feel that they connect to something supernatural beyond the mundane world (McGuire 2008:12–15). They believe that a sacred presence touches them.

It is difficult to comprehend the multidimensional spiritual experiences available at Esalen through words alone (McGuire 2008). Readers can sample an activity related to each chapter in Appendix 1 in order to explore some of the Institute's direct visceral appeal and the immediate rewards of spiritual privilege. These possibilities may add value to the intellectual understanding of Esalen, although their impact is diminished without the many scents and sounds that make simple activities special in Big Sur. The exercises work best in small, informal groups, but most can be done alone or in classroom settings.

Transcendent moments are among the many rewards that Esalen has provided to spiritual seekers. The Institute successfully promoted doctrines and practices that make it possible for people to diversify their allegiances and diminish their commitment to a spiritual path or one place, even the Institute (Iannaccone 1995).

Esalen's many possibilities for enhancing personal and spiritual fulfillment have drawn seekers to Big Sur for six decades. However, diversification also created competition within the market niche that the Institute briefly dominated in the 1960s and early 1970s. The groundbreaking Institute is now an established American institution. Spiritual privilege, the means and desires to reshape personal connections to higher powers, is a resource that has become integral to many Americans' lives. Shortly after cofounding the Institute, in the early 1960s, Michael asked a dear friend to help him liberate America's soul: "George," he said, "let's fire a shot heard 'round the world" (Leonard 1988:167). And so they did.

Plan of the Book

The first chapter of The *American Soul Rush* considers the Institute's central spiritual doctrines. Michael's sojourn at the Sri Aurobindo Ashram in India inspired him to found the Institute with Dick Price and to popularize concepts of everyone's essential divinity/godliness and individuals' ability to maximize their full potential in spirit, psyche, body, and mind.

Chapter 2 describes the Institute's creation narrative and charts Esalen's history through the twenty-first century. In the 1960s and 1970s, many people believed that "Esalen is another world. Probably the most beautiful place, the highest pace, the freest place I'll ever [live]" (Heider 1996:85).

After a period of stagnation from the late 1970s through the early 1990s, the Institute recovered. Its contemporary leaders redefined their mission by emphasizing Esalen's longstanding commitments to personal growth, spiritual exploration, and global social reform and also considering subjects that were mostly off Esalen's radar screen in the 1960s: family life and aging.

Chapter 3 explores the four central dimensions of spiritual privilege: religious affinities, cultural and religious capital, social networks, and economic resources. Esalen diffused spiritual privilege and helped change America's religious marketplace, while it also transformed individual lives.

Chapter 4 describes how four men who have been profoundly influenced by the Institute enact spiritual privilege in different ways. Their personal histories also illuminate the ways that different cohorts interpret and spread Esalen's contributions to spirituality, personal growth psychology, social action, and definitions of masculinity. Gender advantage, the material and interpersonal resources that amplify men's power in American society, augments their spiritual privilege, allowing them to step outside the mainstream in order to reinvent themselves.

Chapter 5 examines how two widely known narratives about Esalen's early years cemented men's centrality at the Institute. Men's narratives and their initial priorities created a space to explore new definitions of masculinity. Over the years, Esalen has remained a place where men can construct and interpret their manhood.

Chapter 6 documents some of the ways that the Institute has made a lasting impact on the wider culture through educational institutions, professional organizations, and media, including books, magazines, and websites dedicated to personal and spiritual growth. Its doctrines and practices of personal divinity and limitless human potential are now embedded in American society and associated with goods and services that are available to most citizens. Sometimes, the Institute's influence is almost invisible, as in the case of the huge best-seller *Tuesdays with Morrie* (Albom 1997).

The final chapter examines the broad impact of spiritual privilege on twenty-first-century Americans. Even in the midst of deep recession, spiritual privilege does not disappear. If anything, it continues to spread, as people seek ways of improving their lives during a painful economic downturn. Critics view alternative spirituality and the optimism that grounds it as futile modes of self-deception (Ehrenrich 2009). Many more people, however, find comfort in the doctrines and practices that first came together at Esalen. The Institute continues to provide a range of spiritual paths and a unifying doctrine to encourage ever wider transmission of spiritual privilege and ever greater participation in the soul rush.

Esalen's Wellspring:
Foundational Doctrines

In the early 1960s, when the philosopher-poet Allen Ginsberg lolled in the hot springs with a group of visiting Episcopal clergy and their wives, he personified Esalen's bedrock doctrine of spiritual inclusivity. Ginsberg was one of many well-known American intellectuals who became an informal ambassador for the Institute during its first decade. He was a luminary in the Beat literary movement and a champion of Americanized Zen Buddhism. In response to his companions' questions about his religious practice, he described a personal credo that captured Esalen's broad spiritual orientation. Ginsberg asserted that he was a Buddhist Jew with attachments to Krishna, Shiva, Allah, Coyote, and the Sacred Heart, and he summed up his own and the Institute's approach: "I figure one sacrament's as good as the next one, if it works!" (Kramer [1969] 1997:23).

Ginsberg never explicitly described Esalen's acceptance of almost every religion that located sparks of divinity within humans and embraced a distant, benevolent supernatural force. Nor did he discuss the Institute's trademark mixture of spirituality, psychology, and physical experience. He didn't need to. The context of his remark—a steaming tub filled with mainstream liberal clergy, their spouses, and a hirsute gay beatnik—embodied Esalen's implicit commitment to bring together disparate kinds of people with enough spiritual privilege to visit Big Sur.

The men and most women sitting in the water were opinion leaders who could augment their prior cultural and religious knowledge by visiting Esalen and spreading the word about the Institute to their networks of friends and acquaintances. In addition, their temporary intimate contact with other seekers so different from themselves expanded their social networks farther and enabled them to carry out new projects (Granovetter 1973). The clergymen's interactions with Ginsberg illustrate how visitors to

Big Sur could easily develop short- and, occasionally, long-term relationships with other spiritually privileged seekers whom they might never meet anywhere else.

Friendships that formed among seminarians often resembled the intense, immediate connections that begin in freshman dormitories or summer camps. Most are temporary, but some survive for decades, adding to participants' social capital, by means of new social networks that complement their old ties. The earnest exchanges at Esalen resembled late night conversations in college dorms, where people engage in serious personal and spiritual exploration, while maintaining a sense of fun and enjoying themselves.

Esalen's commitment to spiritual variety and personal inquiry reflected the guiding assumption that almost every lasting religious tradition could open pathways to divine sparks found in humans, nature, and the cosmos. According to this perspective, the universal spiritual truths shared by all great religions and philosophies are what truly matter (Schwartz 1995:78–80; Spiegelberg 1948). The greatest religion is one that synthesizes diverse approaches to spirituality and draws them together in an ever-changing mixture. These dynamic combinations, however, cannot incorporate hierarchically organized faiths that prohibit continued spiritual seekership and enforce rigid conformity to particular beliefs and practices.

Religions that emphasize inclusivity rest on the assumption that faiths that posit only *one* true god will divide and damage humanity. In contrast, spiritual approaches that define god as a benign supernatural force, not necessarily a recognizable being, embrace spiritual diversity, encourage people to seek personal authenticity by combining varied faiths, and exhort them to work together to advance humankind. The Institute's foundational doctrine of inclusivity, the "religion of no religion," is one of a number of different spiritual traditions that rest on doctrines about individuals' divine essences, their invisible connections to one another, and their hidden links to the cosmos (Kripal 2007a:8–11).

Esalen's commitment to inclusivity reflected Michael's lifelong devotion to the teachings of the Indian guru Sri Aurobindo, who consistently advocated spiritual diversity. Over many decades at Esalen, Michael has changed Aurobindo's arcane Indian philosophy into an Americanized approach to personal growth and spiritual fulfillment. Michael frequently mentions Aurobindo as a profound influence on him and on the Institute, but he does not always articulate the vital connection between his personal history and Esalen's foundational doctrine.

Michael's Passage to India

Michael was born in 1930, and he came of age in the late 1950s, when many young men benefited from relatively easy access to higher education and an expanding labor market. Those advantages allowed some of them to travel and explore different ways of life, with confidence that they could return to good jobs, professional occupational tracks, or graduate education.

He lived in Salinas, California, for all of his first eighteen years, until he traveled north to attend his father's nearby alma mater, Stanford. Throughout his adolescence, Michael hid his intellectual curiosity beneath a façade of enthusiastic conformity, as did many other men of his generation. In his first term in college, Michael pledged Phi Gamma Delta, a prestigious jock fraternity also known as FIJI, where he endured the routine humiliations of pledge week, bonded with his brothers, and caroused with coeds (Anderson 1983:26). And, like many other Stanford underclassmen in the late 1940s, Michael quietly became an atheist, well before he formally left the Episcopal Church to seek meaning elsewhere (Kripal 2007a:56–57).

In the early 1950s, a number of great American universities like Stanford hired respected European intellectuals who had immigrated to the United States in the wake of Hitler's rise to power. Like many other expatriate academics, Professor Frederic Spiegelberg, the man who became Michael's lifelong inspiration, recoiled from the blind obedience that had sustained the Nazi state. In his work at Stanford, he emphasized the importance of intellectual independence and personal growth, and Spiegelberg's perspectives on freedom, tolerance, and self-actualization influenced Michael's commitments to spiritual diversity and democracy at Esalen.

Spiegelberg's popular Stanford class on comparative religion was a turning point in Michael's life because it dealt with general issues about spiritual inclusiveness and introduced him to Sri Aurobindo's philosophy. Although he was a temporary collegiate atheist, Michael had grown up religious and he had a life-long interest in finding spiritual answers to his quest for personal meaning (Schwartz 1995:79–80). His continuing fascination with religious explanations opened him to Spiegelberg's stirring lectures and his evocations of Hinduism's Atman—the highest self—and of Brahmin—the essence of all existence.

After attending his first comparative religion class, in the spring of his sophomore year, Michael enrolled in Spiegelberg's fall-semester Indian philosophy class to learn more about integral yoga and Sri Aurobindo, his professor's spiritual ideal. Michael began to feel that Aurobindo's *Future Evolu-*

tion of Men (Ghose 1963) answered his yearnings to build his own life on a sacred foundation. He meditated for hours, and he moved out of the frat house during his junior year. Around that time, Michael privately vowed to dedicate himself to Aurobindo's vision: "I was sitting by a statue on the Stanford campus meditating, and suddenly the vows just rose up within me" (Schwartz 1995:82–83).

Despite his father's vehement objections, Michael dropped out of Stanford that spring in order to purify his spiritual focus. He spent much of his time reading, meditating, and attending small seminars at Spiegelberg's recent project, The Academy of Asian Studies in San Francisco.

The following year, 1952, Michael took independent reading classes on comparative religion in order to graduate from Stanford on schedule, with a bachelor's degree in psychology. He went into the army that summer and spent two years in Puerto Rico interviewing men suspected of draft evasion by deliberately flunking their psychological examinations. Michael returned to Stanford as a graduate student in philosophy, but his department's emphasis on analytical thinking and Western orientations disappointed him. Michael described graduate school as "the most neurotic time of my life." It was a period when he was totally "off my dharma [righteous path]" (Anderson 1983:29–30; Murphy 1981). He was afraid that he had epilepsy, terrified of getting haircuts that might damage his brain, and obsessed with his uncertain future. He procrastinated about visiting the Aurobindo Ashram but, with Spiegelberg's encouragement, planned a trip to India. His troubling psychological symptoms disappeared soon after he embarked on his pilgrimage.

Michael was in the vanguard of spiritual tourism that grew dramatically in the 1960s (Brown 1998; FitzGerald 1986). Before reaching India, he embarked on an abbreviated two-month grand tour and traveled alone to Rome, Paris, and Rheims. He also played golf on the links at St. Andrews, in Scotland, and visited Egypt. When he finally reached the Aurobindo Ashram, in Pondicherry, Michael unpacked and stayed for sixteen months in order to meditate, read, and live out Sri Aurobindo's integration of mind, body, and spirit.

Hundreds of other spiritually privileged visitors from Western Europe and the Americas joined Indians at Aurobindo's ashram in Pondicherry. Ashram residents played baseball, did calisthenics, and worked in the gardens, and they also attended lectures, meditation groups, and yoga classes. Like Michael, they were attracted to Aurobindo's synthesis of Eastern and Western philosophies and practices and his vision of building a close community of seekers. Although his integral philosophy described human beings in a transitional phase, Aurobindo believed that their personal growth in mind, body, and spirit would eventually stimulate the evolution of all humanity into a more socially and spiritually advanced species.

Aurobindo's father had sent him to England for an elite British education, a common practice among privileged Indian families at the end of the nineteenth century. He returned home as a young man, but, during his years in the West, he absorbed the widespread Western belief in human progress, in contrast to the doctrine of most Asian religions, which posit endless cycles of suffering and rebirth (Stark 2005:8–12). His faith that benign supernatural influences would enable humans to create better lives on Earth and strive to perfect themselves resembled Judeo-Christian convictions about God's wishes for people to act on the full scope of His intentions (Stark 2005:11–12).

Aurobindo's doctrines about spiritual advancement and evolutionary growth meshed with Michael's and other privileged Western devotees' early religious socialization about social progress. Westerners were attracted to his philosophy in part because it converged with liberal Protestant doctrine and therefore enabled them to add to their spiritual capital without relinquishing their previous assumptions.

When he arrived in Pondicherry, Michael discovered that Aurobindo's companion, seventy-eight-year old Mirra Alfassa/Sweet Mother, had taken charge of the ashram and Aurobindo's spiritual movement after the leader's death, almost two years earlier. She had changed the ashram and made it into a rather sophisticated sanctuary that visitors from the West appreciated. Renunciation and denial of physical comforts were not part of her plan for devotees. Sweet Mother had already started a number of new construction projects, and, when he arrived, Michael gasped at the gleaming new athletic complex for calisthenics and its venues for swimming, tennis, and other sports. Aurobindo's philosophy linked spiritual growth to many different sports, and his successor interpreted this doctrine as a mandate for her ambitious construction projects (Brown 1998:158–159; Schwartz 1995:82–83.).

The ashram offered individualized programs to fifteen hundred devotees, just as Esalen would offer personalized programs to smaller numbers of visitors a decade later. There were also group activities such as lectures, audiences with the Sweet Mother, and meals. Sex, alcohol, tobacco, and political activity were strictly forbidden to visitors or residents within the ashram or its guesthouses in Pondicherry, and Michael could easily live without them during his extended visit, even though he was an enthusiastic social drinker back home (Tompkins 1976:34).

While he was in India, Michael began to envision a future religious life for himself that included enjoyment and engagement with many secular pleasures. (Tompkins 1976:33–34). He also deepened his devotion to Aurobindo's teachings, although he had a number of criticisms of the Mother. He found some ashram prohibitions unnecessary, and he was deeply troubled by what appeared to be an emerging cult around the Mother and Aurobindo.

Following Spiegelberg's lead and the general antiauthoritarian ethos of postwar academia, Michael absolutely rejected devotees' blind worship of Aurobindo and their unquestioning obedience to Sweet Mother's interpretations. When people prostrated themselves before the marble plinth on top of Aurobindo's tomb, he cringed. Later, at Esalen, Michael remembered both Spiegelberg's positive lessons and the ashram's negative ones. He and Dick consistently struggled against charismatic Esalen workshop leaders who wanted seminarians to accept their teachings on blind faith (Anderson 1983:172, 262–263).

A spate of suicide attempts in Pondicherry had also bothered Michael. He was concerned that there was not enough theoretical or practical consideration of psychological health and emotional growth at the ashram (Tompkins 1976:34–35). Michael later supported Dick's suggestions for workshops that focused on psychological growth and interpersonal relationships.

Dick's sustained interest in emotional healing and his opposition to mainstream psychiatry reflected a very different set of personal experiences from Michael's. After several psychotic episodes, he had endured involuntary commitment in psychiatric institutions and a horrifying course of electroshock therapy (Anderson 1983:39–42). However, while he and Michael had very different priorities for the Institute, Michael supported Dick and believed that his interest in varied approaches to therapy and personal expansion addressed essential aspects of individual development that Sweet Mother had disregarded.

After spending almost a year and a half in India, Michael returned to his old room in Palo Alto in order to meditate, study, and think more explicitly about possibilities for some type of spiritual retreat in California. He worked as a bellhop and gardener to support himself, while he outlined his novel *Golf in the Kingdom* (Anderson 1983:32; Murphy 1972). In the summer of 1960, Michael moved to Asia House, the integral yoga residence in San Francisco that Frederic Spiegelberg's fellow Aurobindo devotee Harridas Chaudhuri had organized for their advanced students.

When Michael relocated from Palo Alto to San Francisco to explore Asian spirituality in more depth, people from East West House and various other small spiritual study groups in the Bay Area deferred to him because of his stay in Pondicherry. Moreover, they enthusiastically supported his vague plans to start some kind of retreat and meditation center. It was a very different welcome from his parents' stunned reaction to his detour from the conventional road to success.

After his return from India and regular contact with other privileged spiritual seekers like Dick, Michael privately defined himself as an all-American yogi—a smiling preppy who could translate and spread the doctrines and practices of integral transformation to a wide Western audience. In a few years, Esalen would become the launching pad that allowed him to bring Aurobindo's vision of spiritual growth to ordinary Americans. Michael hoped to build a retreat center where visitors could transform their lives and then return to the outside world with greater commitments to personal and spiritual growth.

Americanizing Aurobindo: Spirit, Mind, Body, and Psyche

Aurobindo believed that full spirituality necessarily engaged body and mind, as well as sacred practices like meditation or prayer. Dick and Michael added the psychological dimension to the mix, because they considered feelings and intuitions to be equally important to spiritual growth. They believed that sustained focus on all four areas could open doors to a greater understanding of the meaning of life and improve human abilities, as well. Esalen's eclectic approaches to personal and spiritual expansion reflected Michael and Dick's adaptation of Aurobindo's system of integral yoga, with the addition of an emotional focus that meshed with the emerging field of humanistic psychology.

The Indian philosopher's esoteric wisdom lies just beneath the surface of all of Esalen's eclectic workshops, seminars, and conferences. The Institute's foundational doctrines and practices are grounded in Aurobindo's integral yoga, and they offer possibilities to acquire secret knowledge in a world where human action and natural phenomena may intentionally correspond to one another (Albanese 1977; Hannegraff 1998). In order to fully comprehend this correspondence, seekers must access their personal mystical understandings and sacred experiences like brief feelings of bliss; read and study texts; and develop regular spiritual practices such as meditation.

The emphasis on the divine sparks in both humans and the cosmos places spiritual affinities and personal rituals within a broad religious system. Magic and religion are one and the same at the Institute —even minor coincidences or small pieces of luck, like finding a long-lost ring, take on spiritual meaning when someone believes in a hidden divine essence within and also beyond individuals.

Everyone who works at or regularly visits the Institute implicitly supports its most important doctrines about divine sparks and integral personal and spiritual development. People who identify themselves with Esalen all share in its inclusive, eclectic spirituality and its faith in benign supernatural forces, as well as its goals of facilitating the full development of everyone's mind, body, spirit, and psyche.

While the two central tenets of spiritual sparks and integral development of all four human aspects sprang from Michael and Dick's knowledge of Aurobindo and their personal religious experiences, these articles of faith are very general, and they are compatible with many other approaches to spirituality. Another doctrine of importance to Michael and his current inner circle is much more specific and far less widely shared at the Institute or generally understood by outsiders: the faith in evolutionary human potential that was another cornerstone of Aurobindo's philosophy.

Evolutionary Human Potential

Michael has always hoped that the Institute would become a place where people could cultivate extraordinary human abilities like extrasensory perception or powers of prediction. He believes that the development and spread of greater human powers can contribute to collective biological and social advances (Schwartz 1995:73–116). Evolutionary human potential is central to Aurobindo's optimism about individual and collective human progress. Faith in intentional human evolution rests on trust in human goodness, hope that all aspects of human functioning can improve, and confidence that individual advances will ultimately create a better world for all humankind (Kripal 2007a: 65–67). According to this doctrine, "Every person can join the procession of transformative practice that began with our ancestors" (Leonard and Murphy 1995:xv).

People who are sure of their ability to make a difference in the world and contribute to an evolutionary advance often enjoy the economic and social resources associated with spiritual privilege (Coles 1977:361–412). Their optimism, like spiritual privilege, reflects both personal predilections and social relationships. Hope, tenacity, and willingness to confront challenges ground their efforts at self-improvement. Like Michael, they believe in themselves and their ability to affect others in positive ways.

The doctrine of evolutionary human potential is by no means a scientific interpretation of evolutionary biology (Lewontin 2001; Ruse 2005). It is instead an article of faith that is supported by accumulated anecdotes about personal dedication and individual triumphs (Leonard and Murphy 1995). While relatively few people who pass through Esalen are aware of it, the doctrine enhances the hopeful attitude that permeates the Institute. Michael remains certain that there will be a great leap forward in the near future: "Both spontaneously and through transformative practice, a new evolutionary domain is arising in the human species" (Leonard and Murphy 1995:185).

Esalen has sponsored conferences, offered workshops, and developed research archives about possibilities for transformation of mind, body, spirit, and psyche. The belief in evolutionary human potential lifts personal transformation beyond individualism to public service that advances the collective good.

Michael and his late comrade George Leonard attempted to popularize the theories and practices associated with the development of evolutionary human potential by nurturing local Integral Transformative Practice (ITP) groups throughout the United States (Leonard and Murphy 1995). The network has not grown much, but, for almost a decade, several dozen different groups have started and stopped (Leonard and Murphy 1995).

Some ITP members meet in the Midwest and the border states, but most groups form and dissolve along the Pacific slope. One defunct ITP group began with several people who had participated in an Esalen workshop on personal transformation in the 1990s. They carried the Institute's vision of individual and collective evolution to their social networks on Los Angeles's affluent Westside. Men and women met weekly for close to a year, phoned one another for support, and practiced ITP affirmations, meditations, and physical exercises individually and together. The group disintegrated after most members began to miss meetings because of golf dates, family obligations, travel, and visits to Esalen.

This type of temporary engagement is common because ITP members are usually reasonably affluent and have many options to pursue in their spare time. George and Michael never met their goal of bringing Esalen's foundational philosophy and experiential practices to long-term ITP groups or to large numbers of financially stretched participants who can rarely if ever afford to visit Big Sur.

George and Michael hoped that, "Through the active consideration of transforming ourselves, of becoming consciously involved in our own experience, of becoming consciously involved in our own evolution, we can reawaken to the miracle of existence" (Leonard and Murphy 1995:72). ITP began three decades after the soul rush was under way, and it will probably never be as well known or as influential as Esalen itself. It is, instead, part of the cycle of alternative religious choices that come and go in the spiritual niche that Esalen carved out in the 1960s and 1970s.

The Human Potential Movement and Spirituality

The belief in everyone's sparks of divinity grounded ideas about the importance of discovering a core authentic self through individual and group therapy. During the mid-1960s, Esalen's ties to the broad human potential movement introduced a spiritual dimension to the psychology of personal growth.

The human potential movement that began in the 1960s was a loose configuration of philosophies and practices directed toward people's abilities to improve themselves, their relationships, and their connections to the cosmos. The psychologist Gardner Murphy (1958) developed the concept of human potential, the philosopher Aldous Huxley appropriated it (Kripal 2007a:480), and George Leonard introduced the nascent movement for emotional fulfillment and personal development to mass audiences in a 1966 *Look* article about California, when he suggested that the pursuit of full human potential ought to become a national priority (Leonard 1966).

Esalen's integration of psychology and spirituality to maximize human potential reflected the basic assumptions that everyone's core self-identity and divine sparks could be uncovered and nurtured only after eliminating many layers of social conditioning. According to this perspective, people had to discover their inner authenticity in order to realize their full potential, and self-knowledge was a precondition for full spiritual development.

Esalen's foundational assumptions complemented humanistic psychology and the human potential movement because of their shared emphasis on personal growth and fulfillment. Human potential psychology allowed Esalen to harness its implicit spiritual doctrine to a pragmatic approach to personal happiness through the movement's many branches: humanistic, Gestalt, encounter, existential, and transpersonal psychologies.

Abe Maslow and other well-known academics founded humanistic psychology to create protocols that would help people lead healthy, fulfilling lives and maximize their abilities to contribute to social progress. Humanistic psychologists used words like "truth," "emotional integration," and "wholeness" to describe the desired outcomes of individual and group therapies (Maslow 1961). These goals were part of Esalen's mild humanistic psychology seminars in the early 1960s, but these gentle, intellectual approaches soon gave way to the intense Gestalt sessions and explosive encounter groups that became Esalen's trademark (Litwak 1967).

Gestalt sessions and encounter groups addressed participants' immediate interactions and emotions in order to uncover their past traumas and roadblocks to self-understanding (Litwak 1967). In both kinds of groups, members confronted their personal demons in order to affirm their spiritual bonds to one another and to all humankind. With group support, leaders encouraged conversation and also wordless expression to allow every participant to pursue a personal path to his or her unique authenticity. There was an emphasis on the importance of gestures, voice, and facial expressions, rather than mere words (Litwak 1967; Rakstis 1971).

During Esalen's first decade, Fritz Perls dominated Gestalt at the Institute. Each person in his sessions interacted individually with Fritz or one of his students while others diligently observed them and the therapist-patient relationship unfolded before a rapt audience. Sometimes workshop members came forward to take the role of key people in the patient's life or added their own insights to the interaction, but hierarchical therapist/patient relationships were essential to Fritz's Gestalt methods.

Dick became Fritz's student and later revised his mentor's dictatorial approach. The modifications, which Dick called Gestalt awareness practice, sustained Fritz's emphasis on authentic emotions and personal understanding in the immediate moment, alongside his impatience about self-conscious intellectualization. However, Dick's antiauthoritarian version of Gestalt, which has framed Esalen's recent approaches to emotional growth, made therapists and participants equal partners who joined together to seek meaningful personal truths. He also integrated aspects of Taoism, Zen, and other Buddhist practices into Gestalt awareness practice, emphasizing the need for constant attention to spiritual experience.

In contrast to either Fritz's or Dick's Gestalt approaches, encounter group leaders rarely intervened with members. Instead, they stood back and encouraged participants to relate to one another. The encounters were far less structured than Gestalt and often involved emotional and physical confrontations among their participants.

Esalen became a crucible for humanistic psychology because Michael and Dick embraced almost every groundbreaking approach that could facilitate the expansion of human abilities and spread spiritual privilege to ordinary Americans. Fritz Perls, Will Schutz, and Abe Maslow were the three ambitious, highly competitive human potential movement pioneers who put Esalen on the map and made it famous through the mass media. In their own ways, each of them encouraged individualized spirituality, while at the same time critiquing established religious institutions of every kind (Kripal 2007a:150–151).

Before making their separate ways to Big Sur, Schutz (1967), Perls (1969), and Maslow (1971) had each enjoyed elements of worldly privilege: educational credentials, cultural knowledge, and their peers' recognition of their work in psychology. Esalen staff had sought out Schutz and Perls. Maslow first visited in 1962, when he looked for vacation accommodations at the time when the Esalen property still functioned as a motel, and a surprised and delighted Dick immediately recognized and welcomed him as a distinguished guest (Anderson 1983:67–68, 86–89, 151–152).

Fritz, the Gestalt guru, came to the Institute in 1963 after escaping from Nazi Germany, living in Israel, and later settling in South Africa. Before he traveled to Big Sur, he had spent time in New York City and Miami. Fritz, who was always called by his first name at the Institute, had patients sit on a chair called the hot seat in the middle of his large group sessions. He directed the hot seat's occupant to explore different aspects of his or her life, asking the person to enact various roles in front of other workshop members. People were told to become their father, their dog, their hopes, their breakfast toast, or whoever or whatever was most salient to their internal conflicts and ultimate growth. Emotions rather than ideas were of paramount importance to him, and one of Fritz's often-quoted aphorisms was "Lose your mind and come to your senses" (Perls 1969:no pagination).

A squat, bearded man in his late sixties, Fritz soon gathered a devoted following as Esalen's resident "dirty old man," top therapist, and insightful charismatic leader (Anderson 1983:130–137). He enlivened his workshops with theatrical reenactments of patients' problems, and the press and many visitors adored him. Michael and Dick were ambivalent about Fritz's regular verbal abuse of the Institute's staff and the participants in his sessions, as well as his blatant sexual advances to almost every girl and woman around him. Even though Dick eventually became Fritz's student, Fritz left Big Sur to establish a training center for therapists on Vancouver Island and died there in 1970 (Anderson 1983:203–204).

Will Schutz arrived at Esalen a few years after Fritz, and the two therapists soon became archrivals because they both wanted to define and dominate personal growth groups. In contrast to Fritz, whose undocumented European degrees raised suspicions about his training, Schutz had impressive academic credentials that included a Ph.D. from UCLA and teaching appointments at Harvard and the University of Chicago (Kripal 2007a:166). In the mid-1960s, he accepted Michael's invitation to lead encounter groups at Esalen, and he lived there until 1973, when he moved to the Bay Area to found a consulting firm and develop his own group center (Anderson 1983:243). His best-selling books (1967, 1971) described meaningful, joyful lives as universal prerogatives (Litwak 1967).

Schutz never attracted a large, devoted band of Esalen acolytes as Fritz had, but his well-publicized successes helped make the Institute an important part of the encounter group sector of the human potential movement (Back 1972:109–112, 132–136). Leo Litwak (1967) introduced Schutz's encounters to *New York Times* readers in his detailed personal account of an encounter group, and Jane Howard profiled Schutz in her book *Please Touch* (1970). Schutz's media presence eclipsed Michael's and Dick's in the late 1960s and early 1970s, and he dramatically expanded popular interest in Esalen, helping to make the Institute America's best-known personal growth center.

Liberal religious congregations, businesses, and schools throughout the United States adopted versions of Schutz's encounters (Back 1972). In the early 1970s, the encounter movement was so popular that an enthusiastic reporter contacted an Esalen insider with questions for a feature in *Ingénue*, a magazine read regularly by about three quarters of a million teenage girls. She asked, "How might a girl in a small town locate an encounter group? Providing that none is available in her vicinity, how might she try to increase her own sensitivity and awareness?" (Esalen Institute Collection 1970).

Abe Maslow (1961), the third well-known psychologist associated with both the human potential movement and Esalen, offered lectures and seminars in the early 1960s. Maslow supported the Institute as an important educational institution, but Fritz and Schutz's competitive exhibitionism and the general rowdiness in Big Sur drove him away. The Institute was only one of Maslow's many projects, and he was far more interested in developing the field of humanistic psychology and doing research and writing than competing with Fritz or Schutz (Anderson 1983:176, 184).

As a professor of psychology at Brandeis University, Maslow had assembled vast networks of academic and professional contacts to promote new approaches to academic and clinical psychology that countered both behaviorists and Freudians (Anderson 1983:183–185). Fifty years after he published *Toward a Psychology of Being* (1961), college students in business schools and educational psychology programs still study his influential theories about a hierarchy of human needs, starting with basic physical requirements and culminating with desires for justice and personal authenticity (Maslow 1971). Maslow's ideas about self-actualization and peak experiences dovetailed with Esalen's commitment to help people discover their previously untapped intellectual, emotional, and physical abilities (Anderson 1983:65–70).

Although he was not personally religious and never saw himself as spiritually sensitive, Maslow associated full emotional maturity with frequent peak experiences that offered people a mystical sense of unity with the cosmos. His ideal individual was self-actualized—someone who had explored and developed every ability, including general spiritual sensitivity. Thus, Maslow's vision of human possibilities meshed with the Institute's foundational doctrines of personal divinity and evolutionary human potential.

In 1971, after Maslow and Fritz had died and Schutz was almost out the gate, Michael and Dick deliberately downplayed the intense emotions and dramatic breakthroughs that had captured media attention and attracted troubled visitors along with happy seekers. The two founders forcefully asserted that the Institute was neither a treatment center nor a place for dangerous individualized experimentation of any kind. Instead, it provided a context for personal growth and spiritual exploration. They dismissed false promises of sudden, lasting personal transformation and repeatedly advocated focused long-term practice. (Leonard and Murphy 1995:6–8). However, everyone at Esalen still acknowledges that extraordinary revelations in workshops can open up new possibilities for dramatic personal changes and also deepen an individual's commitment to follow an ongoing spiritual path.

The Power of Groups

Despite Michael's and the CTR's emphasis on theory and research, visitors and massage crew members talk more about their intense emotions and powerful physical responses in workshops, massage, movement groups, and meditations than they do about theory and research. They describe these moments as spiritual because they often discover surprising feelings and emotions that hold personal mystical significance for them. Although they use different terms, everyone, including contemporary CTR members, discusses times when they have felt connected to something ineffable, and they discover ties with the earth, bonds with all humankind, or contact with an amorphous divine force.

They remark on physical sensations, ranging from delightful to horrible, that made them feel that they have temporarily transcended the bonds of everyday time and rationality. Their descriptions echo depictions of mystical experiences across different historical and social contexts (McGuire 2008).

During my research, I found that, after a few minutes of conversation, people at Esalen simply gave up trying to describe their extraordinary moments. Their experiences went beyond spoken language. Wholehearted participation, according to my respondents, was the *only* way for me to discover the full meanings of their spirituality. In order to better understand how Esalen's connection of psychology and spirituality had stimulated the widespread demand for its approaches to personal growth, I joined yoga and ecstatic dance sessions at the Institute, enrolled in a weekend of integral practice at Esalen, and participated in two Southern California psychodrama workshops, where members worked together to explore their personal tensions in brief dramas that they created on the spot.

Some Esalen contexts produced brief sensations for me, while others did not. I sensed fleeting links to something beyond myself while deeply breathing in a yoga group, tapping Ki energy in the workshop on integral practice, and dancing in a wave of Gabrielle Roth's (1998) five rhythms.

My experience could have reflected mystical connections or intense emotion or physical reactions in response to exertion and different patterns of breathing or all of these. None of them offered the sudden dramatic clarity that many people had noted over the decades. Leo Litwak (1967) described how one of Will Schutz's encounter groups produced extraordinary emotions: "that tingling sense of being wide awake, located in the here and now, feeling freely and entirely" (24).

No contemporary Institute workshop that I heard about seemed to reproduce the extraordinary intensity of Schutz's encounters or Fritz's Gestalt performances. Contemporary leaders of workshops that focus on emotional growth at Esalen are often professional therapists who try to make spiritual moments less sudden and dramatic than they were in the 1960s, and group members are calmer and more patient than their predecessors.

A veteran psychologist suggested that I look beyond Esalen and find out more about psychodrama, the therapeutic technique that was a foundation for both Schutz (1971:200) and Perls (Anderson 1983:96–97). Jacob Levy Moreno introduced this approach in the early twentieth century; it involves spiritual elements that Moreno called "a religion of encounter" (Anderson 1983:80). Psychodrama is framed by trust in individuals' abilities to support one another and to affirm their own and others' essential divinity. These groups center on reenactments of highly emotional relationships and incidents in order to deepen participants' personal authenticity.

The director of the two workshop sets that I attended in Southern California described psychodrama's spiritual dimensions on the first day of each group. She stated:

> There are those awesome times—when the entire group—without speaking—is aware of that basic, mythic archetype of human experience. . . .
> And it is at those times that psychodrama fulfills the original ancient functions of drama: the healing and elevating of the human spirit as a religious and communal experience.

The director and her spouse/coleader never guided workshops at the Institute, but a number of their colleagues and students led Esalen groups, and they were close to some key figures from the early decades of the human potential movement. During the three- and four-day workshops in Southern California, I better understood the extraordinary experiences that so many people had tried and failed to describe with words. And I shared the rewards of profound physical and emotional awareness that are at the heart of Esalen's religion of no religion.

Members of the psychodrama workshops that I attended resembled Esalen's constituents, although, somewhat surprisingly, only one had visited the Institute. The ratio of women to men in the two groups was three to two. Participants ranged in age from about thirty to about sixty years old. During the first hour of each workshop, it became clear that all of them were educated, affluent, and attractive people. As the process unfolded, every one of them talked about seeking connections to higher powers and disclosed the personal resources that allowed them to sample and combine different spiritual traditions.

Three members of the first workshop and one more in the second had worked with the director in individual therapy, as well as groups. These two men and two women wanted to become accredited psychodrama leaders themselves someday. They centered their daily lives on nurturing their personal and spiritual growth so that they could serve others. They resembled Esalen's EMBA crew and operations staff members, who focused on their daily practice rather than on the CTR's theories about spirituality and human potential. The psychodrama director supported the aspiring leaders' quests by urging them to remain committed to realizing their full but inevitably imperfect potentials.

One of these four had invited the director to hold the first set of workshops in an elegant Spanish-style house in a fashionable upper-middle-class neighborhood. During the enactments of personal issues and other group exercises in the workshops, I forgot where I was, because the unfolding interactions obscured time and space. I also forgot the less-welcoming hotel meeting room during the second workshop. Scenes from people's lives were so absorbing and the group's bonds were so immediately and profoundly close that nothing mattered but the present interaction and the imaginary worlds that we constructed together.

The two sets of workshops followed the same schedules. After introductions and gentle warm-ups in a conversation with a random partner, we began the psychodrama. The director carefully guided the enactment of dramas from our lives that reflected areas of unresolved emotional conflicts. People acted out scenes from their childhoods, their divorces, or other thorny times, as if they were living them in the immediate moment. We could call upon other group members to play the roles of major or minor characters in our life dramas. Whether we were actors or audiences, our personal disclosures brought everyone in the group together. Sometimes we all laughed. Other times, all eight of us sobbed. The dramatic process involved therapeutic catharsis, ritual, and spiritual experience (Anderson 1983:81; Moreno 1953).

During the first workshop, different participants called on me to assume roles in scenes from their lives. I became a demeaning high school counselor, an ambivalent fiancé, a giggling little sister, and a reticent ticket taker. These assigned roles revealed something not necessarily pleasant about how other group members saw me. However, thank goodness, in contrast to Esalen's original confrontational encounters and Gestalt groups, no one told me why he or she had selected me to play those characters. In the second workshop, when I volunteered to be a protagonist in my own psychodrama, I understood the full impact of the group process. At painful points in the reenactment, my hands turned icy, and I choked and gasped for breath. The scene and the people in them seemed absolutely real. I learned something about my past and a great deal about the force of groups (Back 1972; Schutz 1967). My extraordinary experiences, like those of other members, could be interpreted as gifts from unseen, supernatural powers that allowed each one of us to explore our lives.

Esalen's current workshops and other experience-oriented practices also limit action and feeling to the present moment, while shutting out external distractions. Disconnection from everyday life begins at the Institute's gate and extends to its every corner. The sense of entering another world grows when emotion and physical sensations dominate the structured settings of various activities. Because I could let myself go in psychodrama, without worrying about the effects of personal disclosures on my research, I better understood the feelings of transformation that unfold in many different Esalen contexts.

Although encounters and Gestalt no longer dominate the Institute's offerings, most contemporary workshops that focus on immediate experience still have some power to temporarily transport people away from their mundane lives. During the 1960s, the interdependence between Esalen and the human potential movement built a lasting bridge of doctrines and practices that linked emotional fulfillment to invisible sacred forces. That bridge still stands.

Death: What Happens Next?

During the psychodrama workshops, most of the participants revealed their fears about death, and we also mourned individuals whom we had lost. However, no one described a concrete afterlife. A few people talked about their spirits surviving as bright energy, and some mentioned relationships and deeds as personal legacies. But there were no discussions of a material life after death or places like heaven or hell. No one asked: "Is this all there is?" There was an unspoken assumption that we were in the workshop to improve our time on Earth, because the spirituality that grounded psychodrama did not embrace worlds other than this one.

Almost every vital spiritual system deals with questions about death in some way, but people at Esalen rarely discussed it until the late 1990s (Stark 2001:17–18; Stark and Bainbridge 1996:33–39). For decades, even in the face of personal losses, people in Big Sur behaved as if death would not be a personal issue if they ignored it. The sparks of divinity within and outside offered no specific answers or comfort.

When George Leonard died, at the age of eighty-six, in January of 2010, Michael and other members of the CTR grieved deeply and, for the most part, very privately. Twenty years earlier, Leonard had confronted a blocked coronary artery with a program of rigorous supervised exercise and strict diet, along with meditation and Aikido. The program reversed the arterial blockage (Leonard and Murphy 1995:12–14). He not only healed but also defined his crisis as another affirmation of the connections of body, mind, spirit, and psyche.

In the late 1990s, George received his diagnosis of ultimately fatal esophageal cancer, and initially he seemed to be certain that he could overcome it. For almost a decade, George viewed cancer as another challenge that he could rise above, believing that the unexpected blow could be a gift that allowed him to face death and beat it once again (Leonard and Murphy 1985:152–156). However, George gradually accepted his fate.

Less than a year before his death, he agreed to be honored by 140 participants at an annual celebration of integral practice that was held near San Francisco. Everyone at the conference performed an energy exercise that George had developed especially for the occasion. Touched and pleased by the support and love for him, George viewed a slide show about his long life. The gathering symbolized the ways that his vision and achievements could still continue to exert a posthumous influence on the expansion of human potential.

Shortly after George died, Esalen posted its own tribute to him online. It described what he had accomplished and how he had worked to make the world a better place. There was no mention of any personal deity or possibility of his passing on to a better place or somehow returning to this one (Esalen Institute 2010).

George had tried to transcend death by living his life fully and maximizing his many abilities. He seemed to have cheated mortality when he worked to reverse his cardiac problems, and he rarely mentioned his last battle with cancer. Michael also avoids discussing the ailments and physical problems that he has faced over the years, except to remark on those that he has conquered. When he was in his forties, Michael stated that he planned to rise above physical aging through rigorous physical and spiritual practice. He said, "I just don't believe in that stuff about getting old" (Anderson 1983:260).

Earlier tributes to deceased Esalen figures rarely if ever touched on questions about mortality. Even after the rash of suicides at the Institute in the 1960s and early 1970s and Dick Price's untimely accidental death, in 1985, no one mentioned enduring life except in terms of earthly relationships and worldly achievements. Like George's, the other tributes and celebrations evoked memories of dead comrades and speakers did not speculate about other worlds. Neither heaven nor hell has ever been part of the widely shared worldview at the Institute.

Over the past two decades, however, more CTR members have confronted their own crises with cancer and heart disease, and some of their comrades and family members have died. Not surprisingly, individuals at the Institute's core have grown more interested in death and the afterlife. Since 1998, the CTR has sponsored annual conferences titled "Survival of Bodily Death" in order to explore the topic that was once almost invisible at Big Sur.

There is little consensus about the nature of an afterlife or even the existence of one (Kripal 2007a:442–447). No one at the CTR's conferences discusses concrete punishments or rewards after death, but conversations cover a wide range of issues, from near-death experiences to communicating with the dead to reincarnation. There is a developing consensus that the divine sparks of energy within everyone will not perish. They might lodge in the cosmos at large, in legacies of personal relationships and achievements, or perhaps in a random unborn body, but the sparks will still be part of the evolution of human possibilities.

This relatively recent conversation about what happens after death once again demonstrates how Michael and his inner circle have made their personal concerns into a collective agenda at the CTR. The increasingly frequent discussions about death and the afterlife acknowledge that no one is alone as they pass through the life cycle. Everyone is connected in some way, and Esalen provides a collective context to explore the final, deeply personal life event. George's death deepened members' awareness that death is inevitable, even at the Institute. The hot springs cannot be a fountain of youth.

The baby boomers, who dominated the soul rush and are still the Institute's most loyal constituents, have also started to ponder what, if anything, follows death (Davidson 2007:278–283). More conferences and workshops may soon address the issue. However, for the time being, CTR conversations about afterlife rarely affect the workshops or daily activities within other groups at the Institute.

Although public conversations about the Institute's life or demise are not new, more people have recently asked questions about Esalen's own survival after Michael dies. During the Institute's doldrums in the early 1980s, when it had no clear direction and its finances were precarious, some operations staff and bodyworkers proposed closing down. They described the Sufi mystery schools that shared wisdom traditions and then disappeared after reaching their goals (Anderson 1983:313).

There are contemporary financial issues, as there were in the past. However, new approaches to management and fund-raising put in place by Gordon Wheeler, Esalen's recent president, have stimulated more collective confidence. Esalen continues its mission of transforming the world—one person at a time. Millions of Americans continue to have the desire and resources to seek personal and spiritual fulfillment through alternative spirituality and human potential psychology. The Institute's reputation as the place that first opened up new possibilities for personal growth will probably ensure its lasting position in the spiritual marketplace.

Public Service and Everlasting Life

Esalen's founding generation bound spirituality to an ethic of progressive social change that still shapes varied CTR projects. The people who define the Institute's mission continue to believe that it is both their obligation and their privilege to facilitate a more equalitarian and ecologically balanced world. They can build lasting legacies, like George's, beyond their own or possibly the Institute's lifetimes, by supporting peace, social justice, and environmental harmony. Many people at Esalen feel obligated to give something back to a world that has provided so much for them.

Some Institute insiders have prioritized changing themselves in order to repair the world later on. Others develop seminars and CTR conferences to deal with international relations or religious fundamentalism. And still others look outward to explicit political action at the local, national, or international level. George summed up Esalen's call for social responsibility when he described his personal commitments, stating that he had the need and also the obligation to change the world because "I *was* somehow 'different' and 'special'" (Leonard 1988:108). Therefore, he reasoned, he was obligated to work for social justice.

The Institute's commitment to public service extends themes from the Old Testament Book of Jeremiah (Bruggemann 2007). Liberal theologians interpreted the message in Jeremiah as a call to live simply and to improve the lot of those who were less fortunate. Esalen's elders never mention a biblical imperative, but they describe spreading their message to less advantaged individuals, working for environmental justice, and also creating world peace through their collective influence. These calls resonate with people raised in liberal mainstream faiths that prioritize public service and progressive change (Bader and BSIR Study Group 2006:24). Moreover, Esalen's ongoing calls for social responsibility add to its relevance in the twenty-first century.

Over five decades, the Institute's social missions have varied, reflecting historical opportunities, personal networks, and individual priorities. Throughout the 1960s, George and other core members successfully championed educational reform in public schools through classroom innovations that recognized individuality and also integrated emotions and democratic group process into daily learning (Shapiro 1998). Their approach, confluent education, grounded the Esalen-influenced program in the College of Education at the University of California at Santa Barbara.

Other early initiatives for social justice were far less successful. In the late 1960s, Esalen sponsored a series of black-white encounter groups to confront the racial crisis in the United States. Political differences within Esalen produced deep divisions and generated lasting animosity toward Esalen among some African Americans (Anderson 1983:160–165, 195–198). There were outcries against the ways that social privilege shaped the racial encounter initiative and defined the Institute itself (Cobbs and Brown 1981).

The institute also tried to respond to the rising tide of feminism in the 1960s, inviting visits from major figures like Betty Friedan, well-known writer and a founder of the National Organization for Women (Kripal 2007a:461). The Institute's leadership attempted to develop a feminist agenda in the 1970s, but this project also proved to be a disaster, albeit a less explosive failure than the racial encounters (Anderson 1983:257, 268).

Esalen insiders, led by Michael, still want to change the course of world politics as well as the directions of U.S. society. Since 1971, when three core members visited Moscow to meet with researchers interested in parapsychology topics like extrasensory perception, Michael has cultivated a network of contacts inside Russia. During the Reagan years, as the old Soviet Union disintegrated, Esalen helped organize Soviet-American conferences and supported Boris Yeltsin's visit to the United States before he became president of the Soviet Union and, later, the Russian Federation (Kripal 2007a:231–238). The theme of ordinary citizens as diplomats has also dominated contemporary initiatives for Esalen's Track II Diplomacy, which focuses on peace and common understandings.

The ethic of public service has played out in a number of small, hands-on projects, as well. In the 1980s, Esalen supported an HIV hospice in San Francisco, brought small groups of African American youths to Esalen for special three-day programs, and assisted the San Francisco Zen Center in its brief attempt to enlist disadvantaged youths in a program coached by a former Olympic runner (Downing 2001:209). The Institute continues to develop a political agenda that calls for local social responsibility and service to others who are less fortunate.

Esalen's interpretation of spiritual privilege empowers individuals to try to reshape the world in ways that honor the divine sparks that are within every person. Because of its leaders' commitment to public service, peace, and progressive social change, the Institute has become part of a number of high-profile spiritual responsibility networks that include Dr. Deepak Chopra (1994), a best-selling writer on alternative medicine who founded his own retreat center, and His Holiness the Dalai Lama (1992).

Every aspect of Esalen's doctrine reflects the assumption that people are capable of transforming themselves, their societies, and the Earth. Esalen's founders and their comrades built the Institute to reflect their own yearning for meaningful spirituality and personal authenticity. They assumed all people were basically like them and shared similar abilities and desires to select, combine, and revise highly personal paths to self-actualization and social transformation.

The Institute's underlying principles reflect its founders' life histories, particularly Michael's commitment to Aurobindo's integral yoga and Dick's search for relief from conventional psychotherapy and electroshock treatments that scarred him for life. The doctrine that they popularized and elaborated reached millions of other Americans through Esalen's offerings and its support of other institutions that continue to spread its message.

Many people interested in spiritual and personal growth cannot find the time or money to visit Esalen or someplace like it. They can, however, nurture their own spiritual privilege in other settings and utilize Esalen's foundational beliefs in eclectic spirituality, personal growth psychology, and public service to improve themselves and the world around them.

Life on Earth and service to others, according to the Institute's underlying doctrine, are what matter most. The many spiritual practices and social organizations that Esalen has influenced over the decades all work to maximize people's abilities to take charge of their lives and assume responsibility for helping others. The diffusion of spiritual privilege is central to every aspect of the Institute's doctrine, from the belief in inclusive spirituality that can embrace varied faiths to the emphasis on social responsibility.

Esalen's Reach: A Brief History

California Highway 1 twists south between the Pacific and the jagged peaks of the Santa Lucia Mountains along the unincorporated ninety-mile coastal stretch of Big Sur that begins below Monterey. About forty miles down the highway from Monterey, Esalen's small wooden sign marks a sharp downhill turn toward the Institute's buildings, gardens, and hot springs. There are two timber frame houses, known as the Big House and the Little House, that are left from the 1920s and 1930s, a time when Esalen was the Murphy family's private country retreat. More recent structures include an array of rustic cabins, a cluster of yurts, accommodations for workshop participants, and a central lodge with a bookstore, workshop spaces, and the main dining room. Winding paths lead from the lodge to recently refurbished massage rooms and soaking pools fed by Esalen's hot springs.

Flower gardens, eucalyptus groves, and meadows add to the site's allure. Moreover, every public space either overlooks the Pacific or is a short walk to views of crashing waves, dolphins, and seasonal whale migrations.

Esalen's extraordinary beauty and relative isolation make it easy for visitors to share a sense of inhabiting a sacred place where every activity can take on spiritual meanings (Turner and Turner 1978). The Institute provides liminal space between the sacred and the secular. Here visiting seminarians, short-term residents, and core members can focus on maximizing their spiritual and personal fulfillment.

The extraordinary setting fills most people who visit or live there with a sense of awe. Michael, who came to know the land when he was a child, is no less thrilled by the place than an awkward first-time work-study student who recently unpacked her suitcase. Most people feel pleased and privileged just to be at the Institute.

At Esalen, it easy to discover sacred aspects of nature, and those discoveries add to the affinities for religious meanings that are part of spiritual privilege. There is no well-defined nature religion at the Institute, but instead there is a pervasive sense that the location connects people to invisible spiritual forces (Albanese 1990).

Nature, however, is not always bountiful. Sometimes the setting is challenging, and occasionally it is dangerous. Almost every winter, heavy rains wash out parts of Highway 1 and falling boulders halt travel. At some times during the rainy season, it is impossible to drive in or out of Esalen. During recent summers, wildfires burned near Highway 1, closing off visitors' access, forcing evacuations, and inundating the Institute with smoke and ash. Esalen residents and regular seminarians usually adjust to these inconveniences and dangers, because they believe that they are small prices to exchange for the rare landscape.

The wet winters and dangerous fire seasons also offer some rewards. In the winter, smoke from woodstoves and damp eucalyptus trees perfume the air, blending with salty ocean breezes and the sulphurous scent of the hot springs. The massage crew and staff members savor the pleasures of the rain. They also describe the camaraderie when they are forced to stay inside in winter or come together to take precautions for summer fires. Despite the forest fires that can threaten Esalen, after months of rain and damp fog, people who live and work at the Institute look forward to long, sunny summer days, when their windows stay open and fragrant flowers' scents crowd out almost every other smell.

Bohemian Dreams

Farmers and ranchers homesteaded the beautiful Big Sur Coast in the nineteenth century. In the early twentieth century, a few affluent Californians, like Michael's grandparents, purchased land parcels in order to build their summer homes. The seasonal residents were financially comfortable, but the land remained relatively inexpensive until the 1970s, and the full-time residents and summer people accommodated one another.

A third, more controversial group settled in Big Sur just before World War II, and they became the first generation of the local counterculture. Artists and writers from the Bay Area moved to the rugged coast after Highway 1 opened, in 1937. They began their pastoral adventures with little if any money, and they viewed Big Sur as an inspiring alternative to the relatively expensive Bay Area or big cities in the East and the Midwest. Even with the improved highway that linked the region to other parts of California, it remained isolated and inexpensive. Electricity and running water were uncommon in local cabins until the 1950s, and many sites could be reached only on foot.

Members of Esalen's founding generation sometimes describe the Institute's roots in the bohemian subculture. This imagined connection both adds to their cultural importance and veils the ways that Michael and Dick's economic resources facilitated Esalen's development. Even in the twenty-first century, core CTR members continue to tell stories that connect them directly with a central California artistic lineage that includes Robinson Jeffers, Jack Kerouac, John Steinbeck, and Henry Miller (Kripal 2007a:34). This romanticized link reflects their aspirations more than real relationships.

In the 1950s, bohemian intellectuals, artists, and celebrities who visited the Big Sur coast often romanticized living there, but few of them stayed for long, because of the challenges of daily life (Miller 1957:12–14). For example, in the early 1940s, Orson Welles and his wife, the movie star Rita Hayworth, took a day off from selling U.S. war bonds in San Francisco and drove down to Big Sur. They purchased a small vacation cabin overlooking the ocean for less than $200, but they realized that the place was far too rustic and inconvenient for them, and they never lived there. In 1947, they sold it to the Fassetts, a family with five children. Bill and Lolly Fassett built additions to their cabin, and it became a lasting informal social center for Big Sur bohemians. They called it Nepenthe, after the mythical Greek isle where everyone was free of care.

The Fassett family's restaurant and gift gallery on Highway 1, north of Esalen, is still a hub for the local bohemian subculture and also a destination for tourists (Miller 1957:113–114). Farmers and other, more conventional longtime residents gather at the local grange hall, which was founded as part of a national nineteenth century movement to promote sociability and political solidarity in rural areas, and affluent spiritual seekers go to Esalen, but Big Sur bohemians still gather at Nepenthe. Esalen never supplanted the Fassetts' place as the social center for the local creative community.

In the 1950s, Henry Miller, Big Sur's best-known bohemian writer, described dozens of young men who had served in the armed forces, married, divorced, and settled temporarily in Big Sur. Many years before Michael and Dick founded the Institute, the young bohemians had traded economic security for self-discovery. However, they had no shared agenda for spiritual fulfillment or personal growth. Miller described the young bohemians: "Utterly disillusioned, this new breed of experimenter is resolutely turning his back on all that he once held true and viable, and is making a valiant effort to start anew" (Miller 1957:17).

Most of the bohemian settlers, like Miller or Jack Kerouac, had little or no economic security from their families or from their own earnings. Many were bitter and cynical about their lives, and they viewed their move to the central California coast as their last chance to change course and to salvage their personal integrity. In contrast, Esalen's founders hoped that Big Sur would be a place where they could launch ideas and practices that could make their good lives even better and also allow them to change the world.

Esalen's founding generation differed fundamentally from the bohemians because of the spiritual privilege that nourished their faith in their own possibilities and America's future. While they frequently identified with their bohemian neighbors, who had distanced themselves from mainstream society, the Institute's founding circle could move with ease among intellectual and social elites, because of their prior experiences and resources. They were proud of their knowledge of religion and the psychology of personal growth, and they had the desire and ability to learn more. Spiritual privilege supported their quests, brought them into contact with other affluent seekers, and buoyed their optimism.

Because the Institute's first generation believed that it had embarked on a great adventure beyond the boundaries of conventional values and rules for behavior, it felt a kinship with the cynical bohemians. However, the two groups never merged, and the social distance between Nepenthe and the Institute symbolized their contrasting resources and priorities.

Esalen's Creation Narrative

The stories that link Esalen with Big Sur's bohemian history are among the narratives that define its public identity and symbolic boundaries, although the stories sometimes contradict factual accounts. These tales illuminate what members of Esalen's founding generation wanted to believe and how they depicted themselves to outsiders. Because the inner circle had so many material and cultural resources, its accounts crowded out other tales that were more complicated or critical of the Institute.

The narratives, accurate or not, are an important part of the Institute's identity. Over the years, various writers have interviewed the CTR's inner circle and almost unquestioningly accepted the stories as literal truth (Anderson 1983; Kripal 2007a; Schwartz 1995).

For many years, men who were part of the founding generation have told and retold a handful of stories around fires, at dinner tables, and in print (Anderson 1983; Kripal 2007a; Leonard 1988). The narratives are embedded in the CTR's collective memory, while other groups at Esalen have developed their own, more private narratives with different themes (Halbwachs 1992).

Esalen community members who perform physical labor in and out of doors describe extraordinary experiences during crises like heavy storms or encounters with animals that roam nearby hills. Bodyworkers talk about astonishing physical healing and about the miracles of their children's births. While specific details of these personal stories vary, they are all constructed around themes of collaborating with nature and the processes of birth and healing. The CTR members' narratives are different because they focus on Esalen as an institution and the ways that Michael, Dick, and their comrades became a cultural force (Kripal 2007a; Leonard 1988).

The tale of Esalen's birth is by far the best known narrative (Anderson 1983:12–13). It emphasizes Michael and Dick's friendship and the meaningful coincidences that Esalen insiders refer to as synchronicity and that nineteenth-century Transcendentalists termed correspondence (Albanese 1977; Kripal 2007a:14). Carl Jung (1972), a famed mystic psychologist whose theories about archetypes are still discussed at Esalen, coined the term "synchronicity" to describe magical twists of fate that produce positive consequences for individuals and transform their lives.

The creation story is set in the early 1960s, when the planets aligned and synchronicity brought Esalen into being. It recounts the extraordinary confluence of Michael and Dick's close friendship, their elders' support, the availability of the Murphy family's compound in Big Sur, and the affluent baby-boom generation's collective search for spiritual meaning.

Michael and Dick met after college when they lived at East West House, the relaxed integral yoga ashram on Fulton Street at the edge of San Francisco's Golden Gate Park (Anderson 1983:33; Kripal 2007a:82). Both were Stanford undergraduates during the same period, but they became acquainted only after college, when the moment was right and supernatural forces were in play.

Early in 1961, Michael had casually told Dick that they could each save money by moving into his family's rent-free vacation house in Big Sur, where they might find part-time work, meditate, and see if it was possible to start a small weekend retreat for people who shared their interests in spirituality and psychology (Anderson 1983:9–10, 43; Price 1982). They moved to Big Sur and soon made plans to drive south and meet with various individuals who could offer useful advice about establishing a seminar center.

Before they settled in Big Sur that spring, the two young men had already discussed their vision of a small retreat with writers and philosophers in Northern California, including Michael's mentor Frederic Spiegelberg (1948), the Zen popularizer Alan Watts, and Aldous Huxley, the famous author of

Brave New World (1932). They also spoke to friends and acquaintances in the Bay Area in order to gather support for their nascent venture at Big Sur Hot Springs. This became a more concrete possibility shortly after Michael and Dick moved to Big Sur and Michael convinced his family to give them a favorable long-term lease on the tourist cabins and the two vacation houses on the Murphy property.

Michael moved into the master bedroom on the top floor of his family's vacation retreat, the Big House, while Dick occupied a smaller bedroom on the lower level until he later moved to the Little House just across the way (Price 1982). Before they scheduled seminars, Michael wrote to Huxley to try to arrange a relaxed visit to his house in the Hollywood Hills, where they could talk at length and construct lists of potential supporters. Although he planned to be away all summer, Huxley urged them to drive to Southern California anyway, and he gave them the names of people to look up when they arrived.

Huxley suggested that Michael and Dick visit Gerald Heard, a philosopher and advocate of "gymnasia of the mind," whose small monastic center for spiritual and personal growth, Trabuco College, had operated from 1942 to 1947 (Miller 2005). He also urged them to get ideas about daily operations by visiting Rancho La Puerta, a health spa in Baja California, where they could see how the proprietors combined a holistic weight-loss program with meditation, exercise, and nightly lectures on personal growth (Price 1982).

After meeting Heard in Santa Monica, Dick and Michael drove past San Diego, across the Mexican border. At Rancho La Puerta, they learned about running a retreat, sampled delicious organic food, and tried LSD. The two men talked over their plans for their seminar center when they traveled back to Big Sur to begin months of intense activity. In October 1961, Michael and Dick took over the Murphys' small resort and started to outline a calendar of seminars.

They first scheduled lecturers who already had their own supporters so that the speakers could spread the word about Esalen among their followers. "At the time," said Dick, "we tended to use people who had their own followings, their own mailing lists, their own programs. And we would just provide the place as a conference center for them" (Price 1982:no pagination).

When the seminars started, Big Sur Hot Springs was still a resort motel, but it drew more and more guests who were interested in exploring spirituality and psychology instead of visiting standard tourist attractions along the coast.

Michael and Dick posed for this iconic photograph on the Esalen Lodge deck a few months before Dick died. © Kathleen Thormod Carr, courtesy of Steven Harper

The narrative gains momentum as Big Sur Hot Springs changed quickly because of a series of meaningful coincidences involving unexpected support from elite seekers like Huxley and Heard, as well as stars in the new human potential movement like the psychologist Abraham Maslow and the encounter-group innovator Will Schutz (Kripal 2007a:136–137). Five-day programs soon followed the original weekend retreats, and seekers interested in personal growth and spiritual experience came to live nearby and became Esalen regulars. They encouraged other visitors to come, and the rush to Big Sur began.

During its first year and a half, Esalen offered a variety of seminars and workshops designed to attract support from diverse artistic, intellectual, and spiritual networks. The famed photographers Ansel Adams and Imogen Cunningham co-led a seminar on visual images, and Arnold Toynbee gave scholarly lectures about contemporary history (Anderson 1983:101–102). A momentous workshop that marked Esalen's growing emphasis on direct experience involved LSD's big three advocates. For a few memorable weeks, Ken Kesey, Richard Alpert (Ram Dass), and Timothy Leary (1983) led experiential seminars about psychedelic trips that fundamentally changed the Institute's focus.

Seekers of spiritual experience and self-transformation crowded out the intellectuals at Big Sur Hot Springs, as word of Esalen spread across the country and journalists described their amazing breakthroughs at the Institute (Gagarin 1969; Litwak 1967). In the fall of 1962, Michael and Dick renamed Big Sur Hot Springs Resort Esalen Institute, and, shortly afterward, they filed articles of incorporation as a nonprofit educational institution (Esalen Institute 1963).

The name that they chose acknowledged both the long-vanished Esselen Indian tribe and also the counterculture's growing interest in Native Americans (Kroeber [1925] 2007:377). According to Michael, the land that Esalen occupied was a magnet for spiritual seekers because the Esselen Indians had used the site as a sacred burial ground. He believed that the tribe had recognized mystical power points created by the confluence of three different kinds of water coming together on the site: sulfur springs, a freshwater creek, and the Pacific (Kripal 2007a:30). Michael was certain that it was pure synchronicity that his family owned sacred land.

Amid escalating experimentation, Michael and Dick carefully defined Esalen's mission in the broadest possible terms: "Conduct seminars, lectures, workshops, and conferences of an educational nature and of a scientific quality" (Esalen Institute 1963:1). They hung the first of many small wooden signs marking the sharp turn off Highway I. It read "Esalen Institute by Reservation Only."

Their original small educational and scientific retreat welcomed streams of soulful travelers, teachers, psychologists, dancers, musicians, psychedelic travelers, and celebrities drawn by Esalen's growing reputation for innovation and its beautiful location. By the end of 1963, few visitors came to Esalen to study about spirituality or to participate in tame humanistic psychology groups. Instead, they desired intense moments that might transform their lives. Sex, drugs, Gestalt, and encounter groups made Esalen a magnet for affluent, educated seekers in their twenties and thirties, who would soon be joined by the first wave of baby boomers. Nevertheless, Michael still hoped to fashion a place that could advance human potential in terms of mind and spirit, as well as body and psyche.

This creation story described how Michael and Dick's dream of a modest retreat had spontaneously morphed into the reality of an influential institution dedicated to personal and social transformations. Because of benign supernatural influences emanating from both Esalen's location and more general cosmic forces, the two young men were able to create a hub for spiritual and personal exploration that has survived for six decades. According to the narrative, the stars had aligned so that Esalen could be conceived. Supernatural synchronicity had shaped Esalen's beginnings, and Michael and Dick's road trip ushered in a new era for Americans hungering to expand their lives.

Synchronicity and Spiritual Privilege

The creation tale described two comrades whose road trip in a little red pickup truck marked the birth of a place and a virtual social movement that surpassed their wildest dreams. The narrative emphasized the importance of synchronicity, but, in reality, the key attributes associated with spiritual privilege were what generated and supported their friendship and shaped the Institute.

The resources that Michael and Dick brought to their project enabled them to build Esalen. Their affluence, their longstanding interests in alternative spirituality and psychology, the cultural and spiritual knowledge that bolstered their self-confidence, and their access to elite seekers' networks were far more important than synchronicity.

Social context was also vital to Esalen's success. During the 1960s and early 1970s, middle-class Americans' perceptions of economic security allowed them to seek greater personal and spiritual fulfillment. The Institute's extraordinary early growth also coincided with a growing supply of spiritual choices. University campuses and large cities on both coasts became testing grounds for meditation groups, Asian gurus, and human potential leaders. Moreover, in the early 1960s, newly available, sometimes legal psychedelics like LSD provided personal revelations and moments of instant enlightenment that spurred young adults' demand for expanded spiritual experience (Badiner and Gray 2002; Coyote 1998; Lasch 1978; Miller 1971). The desire to have even headier mystical moments led some to sample alternative religions for drug-free highs (Tipton 1982), at the same time that changed immigration laws had brought new spiritual leaders and their teachings to the United States (Melton 1993). These social changes—not the planets—aligned to enable Michael and Dick to draw on their own spiritual privilege to create Esalen.

Both Michael and Dick were aware of varied possibilities for personal and spiritual growth because of their elite educations at Stanford and their connections to networks of affluent seekers in the Bay Area. However, while their shared interests in spirituality and psychology led them to become friends, Esalen's two founders always had different ways of relating to people and somewhat different goals for the Institute. Friendship alone was not a stable foundation for their enterprise, although the creation narrative implied that it was.

Only a few years after Michael and Dick formally incorporated Esalen, George Leonard became Michael's closest friend and colleague (Leonard 1988:197–217). He supplanted Dick because of his relentless enthusiasm for the human potential movement and because he shared Michael's desire to make the Institute a force for cultural transformation. Dick described George and Michael's close relationship: "George came aboard with Mike in 1965. [He became] the primary partner of Michael, handling programs and media" (Price 1985).

Even before the Murphy compound and small hotel became Esalen, Dick and Michael had created an informal division of labor that reflected their different strengths and priorities. Michael represented their retreat center to the wider world, recruiting potential seminar and workshop leaders and encouraging media attention. Dick took care of Esalen's internal operations, dealing with budgets, maintenance, and the residents' interpersonal issues (Anderson 1983:49–50).

Michael viewed the Institute as a launching pad for spiritual practices and paranormal research that could lead to a more advanced, enlightened world. Dick saw Esalen as a place that could develop alternatives to Freudian or behavioral psychotherapy, while also providing an environment where temporary visitors healed their emotional wounds and fashioned new spiritual practices before they moved on. The two founders' differences became deeper over the years, and by the time that Dick died, in 1985, their interdependent personal and financial stakes in Esalen kept them together as much as their early friendship.

In the late 1960s, a new inheritance cemented Michael's role as the senior partner, while Dick became more marginal in making important decisions. Michael's grandmother bequeathed land parcels that were part of Esalen to Michael, his mother, his brother, and a number of other relatives (Anderson 1983:49–50, 235). Michael now owned segments of the property that the Institute had previously leased from his family.

Dick exercised his authority because he had cofounded the Institute, and he was personally close to the operations staff and massage crew members. He had introduced the Institute's signature Gestalt psychology programs and Fritz Perls to Esalen. His continued leadership role also reflected his financial contributions to physical improvements, publicity, and general maintenance during the Institute's first decade. Dick's father had released some jointly held stock so that it could serve as collateral for business loans and capital improvements that allowed Esalen to grow.

Michael and Dick founded Esalen at a historical moment when the spiritual marketplace was about to expand dramatically. However, without social support from influential figures and financial backing from wealthy donors, Esalen might have remained small and local. Social capital, connections with networks of individuals that furthered their projects, was an essential part of the Institute's success.

Because they knew other privileged seekers from Stanford and San Francisco, Michael and Dick were able to consult well-known men who had influenced American spirituality in the 1940s and 1950s. They relied heavily on Aldous Huxley's suggestions and introductions, although they met together with him only once, during his brief visit to Big Sur in 1962 (Kripal 2007a:86). They had more talks with Huxley's longtime comrade, Gerald Heard, who told them that their Institute *had* to happen. There was a "cosmic mandate" for Michael and Dick to proceed with their project (Anderson 1983:11–13).

In the late 1950s, a friend from San Francisco, Alan Watts (1973), had occasionally talked to small groups about God, Zen, and expanding consciousness at the Big Sur Gallery. He was an established writer on Asian religions, a radio personality, and a local Bay Area celebrity. Watts offered Michael and Dick advice and, more important, the mailing lists from his lectures and seminar series.

They also secured lists from Sequoia Seminars, a spiritual study group that was founded by a wealthy Stanford professor and his wife, who were also Heard's close friends (Markoff 2005:22–26). Their group discussed Asian spiritualities, paranormal phenomena like precognitions, and inclusive ecumenical Christianity, and they were delighted to help Michael and Dick start the Institute (Markoff 2005:21–23).

Beginning in the late 1940s, Sequoia Seminars communicated with similar groups in Southern California and with their counterparts on the East Coast. The East Coast seekers' networks included the founder of Xerox, the head of Fidelity Mutual in Boston, and other wealthy individuals. Many of them belonged to the Vedanta Society, founded by Swami Vivekananda, who had brought his personal version of Hinduism to the 1893 World's Parliament of Religions in Chicago (Miller 2005).

In Southern California, Huxley, Heard, and the writer Christopher Isherwood invited celebrities and rich businessmen to Huxley's home to explore Vedanta (Isherwood 1980; Miller 2005:84–85). During the 1950s, some very rich Southern California families interested in Vedanta and its offshoots even housed their own personal gurus to advise them about every aspect of their lives (Masson 1993).

The East and West Coast networks began to overlap in the 1960s because of easier air travel and the migration of capital to the West as the aerospace and entertainment industries expanded (Davis 1992). Laurance Rockefeller, one of the immensely wealthy grandsons of Standard Oil founder John D. Rockefeller, traveled in elite seekers' circles on both coasts, and, in the 1970s, he became Esalen's major external benefactor.

When Michael and Dick drove their pickup south from Big Sur, they traveled a well-charted social highway that linked Southern and Northern California's elite seekers and also connected with the East Coast. The informal networks of upper-class ascetics who had explored alternative spirituality for decades made it easier for them to found the Institute and to attract well-known speakers and seminar leaders from the beginning.

Esalen was by no means the sudden coincidence described by the creation narrative. It developed because two young men with extraordinary spiritual privilege brought together a growing supply of alternative spiritualities and personal growth psychologies, legitimated them with a doctrine about unlimited human potential that was connected to cosmic forces, and reached out to millions of men and women who also enjoyed some degree of spiritual privilege.

The Institute's almost immediate success was less a matter of synchronicity than the expansion of spiritual paths that had previously been available to relatively small numbers of highly privileged seekers. Social forces, not mystical influences, shaped Esalen's success.

Esalen Through the Decades: A Brief History

Michael and Dick took enormous personal risks and stepped completely out of their families' social orbits when they founded their small seminar center. Both were already in their thirties, without wives, children, or professions. In the late 1950s and early 1960s, young men of their means and talents were expected to be settled into careers and marriage by the end of their twenties (Anderson 1983:32). In their own lives, as well as through their pioneering center, the two founders seemed to usher in the future.

Their first informal seminars on spirituality or psychology drew a smattering of participants from established groups of Bay Area seekers (Markoff 2005:22–26). Skillful outreach and publicity, the breathtaking setting, and the growth of the 1960s quest culture all contributed to Esalen's sudden, rapid development as the flagship of the human potential movement.

In the 1960s and early 1970s, thousands of people passed through Esalen. Some were rich, others economically marginal, but they all were critical of mainstream social institutions and rules for behavior. Individuals who had been involved in the old networks of elite seekers came to Esalen, as did established spiritual leaders, psychologists, artists, and writers. Affluent younger boomers briefly joined the counterculture and took gap years during and after college, traveling to Big Sur to relax and explore diverse paths to personal fulfillment. Less prosperous visitors wandered down from the Big Sur hills or traveled there and paid for their sojourns by working in Esalen's kitchens or tending the gardens (Anderson 1983:239–240).

The Institute prospered for a time because of this free and discounted labor, visitors' fees, and generous donations from both longtime spiritual seekers and new constituents. Leaders like Fritz and Schutz cultivated wealthy California women who contributed support to Esalen, and both therapists bridged the semisacred gulf between professionals and clients (Temerlin and Temerlin 1980). A major Hollywood producer's widow and a beautiful Los Angeles real estate heiress made substantial donations. Money flowed into the Institute from other women with family fortunes founded on toys, department stores, coffee, and life insurance.

However, donations and fees could not support all of the ambitious projects that Michael and his close colleagues envisioned. Michael sought external funding on the East Coast, with the aid of the Twentieth Century Foundation's head, August Hecksher (Anderson 1983:123). George Leonard and George Brown, an academic who founded the Confluent Education Program at the University of California at Santa Barbara, worked with friends in the U.S. Office of Education to secure a Ford Foundation grant for the development of Esalen workshops and seminars that explored new approaches to teaching and learning.

As the Institute grew during the late 1960s, organizational differentiation was inevitable because of the expanded staff, greater public traffic, and increased national outreach. Formal and informal stratification clarified the boundaries between the inner circle composed of Michael, his comrades, and Dick; a second circle of influential teachers, spiritual mentors, and major donors; and a third circle of operations staff, work-study students, and bodyworkers. Some people had ties to more than one group, and there were shifting alliances among Esalen insiders. Nevertheless, there was an obvious hierarchy that reflected individuals' spiritual privilege and affected their power to help shape the Institute (Johnson 1992).

Michael made major decisions in consultation with Dick and George, after they received input from others at Esalen and outsiders whom they respected. When the two founders disagreed, they usually compromised. Because Michael, Dick, and their families owned the Institute and its land, the two founders always held ultimate power. With one or two exceptions like George, the trustees and officers that they appointed were almost always advisers rather than key decision makers.

Esalen's foundational doctrine implied that everyone should be equally free to pursue his or her human potential and connections to the cosmos, but the Institute was *never* an equalitarian community or a democracy. Different levels and combinations of spiritual privilege often determined someone's position in the informal hierarchy.

Michael and Dick enjoyed extraordinary spiritual privilege in terms of all four elements: spiritual affinities, religious and general cultural knowledge, connections with elite networks, and economic resources. Others members of Esalen's core might not have possessed all four elements to such a degree, but they usually demonstrated extraordinary strength in one or two areas. George, for example, was by no means wealthy. However, as a long-time senior editor of *Look*, he was crucial in bringing Esalen insiders into his loose social networks of media leaders and celebrities , as well as networks of other spiritual seekers.

The two founders assumed that almost every workshop leader, massage crew member, and building and grounds worker would eventually leave and spread the Institute's doctrines and practices to other venues (Carter 1997:68). Financial considerations motivated people to leave Big Sur and go back to school or enter the workforce, but at Esalen in the 1960s and early 1970s, the Institute's flexible rules made it plausible for all of its varied stakeholders to believe they might remain there permanently.

Michael and most of his inner circle paid little attention to the bodyworkers, operations staff, or hangers-on, so long as there were no rebellions or major problems. Dick was more engaged, but he usually focused his attention on pet projects and new enthusiasms. There was a profound social distance that separated Michael's Big House and Dick's Little House from the rustic cottages housing resident teachers and from the yurts, teepees, cabins, and crowded collective living spaces in the hills around the Institute. Both physical and social detachment insulated the founders and their inner circle from questions about power and ownership.

Staff members and bodyworkers who have been at Esalen for decades fondly remember the minimal organizational structure as a space for

Contemporary Esalen massage tables connect to the hot springs enclosure and overlook the Pacific. © Lori A. Lewis

extraordinary innovations. For example, the massage crew came together spontaneously at the hot springs in Esalen's first years, when people soaked and later massaged one another in the open air. They occasionally threw towels around themselves, but usually both practitioner and receiver were naked. Bernie Gunther (1971), a showman who borrowed shamelessly from his teachers Charlotte Selver (1979) and Ida Rolf (1978), organized the massage crew before he moved on to other things at Esalen and then to the Shree Rajneesh Ashram in India.

The grandest of all of the projects that Michael supported in the 1960s was a residential living program where twenty carefully selected fellows could work together for a year in order to develop every aspect of their potential. One of its leaders, a pioneering humanistic psychologist, described these seekers as "psychonauts" who conquered new dimensions of inner space, much like astronauts explored outer space (Bugenthal and Michael 1980). The projected budget was at least $150,000 in 1966 dollars, with a maximum of $60,000 generated by tuition from residential fellows. Esalen could not raise anything close to the additional $90,000 or more that was necessary to fund the project and to pay its well-known visiting faculty, although Michael approached more than thirty private foundations (Anderson 1983:123–125).

Although there were shortfalls, seventeen people participated in the first residential program, which was launched in the fall of 1966 and lasted for nine months. There were twenty participants the following year. Later programs became smaller and shorter before they were discontinued in 1971 (Kripal 2007a:167–168). Michael was disillusioned with the whole concept of advanced fellows at Esalen, the residential programs were costly, and Schutz, the program's leader, had become marginalized at the Institute. Moreover, from the beginning, Dick opposed the residential program because it was far too ambitious (Anderson 1983:127).

Other internal strains foreshadowed Esalen's diminished vitality and shrinking public influence. In the late 1960s and early 1970s, at least nine people closely associated with Esalen committed suicide. Four suicides occurred at or near the Institute, and the others were off the property. All of the deaths deeply affected Esalen's core members, staff, and bodyworkers (Anderson 1983:199–202, 234–237; Doyle 1981). In his personal journal, Esalen encounter leader John Heider (1996) wrote, "Too much suicide." After the wave of deaths, leaders toned down the intensity of their groups, and Esalen catalogues spoke forcefully about an ethic of self-awareness and self-responsibility at the Institute.

Fritz, who had goaded two despondent women to suicide, departed to his own Canadian institute in 1969 (Anderson 1983:199–203). Schutz, unhappy with his diminished influence, left in 1972. Michael also moved, although he continued to function as a principal in the Institute's governing circle. Encouraged by George and by former Episcopal bishop James Pike, of San Francisco's Grace Cathedral, Michael established an Esalen San Francisco branch on Union Street in the fall of 1967. Seminarians could now attend lectures, workshops, and encounter groups without going to Big Sur (Anderson 1983:147–160).

Although it was more accessible than the mother ship in Big Sur, Esalen San Francisco could not compete successfully against all of the nearby individual practitioners, alternative religions, personal growth organizations, and university extension programs. Moreover, factions from the Bay Area's radical political culture publicly sniped at Esalen San Francisco. Questions of racism surfaced in relation to staff pay and preferential treatment of white employees in Esalen's racial encounter project (Anderson 1983:195–198; Cobbs and Brown 1981). Feminists picketed the Institute's 1973 Spiritual Tyranny Conference in San Francisco, because no women were invited to be presenters or conveners (Anderson 1983:266–268).

In the wake of these conflicts, Michael retreated from the San Francisco branch and withdrew further from Big Sur in order to write his novel *Golf in the Kingdom* (1972) and to concentrate on his relationship with another privileged spiritual seeker, whom he married in 1972. He finally closed Esalen San Francisco in December of 1976 and moved its files to his house in Mill Valley, across the Bay from San Francisco. Dick tried his best to manage things at Big Sur.

Under Dick's stewardship, Esalen turned inward in the mid-1970s. Outreach, public relations, and the grandiose intellectual projects that Michael had envisioned almost vanished. The rustic buildings began to sag, and Esalen's residents and staff worked together with little or no guidance. Dick wanted to nurture a cohesive, albeit impermanent community dedicated to Gestalt awareness practice, and he invited like-minded individuals to come and work at Esalen (Price 1982).

Most massage crew members participated in Dick's Gestalt workshops and looked to him for individualized guidance. In spite of his regular exhortations to move on, they nevertheless constructed their lives around their work and spiritual practice at Esalen. Their children played together at the Institute's Gazebo Preschool and later attended local public schools or studied at home. When their children grew up, most of them became involved with bodywork, earning their livings by doing massage, teaching yoga, or facilitating ecstatic dance in Big Sur and other venues.

While Dick was in charge at Esalen, members of the operations staff were underpaid, sometimes unpaid, and often confused about their roles. For example, when someone asked for a regular salary in order to buy warm clothing, Dick paternally offered to purchase a woolen coat for her, while avoiding the issue of pay. Dick's leadership style reflected the priorities he placed on handling his own emotional troubles and seeking spiritual fulfillment. He left Esalen for three months in 1971 to stay in New York City and study Arica, a psycho-spiritual process that was developed by a charismatic leader, Claudio Naranjo.

When Dick went to New York, a clinical psychologist with a background in consulting and organizational development, Julian Silverman, became the director at Big Sur. Despite resistance from many old timers, he brought more explicit organizational arrangements and financial accountability to Esalen. After Dick's return, later in the year, there was a triumvirate of Dick and two senior directors that Michael trusted to implement ongoing plans for fiscal and organizational responsibility.

Then, in 1977, Dick and a number of staff members briefly became devotees of the Indian charismatic Bhagwan Shree Rajneesh (*Time* 1978). Shortly after the Rajneesh interlude, one codirector resigned from her post to concentrate on early childhood education at Esalen's Gazebo School. The psychologist who had reorganized Esalen's administration made plans to leave Big Sur. Seeking guidance, Dick persuaded his management team to consult a resident Esalen psychic and to take advice from the "Nine," a collection of spirits that the psychic channeled (Anderson 1983:302–305; Kripal 2007a:366–368). This strategy was brief and, to say the least, highly controversial among most of Esalen's residents and also Michael's circle in the Bay Area.

The Institute moved toward financial stability in the 1980s because Michael, his close comrades, and sympathetic Esalen residents came together to banish the Nine and to develop a relatively long-term organizational strategy. Affluent individuals who had come to Esalen since the 1960s pledged long-term loans. Nancy Lunney, who is now married to Gordon Wheeler, the Institute's current president, developed workshops and designed catalogues to attract a broader range of visitors and generate more income (Kripal 2007a:376–379). Moreover, the Institute gradually benefited from formal legitimation and an influx of new visitors after 1982, when the California Board of Registered Nursing and the California Medical Association certified some of its massage and personal growth programs, enabling participants to fulfill requirements for professional continuing-education units.

During this period of reorganization and increasing stability, Dick died, at age fifty-five, in November of 1985. A falling rock hit him while he hiked in Hot Springs Canyon. His widow, Christine, stayed close to the Institute. She served on the Board of Trustees during the late 1980s and 1990s, and she continues to offer occasional Gestalt workshops in the twenty-first century. The power at Esalen, however, shifted even more significantly toward Michael and his inner circle.

When Dick died, the massage crew and a number of other old timers grieved deeply. Many of them still believe that Dick's vision and his contributions to the Institute have never been fully acknowledged, although there was a four-day Esalen celebration to honor his memory in November 2010 (Carter 1997:68). One of the crew's longtime members observed, "He [was] truly a leader, loved, respected, a spiritual master with compassion."

Michael briefly moved back to Big Sur from the Bay Area after Dick's death. He attempted to become an active manager, while ceding most strategic decisions to Steven Donovan, who became the next Esalen president. The transition was eased because, shortly before he died, Dick had agreed to a second leadership triad, with Michael and Steven.

Steven was another Esalen leader with substantial spiritual privilege. He was a skilled manager with an M.B.A. from Columbia University, who had embarked on his own spiritual quests and belonged to networks of elite spiritual seekers. However, he lacked Dick's historical connection to the Institute and its longtime operations staff and bodyworkers. Dick had been comfortable making ad hoc decisions about almost everything, and the mutual financial obligations he had discussed with people living or working at Esalen were at best casual. Steven had to sort those out.

One of his first tasks was to renegotiate the complicated informal arrangements and promises that Dick had made to both Esalen's residents and its nonpaying visitors with decades-long connections to the Institute. Some of them lived on property owned by Esalen or the Murphy family trusts, others traded services for dining-room meal privileges, and still others simply felt that they were entitled to access to the hot springs and meals at any time because of their relationships with Dick (Kripal 2007a:391–392). Negotiations took more than three years, and a number of bodyworkers and staff still resent them. Describing that period, one Esalen old-timer said, "*everything* here is nebulous, conditional, lacking uniformity, relational, and personality driven" (Carter 1997:70).

Because they were central to the Institute's identity and attracted professionals to workshops that provided continuing-education units, the massage crew and bodyworkers bargained from strong positions. However, the new director also made deals with old-timers who had fewer resources and options (Kripal 2007a:389–390). Michael had asked Steven to take care of them. And he worked compassionately to find places at Esalen for people who would have had trouble functioning beyond Big Sur.

Contemporary operations staff and work-study students describe half a dozen emotionally fragile people who found essential social support at Esalen and who have continued to work and live there for more than thirty years because of Steven's and Michael's flexibility. Their supervisors adjust to their moods as much as possible, silently acknowledging decades of loyalty to the Institute.

Donovan brought both his money and his business expertise to the table. He was one of the founders of the Starbucks Coffee empire, where he had already learned to negotiate delicately with old-timers. While shepherding the Institute, he worked half time in Big Sur and also maintained his day job in San Francisco, transforming Peets Coffee from a local Berkeley tradition into a lucrative, nationally recognized chain that competed with Starbucks.

A talented administrator and fund-raiser, Steven steered the Institute away from demoralization and debt. When he stepped down, early in 1993, Esalen was $500,000 in the black (Kripal 2007a:389, 432–433). After he left, Michael tried to spend most of his time in Big Sur, and he managed the Institute for about a year afterward. Even in this relatively calm period, however, he was unsuited for day-to-day leadership. His handpicked successor had little success, and she had bitter disagreements with various staff members, who characterized her as a "drama-queen figurehead."

During the "drama queen's" reign, the massage crew organized the Esalen Massage and Bodywork Association, which became an official group in the late 1990s. The EMBA now negotiates with Esalen's Board of Trustees for wages, living arrangements at Esalen, off-site living allowances, and the freedom to develop its own outreach programs.

In the mid-1990s, Dick's son, David, returned to Big Sur, and he soon became Esalen's operations office, sharing day-to-day management decisions with the Institute's personnel director. There was another new president, whose primary task was to raise funds in the wake of the 1998 El Niño storms that virtually destroyed the site of the hot-springs baths (Kripal 2007a:236–237).

At the turn of the twenty-first century, Michael began to consider his own death and Esalen's future. He briefly talked about George as his obvious successor, although George was older than Michael and already in poor health. Then he recruited new leadership, Gordon Wheeler, who had recently married Nancy Lunney, the woman who had scheduled workshops for four decades (Kripal 2007a:377–378, 437–438). Gordon first came to Big Sur because of his work as a Gestalt psychologist, and he joined Michael's inner circle as his relationship with Nancy deepened. Moreover, he brought his own economic resources to help sustain Esalen.

Gordon restructured the Institute's internal organization to include clearly delineated departments for operations and facilities, guest services, finance, fund-raising, and community services. The organizational changes remain true to Esalen's original traditions of creating a space where work becomes a meaningful vocation. Job descriptions for every post stress empathy, common sense, and self-awareness, along with more typical professional qualifications.

He has also underscored the importance of Esalen's commitment to draw together public service and spirituality. He and Nancy attend national and international meetings that position Esalen in international groups committed to environmental sustainability, social justice, and world peace.

The Institute's Board of Trustees expanded to include representatives from the community of operations staff and bodyworkers. Michael and a few core members of the Center for Theory and Research, however, still chart the Institute's broad course, although Gordon tactfully redefines goals and relationships within and outside Big Sur.

Generation Gaps

Gordon identifies with the generation of boomers who first flocked to Esalen in the mid-1960s. However, he struggles to make the Institute attractive to younger constituents, as well as to boomers who are now much older and more affluent than they were during the Institute's glory days. There is some current tension between sustaining Esalen's core doctrine and aesthetics of simplicity and appealing to twenty-first-century tastes in style and spirituality. Nothing illustrates this dissonance more than questions about food in the dining room, its preparation, and its relationships to social responsibility.

Michael has often discussed the importance of "conscious eating" (Leonard and Murphy 1995:135). However, "conscious eating" has different meanings for different people in terms of the relative importance that they attach to their food's simplicity, sensuality, or environmental sustainability. Staff and work-study students raise thorny political and spiritual questions about whether it is acceptable to eat meat or even cooked food of any kind. Two contrasting cookbooks illustrate how eating and personal style have changed at the Institute, although neither book requires that one choose between minimal and indulgent consumption or between vegan and omnivorous eating.

When Esalen turned inward under Dick's leadership in the 1970s, his wife, Christine, edited and self-published a small paperbound collection of Esalen community recipes, *Food for the Senses* (1980), with charming hand-drawn illustrations, instructions, and anecdotes from residents and longtime workshop leaders. Twenty-six years later, a well-known cookbook publisher released a former Esalen chef's book in a handsome format with glossy photographs of tempting dishes like pecan-encrusted chicken (Cascio 2006). The dramatic contrasts between the early 1980's *Food for the Senses* and the twenty-first century *Esalen Cookbook* indicate some of the ways that Esalen's original constituents have become more obviously privileged. Younger guests and work-study students, however, often ache for more simplicity and earthiness, as they imagine Esalen during its early years.

This Buddha is one of many different material signs of Esalen's commitment to spiritual inclusiveness. © Lori A. Lewis

Like all religious organizations, Esalen faces the problem of building new generations of leaders, members, and constituents. Many of the children who grew up around the Institute have moved on, and the younger staff members are relatively recent arrivals. Because it is not directly tied to present-day political or cultural movements, Esalen fails to excite college students and other young adults in the ways it did in the 1960s and early 1970s.

Generational divides deepen the schism between CTR members and the other two subgroups at the Institute. Almost everyone at the core of the CTR is past sixty, and many of Michael's close advisers at Esalen and in his broader networks are in their seventies and eighties. This disconnect is almost immediately visible in the Esalen dining room, where work-study students and staff cook, serve, and wash dishes for older guests. On the decks surrounding the hot springs, massage students, apprentices, and younger EMBA members knead sagging flesh. Even Peyote, the Gazebo School's gentle pony, grayed along with the rest of Esalen and died in 2007 at age twenty-nine.

Work-study students and younger staff members joke about the generational divide, replicating some of the gentle rebellions that characterized the first generation of Esalen seminarians, teachers, and workers. They smoke weed, ingest magic mushrooms, try out Tantra, and experiment with casual sex as their forefathers and foremothers did. They also critique office politics in guest operations and the apparently arbitrary regulations at their work-sites and in their living quarters. They also feed on the decades of resent-ment about the CTR and Michael's privileged inner circle

So long as they do their thirty-two-hour-a-week jobs like dishwashing and laundry and attend the workshops and counseling sessions designed for them, the work-study students' month-long passages through Esalen are smooth. Some remain as extended students for a few more months or longer, and they may be reassigned to pleasanter tasks, such as doing office work or assisting at the preschool. Occasionally, work-study students with credentials for jobs such as computer repair or early childhood teaching are recruited to become regular paid staff members.

Until a few years ago, Michael occasionally led workshops that fused golf with spirituality and meditation. Avid golfers traveled to Big Sur, lured by Michael's reputation as a novelist and the Shivas Irons Society, which formed as a response to his second novel, *The Kingdom of Shivas Irons* (1997), a book that addressed esoteric phenomena, Zen, and golf.

One work-study student's observations about an Esalen golf workshop capture the resentment of privilege and hierarchy that is the product of decades of differentiation at the Institute. It is a visceral response to the ways that spiritual privilege and its rewards are unevenly distributed:

> Golf in the Kingdom [workshop] was like a bunch of aliens had dropped out of the sky and showed up in the Esalen kitchen. They would have golf early in the morning. They had tee times in Monterey. So we would be told that we had to have nuts and breads and fruits ready for these rich people.
>
> Guys in polo shirts and chino slacks, and it was just different . . . it was almost like Golf in the Kingdom just didn't fit in with Esalen. They were thoroughly enjoying the Esalen experience, but they felt that people [staff and bodyworkers] isolated them.

The critical work-study student enjoyed his own version of spiritual privi-lege, so he could drop out of the workforce, live at Esalen for a few months, and cultivate his emotional and spiritual growth. Nevertheless, he chafed at the golfers' obvious affluence and expectations of deference. After the stu-dent left Big Sur and looked back on his months at the Institute, however, he recognized mutual bonds of seekership that connected him with other staff and with visitors, even the golfers. Like many of the polo-shirted sportsmen, he has returned to Big Sur from time to time over the past several years. As he grew older and more economically secure, the young man came to believe that Esalen offered unforgettable lessons to him and to all who are open to them, regardless of the levels of spiritual privilege that they bring with them.

Unlike people who live or work at the Institute, casual visitors often depart unaware of the CTR or its arcane theories about evolutionary human potential, although most are intrigued by the implicit doctrines of core sparks of divinity and personal possibilities. The extraordinary landscape, the massage and bodyworkers, the staff, and the workshop leaders enable them to develop more self-awareness and add to the spiritual privilege that initially motivated them to visit Esalen. Those rewards are more than enough.

Esalen provides space to enact and amplify spiritual privilege. Almost no one has ever departed from Big Sur with diminished spiritual privilege. The dynamics of an individual's privilege can change, however, as someone's dramatic mystical experiences or newly forged relationships with important figures and networks in the spiritual marketplace add to their existing privilege, although they may sacrifice income to stay at Esalen for several months.

The Institute's remarkable early impact reflected its leaders' determination to offer innovative spiritual options to every American. Esalen transformed the religious marketplace because it developed and spread new combinations of spiritual practices and techniques for personal growth. Over the years, thousands of people have passed through Big Sur and come away with new possibilities and enhanced spiritual privilege.

Spiritual Privilege and Personal Transformation

Esalen's founders and most of their close comrades enjoyed enough economic security to devote their lives to spiritual and personal transformations. They have relied on combinations of family resources and fees for teaching, writing, and counseling about self-actualization. The Institute's first generation helped found informal guilds, formal professional organizations, and alternative institutions to maximize their impact on society and to share emotional support and financial resources with other spiritual entrepreneurs.

Different kinds of guilds and institutionalized groups of privileged spiritual practitioners have existed for centuries in varied social and historical contexts. In ancient Greece, Egypt, and Rome, magicians organized professional associations to support one another, share techniques, and enlarge their clienteles (Durkheim 1915:43-45). They offered their patrons rituals and spells for earthly rewards such as love or healing. Priests in the same societies, however, elicited more extensive commitment from their loyal followers than magicians, because they went beyond solutions to worldly problems and grounded their magic in comprehensive doctrines that explained the sacred and the afterlife (Weber [1922]1964:20–31). The priests set themselves apart from the surrounding culture and entirely dedicated themselves to their spiritual vocations (Stark 2001:44–45).

Theorists, teachers, and practitioners involved with Esalen differ from the ancient priests because they neither separate themselves from society nor develop formal, inflexible hierarchies. The Institute's inner circle has encouraged spiritual specialists such as humanistic psychologists and holistic health practitioners to organize their own professional guilds and to serve consumers in the wider society, much as magicians did in the ancient world. Many of these professionals and their clients return regularly to Big Sur for social support and to further embed their practices in the Institute's doctrines of individual divinity and limitless possibilities. Esalen thus brings spiritual meaning to contemporary, results-oriented magic, blurring the practical boundaries between religion and magic.

Since the early 1970s, after Fritz and Schutz left Big Sur, Michael and his comrades have emphatically cautioned seekers to trust their own intellectual and emotional responses to every spiritual path and mentor. They urge people to try something else if a leader or practice feels too demanding or problematic in any way. Over and over, Michael, Dick, and George asserted, "Transformative practices are best guided by several mentors rather than a single, all-powerful guru" (Leonard and Murphy 1985:17).

By advocating omnivorous spirituality, they have promoted loyalty to the Institute and its foundational doctrines, rather than to any single individual or spiritual path. Changing allegiances and personal priorities are not defections in this schema. Instead, they are extensions of Esalen's doctrine and practices. The emphasis on choice and combination meshes with the Institute's commitment to spread spiritual privilege as widely as possible. Spiritual privilege is now part of the consumer culture that almost every American can sample in some way, as this seeker's reminiscence suggests:

> Since my twenties, I've been walking what Joseph Campbell calls "the pathless path," cutting through teachings and traditions, trusting personal experience. . . . As with designer pizza, people can mix n' match, create their own, or stick with straight tomato. (Davidson 2007:245)

Chic pizza is not available to everyone, but most Americans can make some choices about toppings on their mass-produced pies. The widespread sampling and combinations of doctrines and practices mark the diffusion of spiritual privilege that began at Esalen in the mid-1960s. However, when Michael and Dick started the Institute, access was far more limited, and most Americans had not yet tasted a wide range of "sacred toppings."

Democratizing Privilege

Throughout history, full- and part-time spiritual innovators have usually been social elites, who were able to explore religious alternatives because of their wealth or special status. Siddhartha Gautama, known as Buddha, represents the ultimate privileged seeker who founded his own religion. As a young man, he gave up his personal fortune and joined a wandering group of ascetic monks. His approach to spirituality closely resembled Esalen's doctrine, because Buddha viewed all deities as worldly illusions, and he sought sparks of divinity in everyone and everything. After attaining his own enlightenment and taking the name Buddha, he founded a new traveling order (Collins 1998:228).

The first generation of itinerant Buddhists relied on donations from members of the upper class (Lester 1993:866–867). Buddha himself was a prince, and fifty-five of the first sixty members in his original coterie also came from prominent families (Lester 1993:867). Other elites who resembled the monks in terms of their education and class positions were drawn to early Buddhist philosophy, rituals, and meditations (Stark 2001:44–50). They did not need a supernatural being to supply them with material benefits but instead sought more abstract doctrines that offered meaningful explanations of life on earth and affirmations of their personal possibilities (Stark 2001:10).

Michael and Dick used their affluence to change the spiritual landscape in America and in Western Europe, whereas Buddha initially set aside all of his riches and social power in order to uncover great truths about the cosmos and to experience personal enlightenment. In contrast, Esalen's two founders were content to explore and share spiritual truths that others had already discovered. They believed that spreading their discoveries as widely as possible was inseparable from their own enlightenment.

Early Buddhism in India unfolded thousands of years and thousands of miles away from California in the 1960s, but the story of Buddha's life illustrates the deep connections between social power and spiritual privilege that had characterized most quests for individual and collective spiritual fulfillment in the East and the West until Michael and Dick founded the Institute (Stark 1996:29–48). They broke away from the centuries-old elite monopolies of spiritual privilege and the closed networks of spiritual seekers. Michael and Dick democratically shared the possibilities to select, revise, and combine varied practices for religious and personal growth by providing access and encouragement for every American to fulfill his or her full spiritual and human potential.

When they first began to envision their small center for spiritual and personal exploration, Michael and Dick sought guidance from the well-known philosopher and novelist Aldous Huxley (Anderson 1983:10–12). Over many years, Huxley had introduced small groups of rich, famous, or socially influential Californians to new kinds of spiritual experiences and mind-altering drugs (Isherwood 1980:201–202, 219–220; Miller 2005:85–87). He had also counseled a number of accomplished young men, like Michael and Dick, holding fast to his conviction that all spiritual advancement rests on the efforts of a select minority of highly privileged seekers.

The writer and philosopher Aldous Huxley encouraged elites to sample alternative spirituality and mind-enhancing drugs. (Center for the Study of Democratic Institutions Collection at the University of California at Santa Barbara Davidson Library)

In the early 1960s, about two years before Michael and Dick founded the Institute, Huxley met regularly with Tim Leary, the former Harvard professor who soon became America's best-known advocate for psychedelics, especially LSD (Leary 1983:40–43). As Huxley and Leary ingested hashish and hallucinogens together, Leary disclosed his desire to make mind-altering substances accessible to ordinary people. Huxley attempted to dissuade him from tendering powerful drugs to a mass audience. He said, "In the past, this [type of] spiritual knowledge has been guarded in privacy, passed on in the subdued, metaphorical obscurantism of scholars, mystics, and artists" (Leary 1983:44).

However, Huxley also acknowledged that psychoactive drugs might bring about vast positive social changes, leading to the evolution of collective human potential. He suggested a middle ground, urging Leary to quietly search for socially and politically important advocates. Later, those spiritually and psychologically evolved individuals might spread the word to wider audiences. Huxley asserted, "These are evolutionary matters. They cannot be rushed. Work privately. Initiate artists, writers, poets, jazz musicians, elegant courtesans, painters, and rich bohemians. And they'll initiate the intelligent rich. That's how everything of culture and beauty and philosophic freedom has been passed down" (Leary 1983:44). Despite Huxley's strong recommendations that he focus on privileged spiritual seekers, Leary soon promoted LSD indiscriminately, dreaming that he could spread peace, love, and instant mystical experiences by supplying every American with a tab of acid.

Huxley offered similar advice to Dick when they corresponded about the possibility of developing a spiritual retreat in Big Sur. Michael and Dick first sought out influential patrons who were part of Huxley's social networks, inviting well-known intellectuals and wealthy spiritual seekers to attend their seminars at Big Sur Hot Springs. However, they soon reached for much broader support, as the expansion of higher education and the spread of economic security produced new cohorts of middle-class spiritual seekers who were no longer satisfied with their parents' faiths (Roof 1999).

During Esalen's first year, Michael courted reporters, inviting them to Big Sur to write about the new possibilities that the Institute offered ordinary Americans. And, when George became Michael's closest friend, a few years later, he made sure that Michael and Esalen appeared in *Look* features about "turned-on" Californians (Leonard 1966, 1988). Because of their efforts, the Institute became a resource for writers and reporters looking for colorful stories.

Although they have intentionally reached beyond networks of elite spiritual seekers, Michael and his circle have always been somewhat isolated by the privilege that they rarely acknowledge. They have defined themselves as nonconformists and iconoclasts, rather than as entitled seekers, because they have renounced some of their possibilities for wealth and political power.

First, second, and even third generations of Esalen insiders identify themselves publicly and privately with artists, intellectuals, and poets, rather than with their affluent relatives and friends. This bohemian ethos allows them to think of themselves as cultural rebels and to downplay the entitlements of money or education that have made it emotionally and materially possible for them to reject conventional careers and pursue spiritual vocations.

Dynamics of Privilege

A wide variety of contemporary Americans, ranging from full-time religious devotees and professionals to casual dabblers, also enjoy some degree of spiritual privilege that they may not fully acknowledge to themselves or others. An individual's privilege reflects the intersection of the desire and personal ability to pursue spiritual solutions in daily life with the social and economic resources that empower active seekership.

An expanded definition of spiritual privilege: *Spiritual privilege is an individual's ability to devote time and resources to select, combine, and revise his or her personal religious beliefs and practices over the course of a lifetime. It is shaped by a mixture of four attributes—affinity for supernatural meanings, experiences, and explanations; cultural resources that include broad education and more explicit religious knowledge; participation in supportive social networks of like-minded spiritual seekers; and economic wherewithal. Possibilities to enact spiritual privilege increase in societies that encourage religious pluralism.*

The concept of spiritual privilege reflects some of the sociologist Pierre Bourdieu's (2005) more general ideas about cultural capital and its accumulation. Knowledge about religion and spirituality is one element of cultural capital, a classification that includes language, education, taste, and other significant markers of status within a society (Verter 2003).

Different aspects of someone's spiritual privilege can be placed in two related categories: cultural resources and social/economic assets. The cultural resources are individual affinities for religious meanings and sensations, along with more general personal knowledge that is derived from education and social interactions. In the lives of real people like Michael and Dick, cultural resources are intertwined with the social/economic assets of interpersonal networks and economic wherewithal. However, consideration of cultural and socioeconomic assets as independent categories illuminates the different ways that some degree of spiritual privilege can be part of most Americans' lives, regardless of their educations, incomes, or occupations.

Someone may have few material resources or little education, for example, but enjoy a great deal of spiritual privilege because of personal affinity for religious experiences and contacts with networks of likeminded seekers. An affinity for spiritual experiences and ideas, the element of spiritual privilege that often defines charismatic leaders and totally engaged seekers, is not necessarily tied to economic or cultural resources (Orsi 2005). In fact, some contemporary American spiritual leaders like the famous channeler JZ Knight (2004) boast about their early poverty and lack of education.

People who are highly sensitive to spiritual ways of looking at the world and who regularly have direct experiences with powerful supernatural influences are known as spiritual virtuosi (Weber [1922] 1964:20–31,162). These virtuosi are uncommon, but other spiritual seekers with less sensitivity to the sacred share some of their sustained desire to discover and nurture their own personal sensations of powerful supernatural forces.

At Esalen, almost all residents and many visitors describe mystical moments that they encounter in their daily routines, as well as in religious practice. Alone and in the company of others, they strive for transcendent feelings that remove them from their everyday lives. They remember the feelings later and can re-experience them at other times and in other places (McGuire 2008). Once they discover powerful rewards such as trances, enhanced physical powers, or a dramatic sense of oneness with the universe, they can recapture the feeling and enlarge their capacities for spiritual experience even more. Affinities for spiritual experience lead to rewards that lead to greater affinities for spiritual experience on a potentially endless trajectory of transcendence.

Religious leaders such as clergy or charismatics usually develop their innate capacity for spiritual experience during their childhoods (Weber [1922] 1964:20–31, 62–63). Over the years, their experiences become more intense and rewarding as they nurture them through daily practice. Even before they founded the Institute, Michael and Dick occasionally rose beyond their mundane lives through spiritual practice, emotionally intense group encounters, and the use of mind-altering drugs. Later on, they did so more frequently. Discussing his lifelong dedication to daily practice, Michael playfully observed, "If you sit in meditation as much as I did, you could almost say by the law of averages, you're bound to have an epiphany now and then" (Schwartz 1995:82).

Workshops, rituals, study groups, books, seminars, and websites can provide seekers with both spiritual experience and religious capital—cultural knowledge that increases their familiarity with many spiritual options and piques their desires to explore new doctrines and practices (Verter 2003:151–152). At Esalen, the massage crew and operations staff members accumulate cultural and religious capital that is often quite different from CTR members' theoretical understanding of evolutionary human potential. The individuals who are deeply involved with either bodywork or operations have stores of specialized information regarding things like natural healing or influences of the moon on people and plants that both augment their general spiritual privilege and fuel their desire for more knowledge and spiritual experience.

Economic resources are extremely important to spiritual privilege because they often determine which networks people will join and the kinds of cultural resources they bring and take away from Esalen. Financial security makes it easier to devote time to pursue the development of full human potential, and it also contributes to someone's confidence that life on Earth can produce immeasurable rewards. Therefore, affluent people are better equipped to explore diverse alternative spiritual paths and to join with others in their searches. Their economic resources enable them to pursue varied spiritualities, to change directions if they wish, and to diversify their commitments to numerous religious perspectives and practices (Iannaccone 1995).

As we noted earlier, middle- and upper-class Americans are particularly likely to be interested in alternative spirituality and in established religions that focus on ephemeral spiritual essences (Stark 2001:9–30). Affluent, educated parents can offer their children access to cultural and religious opportunities and to social networks of people who are equally empowered. For example, their fathers' wealth and cultural knowledge enabled Michael and Dick to attend Stanford, where they explored philosophy, comparative religion, and psychology in classes and campus activities, adding to their cultural capital. During their university years and, later, in the wider Bay Area, their families' financial help and their own elite educational backgrounds enabled the two young men to join informal networks of affluent, highly educated spiritual seekers like themselves. Their trust in the amorphous sparks of divinity within everyone reflected the self-confidence that flowed from their families' economic comfort, their own social skills, and their families' great expectations for them (Coles 1977). They could easily believe that everything in their lives would eventually turn out for the best, because they had the material resources to ride out difficulties and explore different possibilities.

Social Class and Spiritual Privilege

The people dedicated to the CTR and its vision for humanity follow a Western historical tradition of rational sacrifice that does not require total rejection of their material resources and comfort (Stark 2003:7). And people in the other parts of Esalen—the EMBA and operations—also make some sacrifices without foregoing many earthly delights.

The Esalen insiders' faith in themselves and in their futures connects to but remains separate from their social class. Throughout the Institute, almost everyone has an intuitive understanding of the sociological maxim that there is no absolute empirical measure of social class in the United States. In fact, many people at Esalen believe that an individual's social class primarily reflects self-definition. Class, however, is grounded in material resources and, like spiritual privilege, is an interactive mixture of economic assets, cultural capital, social networks, personal preferences, and future prospects (Wright 1997).

Generally, occupation is the first and most important element that defines someone's social class. Income, another important part of social class, is tied to occupation. Invested wealth that generates income, however, may make it possible to forgo a job or to take one that offers minimal financial compensation, as Michael and some members of his inner circle have. Education is strongly related to occupation and income, and it also connects to more individual but nevertheless class-related cultural elements such as knowledge about comparative religion or tastes in art or music or sports. What people buy, how they spend their leisure time, and what they hope for themselves and their children usually signify their educational levels and their aspirations, along with their material resources (Brooks 2001).

Whatever their occupation, income, and education, most Americans see themselves as part of the broad middle class. Almost everyone who lives, works, or visits the Institute defines himself or herself as middle or upper middle class even if he or she comes from an upper-class family or earns millions of dollars yearly. "Wealthy," "rich," and "upper class" are terms that sometimes imply arrogance and hierarchy, and they do not mesh with Esalen's foundational assumption that everyone has prospects for spiritual and personal growth, although their abilities vary.

Esalen's rustic West Coast location distanced it from the established American upper class during the 1960s, although a member of the Eastern establishment, Laurance Rockefeller, helped support the Institute for decades. In 1962, when Michael and Dick began their project, a national

Protestant elite on the East Coast still dominated American economic and political life (Baltzell 1964; Domhoff 1974; Mills 1956). They were the nucleus of the hidden networks of seekers that had explored alternative religions and philosophies for more than a century.

However, despite their apparent cultural power in the late 1950s, the old American upper class was already giving way to both a new technocracy and an emerging global group of far wealthier elites (Brooks 2001:29–30). California's rising networks of moneyed seekers with ties to international finance supported Esalen and other new centers of spiritual privilege.

Although Michael and his extended family own hundreds of acres in and around Big Sur and also have other sources of investment income, he still thinks of himself as upper middle class because of his distance from the East Coast Protestant establishment of this youth (Schwartz 1995; Tompkins 1976). Albert, another of the four Esalen men who are the subjects of the next chapter, has almost no personal wealth, but he also defines himself as upper middle class because of his own educational achievements and his father's respected professional role as a physicist. Throughout Esalen, even people whose incomes are close to the poverty line believe that they belong to the middle class. A few of them expect generous bequests in the near future, but others see themselves as middle class because of their faith in a generally benevolent universe.

People who center their lives at Esalen—CTR members, bodyworkers, and operations staff—all share a common sense of entitlement, an important psychological similarity among Americans who perceive that they are well off (Coles 1977). Entitlement involves feeling that financial security is not problematic and that life will ultimately provide happiness in spite of occasional setbacks (Coles 1977:363–364). This sense of security is related to but distinct from social class, and people who cultivate their inner divinity and emotional potential at Esalen, in the aisles of bookstores, and elsewhere believe that they are entitled to meaningful, joyful lives and that they will attain their entitlements. Faith in an inalienable right to spiritual and personal fulfillment is the foundation of spiritual privilege at Esalen and in contemporary America.

Privilege to Grow

Anne, a woman who had once been part of the massage crew, sometimes visits her old friends at Esalen. In stark contrast to Michael and many others at the Institute, she can barely scrape together money for her essential prescription medication and other necessities: her friends help pay for her medical care. However, she is also spiritually privileged, and she makes sure to read Jung and the Greek myths regularly in order to expand her soul. Although she bemoans living on the edge of poverty, Anne still sees herself as entitled to spiritual and personal fulfillment. Like Anne, most people at Esalen define their privilege as having the resources to maximize personal possibilities and not as financial abundance or social recognition.

Nevertheless, money is still a persistent, vexing issue for many people who are closely associated with the Institute. Unequal economic resources play out most dramatically in the strained relationships between the CTR's core members and the small band of artisans and workers who created their own informal community at the Institute in the 1960s and early 1970s, with the hope of remaining in Big Sur for life. Neither Mike nor Dick wanted anyone to live indefinitely at the Institute, and Dick compared Esalen to a greenhouse where plants could be nurtured in order to bloom in distant gardens (Carter 1997:68).

Yet, a few dozen Esalen pioneers still tend the gardens, fix leaks, lead occasional workshops, and perform other tasks. They live on site or close by. These longtime community members supplement their meager incomes with housing arrangements at Esalen and with assistance from affluent friends with historic ties to the Institute. Although they are often poor enough to qualify for government assistance, like the old massage crew hand Anne, the longtime community members enjoy the rare privilege of devoting their lives to pursue spiritual and personal growth in Big Sur.

All of Esalen's most committed people—the community residents, operations staff, EMBA bodyworkers, and core members at the Center for Theory and Research— assume that they possess rights, perhaps even obligations, to pursue their personal growth and spiritual development. Residents and visitors alike endorse equal opportunities for self-actualization for millionaires and for the merely middle class, for women and for men, for heterosexuals and for others, and for whites and for the very small number of minorities who visit Esalen. Easy camaraderie, casual use of first names, and Esalen's informal dress code of simple, natural-fiber clothing symbolize the Institute's equalitarian ethic.

Despite these democratic intentions, the veneer of equality chips quickly. At the end of a workshop, someone looks at her battered Timex while another woman checks a solid gold Rolex. In a casual dining-room conversation between two forty-something men, one describes enjoyable tennis games on public courts near his home. The other, seeking a common bond with his lunch partner, responds enthusiastically, "Yes! We have a champion-ship north/south tennis court at our house." A member of Michael's inner circle speaks disparagingly of the bodyworkers at the EMBA and their criti-cisms of the invitational conferences at the CTR. He asks me, "Would you want the gardeners to govern the university?"

In order to promote wider access to Esalen, there is institutionalized short- and medium-term support for less advantaged seekers, who neverthe-less resent the obvious class inequalities at the Institute. Esalen offers partial scholarships; very basic, relatively inexpensive sleeping bag housing options for visiting seminarians; and work-study programs of one to three months. These opportunities make the Institute available to a wider range of people, some of them younger than thirty years old. Despite their vocal resentment, individuals who stretch their finances to participate in a few months of work-study or attend a week of workshops are still privileged because they, like Anne and other old Esalen hands, hold rich visions of their own spiritual possibilities and personal transformation.

Gender and Spiritual Privilege

Women and men alike enjoy access to spiritual privilege in varied contexts. Men, however, have dominated Esalen's leadership and the CTR because of historic advantages that continue to affect life at the Institute. Women are the majority of participants in Esalen workshops and make up most of the rank and file in almost every mainstream and alternative religion (Miller and Stark 2002). Men, however, perform leadership roles in nearly all religions and at the Institute because of their greater access to economic and political power in the wider society and their historic roles as spiritual leaders.

Michael, Dick, and their comrades created Esalen—its implicit doctrine, formal organization, and public offerings—without recognizing that women might have different priorities. As the Institute grew, most of the women who lived and worked there gravitated to massage or bodywork like ecstatic dance and sensory awareness or worked in guest services, on the grounds, and in the dining hall. There was no formal division of labor based on gen-der, but power at Esalen remained in the hands of Michael, Dick, and their mostly male comrades.

Through the 1960s, men like Alan Watts (1973) or Aldous Huxley shaped the social networks that explored alternative spirituality. Until the early 1970s and the rise of the second wave of American feminism, few people inside or outside Esalen questioned the fact that men led the Institute and most of its workshops, because men were central to almost every other spiritual venue, both mainstream and alternative. The gap between men's power and women's participation unfolded at Big Sur and in the ways that Esalen's public outreach almost always highlighted men's contributions. For example, men wrote sixteen of the seventeen books published in the short-lived Esalen/ Viking series between 1969 and 1975 (Kripal 2007a:527–528). No one seemed to care that there was only one female author in the series and that men represented the Institute to the public in print and in person.

Gender roles at Esalen continue to reflect the Institute's early division of labor, as well as the ongoing financial and cultural inequalities in the wider society. Men steer the CTR, and women are still most active in bodywork. Although Gordon has worked to make people at the Institute more sensitive to differentiation, men's advantage is still a subtle, complicated dimension of spiritual privilege at Esalen, as it is in other religious contexts (McGuire 2008:159–184).

Because the founding generation of men assumed that deep down *everyone* could cultivate divine sparks and maximize his or her full potential, women were always included in the Institute's ventures. However, the founders collaborated with comrades and mentors to create practices and spiritual doctrines that mirrored their own concerns, rather than those of most of the women who also lived and worked at the Institute. Thus, for example, the CTR and Michael's earlier inner circle rarely dealt with questions about children or familial spiritual practices or the ways that ideas about dance and massage might add to theories about evolutionary human potential.

Golf, tennis, running and other sports are essential elements of Michael's spiritual vision, and they exemplify the ways that the innocent implementation of gender advantage still frames many aspects of the Institute. During the 1970s, there was a short-lived Sports Center at Big Sur and an Esalen Athletic Club in San Francisco (Anderson 1983:259–262; Kripal 2007a:285). Although these departments quickly closed, beginning in the 1970s and into the present, men have usually led the workshops that deal with active sports. Michael tied sport and spirituality together when he asserted, "Success in sport elicits inner harmony" (Murphy 1974:7). While there is now far more equality in sport than there was in the 1960s, it is still widely perceived as a male domain, and it exemplifies the subtle distribution of men's power at Esalen.

Sexual experimentation with different partners and different positions at Esalen was another reflection of gender advantage that became less obvious over the decades. Pressures for promiscuity were built into some of the Institute's workshops in the 1960s and early 1970s and also into its informal social norms. And men tended to benefit most from this emphasis (Miller 1971). Even in the twenty-first century, men at Esalen have not had to abandon sex and sports in order to become more spiritually and emotionally aware. They embrace those traditional hallmarks of American masculinity and also add other dimensions of spirituality and psychological sensitivity to their definitions of being truly manly (Stark 1996:55–59). This relatively recent emphasis on men's nurturing roles and the importance of gender equality has not erased the enactment of gender advantage.

Esalen was one of the first places in America to promote men's emotional awareness and their expression of strong feelings in private and in public. However, being a man at the Institute often, although not always, adds even more weight to other resources that facilitate spiritual privilege.

Wealth and Institutional Survival

During the 1960s, long-range financial planning was completely off the radar at the Institute. Few members of the founding generation seriously considered Esalen's prospects for long-term funding, because they came to Big Sur at a time when their own futures seemed to be unbounded by economic constraints or their past personal commitments. The skies, land, and ocean were so vast and forgiving and the Institute's genteel bohemian ethos was so strong that there seemed to be no need for strategic planning.

From Esalen's beginning, however, rich or famous people have almost always received special recognition and access to the Institute's varied resources. Currently, they may be invited to have drinks with members of Esalen's Board of Directors or to attend select fund-raising events featuring some of the Institute's best-known supporters. This extra attention is not about money or celebrity connections alone. Some of the CTR's core members still see highly accomplished people as unique agents for social change, and they want to create the kinds of elite networks that Aldous Huxley advocated fifty years ago, while still reaching out to mass audiences.

Connections to individuals who have the power make a difference in society are as important to Esalen's leaders as their desire to enlist the rich and famous as donors. Michael and many members of his inner circle believe that those who excel can become models for others' growth and implicitly encourage members of the general public to cultivate their own human potential (Leonard and Murphy 1995:10–15). The fact that these role models can also offer Esalen financial support or publicity, however, adds to their luster.

For many years, Michael tried to avoid systematic fund-raising and preferred to develop extended informal networks of private donors, which have now become formalized as Friends of Esalen. During the Institute's first decade, he quietly, almost surreptitiously, sought financial support from people like Laurance Rockefeller (Anderson 1983:123–124). Michael was very reluctant to become a public fund-raiser because he grew up in a time and a social class where conversations about money were fraught with embarrassment. However, he changed and actively sought donors to Friends of Esalen when the 1998 El Niño storms and floods ravaged the Institute's buildings and gardens and destroyed the bathing sites at the hot springs.

In order to rescue the Institute, Michael set aside his reservations about soliciting financial support and jumped into public fund-raising with growing enthusiasm. Esalen's Ninth Annual Benefit weekend in 2010, which cost $3,000 a couple to attend, honored Michael's eightieth birthday and celebrated his inspirational life.

Two years earlier, in 2008, a massive summer wildfire in Big Sur reached Esalen's edges but burned no buildings on the grounds. The Institute closed for almost three weeks and lost at least a quarter of a million dollars in revenue in its busiest season. During the most dangerous period, when the fire raced unchecked, staff and many Big Sur neighbors volunteered to clear brush, hose down buildings, and help fire crews with food, lodging, and other resources. As the smoke cleared, calls went out for donations of labor and money so that the Institute could recover from the disaster that had depleted its resources.

Rich benefactors, infrequent visitors, marginally employed work-study students, members of the massage crew, and staff members all responded to the call for assistance with heartfelt gratitude that the Institute was still standing and that they could help ensure its future in large and small ways.

Subtle Privilege

At Esalen and elsewhere, people who enjoy spiritual privilege often take their advantages for granted because they are so deeply embedded in their lives. The subtle, pervasive impact of spiritual privilege at the Institute first came into focus when I attended a select invitational conference to review and promote Esalen's significant contributions to American cultural history (Kripal and Shuck 2005). The CTR-sponsored conference, "On the Edge of the Future," revealed many of the dimensions of personal entitlement and spiritual privilege that sustain Esalen and nourish the broader markets for alternative religions and personal fulfillment.

At the beginning of April 2003, about twenty people, a mix of academics, core Esalen CTR members, and others who had been associated with Esalen for decades, responded to invitations to Big Sur in order to locate the Institute in the history of American spirituality. It was a working symposium with invited papers that would be published in a collection co-edited by one of the organizers (Kripal and Shuck 2005). Only four out of twenty presenters were women, and only one of the four was formally affiliated with Esalen and the CTR.

The symposium took place in the Big House—Michael's grandparents' refurbished vacation retreat, on the north end of the property. It was physically and symbolically set apart from most of Esalen. The white wood-frame building was originally built in the late 1930s for Michael's grandparents and the extended Murphy clan. It continued as a private family retreat until the late 1950s, a few years before Michael and Dick moved to Big Sur (Anderson 1983:22–23).

In the 1960s and 1970s, the Big House sheltered various staff, offices, and activities, but Michael always reserved a bedroom for himself. During the 2003 conference, however, he occupied the private Little House across the road, where Dick and his family had lived and which became Michael's domain after Dick's widow and her daughter moved away from Esalen.

Early in 1990, Laurance Rockefeller donated a quarter of a million dollars toward total renovation of the Big House. The changes eventually cost close to four times that amount, and Michael privately tapped Rockefeller again, found other donors, and dipped into the Murphy family trusts (*Esalen Catalogue* 1991:3–4). Workers gutted the old structure and reconfigured it into a comfortable retreat center with ten bedrooms, nine baths, and an enormous commercial kitchen. It was the site of many CTR conferences, but outside groups that shared Esalen's liberal spiritual and political philosophies could rent it for their own conferences and retreats.

In 2003, the Big House's impersonal conference-center décor and ambiance exuded subdued good taste and reflected assumptions about visitors' aesthetic preferences. The muted blues, grays, and mauves on the walls and the neutral furnishings mirrored the upper-middle-class culture shared by the educated people who designed the house and also those who used it. Lush green lawns and views of the Pacific enhanced the tasteful casual ambiance.

There were no obvious indications of wealth, but, like the rambling summer cottages overlooking the Atlantic in Maine or the few remaining rustic retreats on the shores of Lake Tahoe, this simple house cost a great deal to build and maintain. Few of the academics or other guests invited to present papers could afford to buy or even pay a full season's lease on a comparable retreat. But we all were equal within the conference boundaries, and we all knew how to behave appropriately in that refined setting.

Participants rarely raised their voices, even in heated debate. Dress was Brooks Brothers casual, with shades of gray, beige, navy, and black predominating for men and women alike. There was a sprinkling of bright colors and billowing shirts, but, overall, our clothing was simple and restrained. All of the participants' dress and demeanor meshed with the organizers' earnest commitments to develop deeper understanding and wider pubic recognition of the Institute's historic mission to bring doctrines of essential divinity and human potential to all Americans.

On March 18, 2003, President George W. Bush threatened Saddam Hussein with a full-scale American invasion unless he left Iraq within forty-eight hours. The same day that President Bush issued his ultimatum, final conference schedules were mailed, along with a letter announcing the importance of our Esalen project. The chief conference organizer wrote:

> We plan on going ahead with the conference in spite (indeed because of) whatever transpires in the next few days. Esalen, as we all know, has a rich and honorable history of addressing just these sorts of cross-cultural conflicts. It thus seems like an act of hope and humanity to proceed with the intellectual matter at hand, the history of Esalen, in the midst of so much fear and anxiety.

The letter, along with the conference's general theme, underscored the extraordinary importance that core members of the CTR have attached to intellectual discourse about the Institute. A handful of participants, Esalen insiders and invited academics alike, privately questioned the great significance that the letter writer had attributed to Esalen and the conference. However, as we proceeded with our agenda, everyone genially acknowledged the overall value of our presentations and discussions.

The core CTR members at the conference embodied spiritual privilege, although they did not fully recognize the personal entitlements that had allowed them to focus their lives on theory, religious practice, or personal fulfillment. All of them had enjoyed materially secure childhoods. A few had grown up in wealthy families like Michael's, most were comfortably upper middle class, and only one or two had working class childhoods. But while they were growing up, none had gone hungry or realistically worried about having shelter or clothing. Both the boomers and those who were born during the Great Depression were raised in homes with real and symbolic mirrors, where they could look at themselves and believe that they had the potential to make their marks on the world (Coles 1977).

College and graduate school had expanded all of the participants' opportunities and inflated their expectations about the potential social impact of their work. The CTR insiders, not the invited academics, casually referred to their years at elite universities: Harvard, Yale, Duke, Stanford, and the University of Chicago. The academics took one another's educational credentials for granted, while CTR members seemed to want to show the professors that their cultural capital equaled the scholars'.

The Esalen insiders wore their academic achievements like amulets that could both protect them from possible material deprivation and confirm their unique place in the world. They appeared confident that their university degrees and their studies of psychology and spirituality had validated their intelligence and also lent authority to their deeply held beliefs about Esalen's extraordinary importance. Their credentials also differentiated them from the bodyworkers and from the Institute's operations staff, who might have graduated from college but seemed to be unconcerned with general theory or research.

Gordon noticed that no one had invited representatives from the Esalen Massage and Bodywork Association to the conference. Several CTR members suggested that the EMBA group, predominantly women, rarely engages in the intellectual discourse that defines the CTR. Instead, its members had other, less important priorities. In a different discussion, another CTR member asserted that the massage workers and the bodyworkers were merely skilled craftspeople who needed theory and ideas generated by the CTR to contextualize and expand the impact of their work.

At the time, Gordon was a relatively recent arrival to the CTR's core, and he was very tactful as he questioned some of the other ways that his Esalen colleagues enacted their spiritual and social privilege. He described himself as a steadfast advocate for the Institute, but, at the same time, he commented about the CTR's exclusivity and the ways that education and economic resources had empowered the Institute's founders and members of the current inner circle.

Gordon questioned privilege when he asked the whole group, many of whom were draft eligible in the 1960s, whether they had any friends or relatives who had died in the Vietnam War. None of us did. Nearly sixty thousand Americans had died in that conflict, and an estimated two million Vietnamese had perished; yet *no one* at the conference knew any combatants well enough to mention some relationship. The symposium went on to other topics, and we did not dwell on our collective economic advantages or cultural and material capital.

Although all of the participants had avoided military service during wartime, some CTR members and also a few outsiders quietly observed that their gifts, personal and material, required them to make a difference to the world in other ways. CTR insiders articulated their desires to be involved with national policies and international negotiations in order to fulfill their personal obligations to create ecumenical understandings that could lead to world peace. They reasoned that their commitments to the common good exempted them from varieties of painful experiences and daily obligations such as military service or employment in frustrating, alienating jobs.

Gordon had quietly commented on gender issues when he mentioned the absence of representatives from the EMBA, and he later questioned gender advantage more explicitly after a longtime CTR member's brief description of Esalen in the 1970s. The presenter portrayed the Institute's early years as an era of idyllic community, and his view of Esalen reflected his early position in Michael and Dick's inner circle. He said, "Esalen is a Renaissance court with its geniuses and fools, its royalty and peasants, its knights and ladies, its musicians and scholars, its astrologers and ministers, its rogues and lovers" (Tarnas [1978] 2007).

Gordon raised a number of eyebrows when he talked about feudal hierarchy with active knights and passive ladies. The presenter responded that knights and ladies were simply a metaphor for the stylized relationships and role playing in Big Sur. Like most other core members from the early days, he took differentiation and inequality at Esalen for granted. Older CTR members viewed their dominance in the Institute's heyday as part of a graceful dance that partners enjoyed together, whereas women often wanted to avoid dancing when men consistently led them.

Over the years, other men at Esalen have also used courtly metaphors to explain the prerogatives of their spiritual privilege. Will Schutz routinely ended his emotionally charged encounter-groups with the song "The Impossible Dream," from the Broadway musical *The Man of La Mancha*. He utilized the song's lyric to inspire participants to "fight the unbeatable foe" and "be far better than you are" (Litwak 1967; Schutz 1967:220). Spiritual privilege allowed people at Esalen, men and women alike, to become heroes of their own lives and to go forth and spread the ideal of heroic quests for personal and spiritual growth far beyond Big Sur.

Gordon's comments about privilege reflected his desire to change the Institute from within by clearly defining jobs and responsibilities, while at the same providing more economic support and recognition for the EMBA and for the resident Esalen community. He also hoped to develop workshops and seminars about issues such as environmentalism and globalization and to affirm Esalen's doctrines of social responsibility in other ways.

His recognition of the inequality at the Institute and his desire to increase personal accountability within Esalen reflect the generational shift in leadership from Michael and his colleagues to others who are a decade younger and who are more aware of the ways that the CTR is a vortex of spiritual privilege. However, even though the Institute has become somewhat more egalitarian and dedicated to social justice since the turn of the twenty-first century, the related resources of spiritual affinities, cultural capital, social contacts, and economic security still determine who holds power there, as well as what kinds of people are drawn to Esalen and its foundational doctrines of spiritual and personal fulfillment.

Living Privilege: Four Esalen Men

Michael, Gordon, David, and Albert illuminate the dynamics of spiritual privilege and how it changes and combines in different ways. They responded to Esalen's doctrines and practices because of their personal needs and hopes, just as other spiritual seekers select, revise, and combine their beliefs and practices in terms of their own primary concerns.

When I asked twenty-three respondents to identify a few people who embodied the Institute for them, individuals from the CTR, the EMBA, and the operations staff mentioned these four men because of Esalen's centrality in their lives and their many contributions to the Institute. Their extraordinary dedication to actualizing their full human potential made them exemplars of spiritual privilege in Big Sur.

With the exception of Albert, whose brilliance in science and mathematics set him apart at an early age, none of the others was uniquely talented. Although they were bright and engaging, the men became extraordinary because of their passionate pursuit of spiritual privilege and not because they were gifted to begin with. Their focus on self-actualization throughout their adult lives set them apart and allowed them to shine.

Michael and Gordon came from wealthy families, and David and Albert were upper middle class. They assumed that they would always be able to support themselves in some way, so they focused on maximizing their full potential and making a difference in the world. Their confidence in their talents and survival skills also reflected their parents and other adults' validation and encouragement while they were growing up.

They paid a high price for adult approval, however. As boys, Michael, Gordon, David, and Albert believed that they had to live out their parents' hopes and dreams for them. Consequently, they often ignored their own feelings and desires (Miller 1981). When they left home as young men, they sometimes had staggering self-doubts about who they were and what they wanted (Goldman 1999:235–242).

This is the other side of spiritual privilege. Searches for personal and spiritual fulfillment often begin with intense emotional turmoil, and the immediate rewards of mystical experience temporarily erase debilitating self-doubt (Goldman 1999). In order to discover a core identity that did not reflect others' priorities, Michael, Gordon, David, and Albert all sought sparks of divinity within themselves and connections to larger, amorphous supernatural forces.

Trade-offs are built into the dynamics of spiritual privilege. No matter how many different resources people have, they inevitably give up something that matters to them as they pursue self-actualization. There are always costs to prioritizing spiritual options, and they are far more complicated than simple monetary exchanges or deferred income. Quests for spiritual meaning can estrange family members and old friends, destroy intimate relationships, or simply eat up discretionary time to go to movies or play basketball. Spiritual seekers make choices that involve their perceptions about what will be most rewarding to them in the short- and long-run (Iannaccone 1995).

Esalen developed and spread possibilities for spiritual and emotional growth that made self-actualization a reasonable goal for millions of Americans. Thanks to the Institute's lasting contributions, people less advantaged than the four men can pursue their full potential without major sacrifices of time, money, or relationships.

Dedication and Devotion

Because of their deep, lasing connections to Esalen, Michael, Gordon, David, and Albert men do not typify most Americans who exercise some degree of spiritual privilege or even those who invest a few months or years at the Institute. Their extraordinary devotion to the Esalen and its goals, however, reveals some of the ways that less dedicated men and women explore their possibilities in varied contexts. The men represent extreme cases of spiritual privilege.

The sociologist Erving Goffman (1963) developed the extreme-case approach when he examined routine ways that Americans cope with feelings of shame about their physical appearance. Each Esalen exemplar's personal history is unique, but each one has general implications for understanding individuals with less privilege and less commitment to self-actualization who also pursue personal and spiritual growth. The four men's search for meaning and value in their lives reveals something about millions of other spiritual seekers' quests.

Biography and History

All four men grew up with material comfort and emotional distress. They were eldest sons, burdened and also motivated by their families' hopes that they would become extraordinary people whose endeavors could change the world. Their parents encouraged them to be great but failed to empathize with their sons' emotions or independent goals (Miller 1981). When they came of age, each of the young men discarded his family's expectations in order to construct an individual path to personal and spiritual fulfillment. And, over the years, they all accumulated enough spiritual privilege to pursue their desires for self-actualization by means of the doctrines and practices that the Institute had popularized.

Michael linked himself to the Institute throughout his adult life, but the others changed directions a number of times, although spiritual and personal actualization were always their ultimate goals. Michael's and Esalen's stories are nearly indivisible. His affinity for spirituality, his education and knowledge, and also his bonds to influential fellow seekers allowed him to use his family fortune to help found and steer the Institute for five decades. Gordon, who is fourteen years younger than Michael, didn't visit Big Sur until the late 1990s, but the Institute's innovations nevertheless transformed his life. His story illustrates how the spiritual alternatives that Esalen popularized enlarged people's options throughout America.

David, Dick Price's oldest child, represents Esalen's second generation, whose central spiritual practices might include long-distance running or dancing or drumming. In the 1960s and 1970s, children raised in spiritually privileged families learned that all kinds of personally important activities could hold sacred meanings and facilitate transcendent moments. David grew up in the Northern California counterculture, although he always thought of Esalen as his real home. He was in charge of the Institute's internal operations for eight years, until shortly before a relatively small settlement from his father's estate facilitated his move to Europe in the mid-2000s.

Albert, the youngest of the four, left a prestigious graduate philosophy program at the University of Michigan to pursue personal growth and spirituality at Esalen in the 1990s. He moved to Los Angeles after five years in Big Sur to work in a new think tank funded by one of Michael's many friends. However, Albert soon redirected his energies to become an actor and an adjunct professor, bringing Gestalt and spirituality to his dramatic work. Despite some successes, Albert could not earn a steady income in the entertainment industry. He returned to graduate school in order to become a clinical psychologist, incorporating Esalen's approaches to healing and personal growth into his new profession. He also founded and manages Esalen's grassroots social-networking website, www.ithou.org, where members recreate elements of the Institute in cyberspace.

Each man's life history reflects the increasingly wide diffusion of Esalen's approaches to maximizing human potential. Their personal stories mark the ways that the Institute's inclusive definitions of spiritual practice have created varied avenues for people to engage the sacred. David and Albert lack the economic resources that supported Michael's and Gordon's quests, but because of the ways that Esalen democratized spiritual privilege, they entertained a variety of choices that had rarely been available to people like them before the 1960s.

All four have focused their lives on the sacred through a gradual process that resembled the ways that people develop enduring commitments to diverse alternative religions (Lofland 1977). In childhood, they felt a lasting tension between their ideal lives and their family milieus, and that tension plagued them until they deliberately embarked on paths to personal and spiritual fulfillment.

When the men reached college age, they searched for emotional comfort and a sense of purpose by reading and talking about religion and philosophy and sometimes sampling different practices like yoga, meditation, or Gestalt. That was the point when each of them defined himself as a spiritual seeker and began to form bonds with like-minded comrades and mentors. They sought self-transformation in many different places, but, ultimately, each one found what he wanted at the Institute. Michael and Gordon are seldom far from Big Sur, and David and Albert regularly return there. Wherever they are, they carry images of Esalen with them.

Michael's Path

Some years ago, Michael described himself as the Toots Shor of the metaphysical circuit (Downing 2001:248). Toots was a famed Manhattan saloonkeeper from the 1940s through the 1960s, who welcomed sports stars, politicians, and well-known gangsters to his establishment (Considine 1969). Michael saw himself as Shor's counterpart in the spiritual marketplace because of the genial ways that he connected networks of religious leaders, celebrities, psychologists, wealthy seekers, and intellectuals at Esalen and beyond.

When he laughingly spoke about Shor, Michael unintentionally disclosed his assumptions about the lasting fame of almost forgotten Americans. Shor's chophouse closed in the early 1960s, and few people born after World War II have any idea who Toots Shor was or that his friends included notables from Chief Justice Earl Warren to Mickey Mantle (Considine 1969). Michael remains a mid-twentieth-century man. Despite his hope of creating a greater future and exploring new frontiers of human potential, he is still grounded in the 1950s.

Although he was born at the beginning of the Great Depression, Michael always enjoyed the economic resources that often accompany extraordinary spiritual privilege. His grandfather was Monterey County's leading physician, and his grandmother successfully developed real estate worth more than a million dollars in the 1930s (Schwartz 1995:77). Michael's father John, a member of San Francisco's exclusive Olympic Club, briefly practiced law before he married into a successful Basque immigrant family.

In 1927, the newlyweds moved from San Francisco to John's hometown, Salinas, where he oversaw his family's real estate empire. Michael grew up in the midst of an extended old California family that was insulated from the nearby Watsonville anti-Filipino race riots and the incarceration of Japanese Americans in the Salinas Fair Grounds in 1942 (Pascoe 2009:93). Like local racial tensions, the economic hardships of the Depression era and World War II barely touched him.

Class and racial struggles simmered in neighboring communities, but Michael's childhood revolved around long family vacations in Big Sur, visits to San Francisco, and Saturday afternoons at Stanford football games. Conflict and tension, however, were part of his life because his parents' recurrent confrontations shook the household. Michael tried to ignore their raised voices and told himself that their fights were simply mild disagreements. He also laid low and withdrew when his volatile father became frustrated and upset with him or his younger brother.

While he was growing up, Michael learned to dissociate himself from his surroundings, and he developed surprising capacities for private spiritual experience that he would later cultivate intentionally in church, on the golf links, and in meditation. His early desire to withdraw and to avoid conflict also characterized his leadership at the Institute. A longtime friend described how he circumvented potential confrontations:

> I used to sit in Michael's office [in the late 1960s] smoking and putting my ashes in these very interesting ashtrays. I would put my ashes in the ashtray, Michael would come and take my ashtray and empty it and then put it down. And I thought, "Well, my goodness, that's a little strange, being so formal and clean here."

These exchanges continued until another comrade informed the smoker that the "ashtrays" were actually sacred Zen tea bowls that were gifts from a revered Buddhist teacher. Throughout his life, Michael has waited diffidently until people eventually agree with him, withdrawn his attention from an issue, or simply gone ahead and done what he wanted without much consultation. He keeps his own counsel because of his personal style and also because of the many economic, social, and cultural resources that enable him to go his own way.

Michael's mother favored him because of his sunny smile and his remove from family battles (Schwartz 1995:78). His later self-confidence and inner strength may have reflected her almost unconditional support. As Sigmund Freud noted, a mother's favorite son develops triumphant convictions that his projects will inevitably succeed (Gay 2006:506–507).

During adolescence, Michael escaped from family turmoil by participating in organized sports at school and joining activities sponsored by the Episcopal Church in Salinas, including summer camps and religious retreats. When he trained alone before high school golf tournaments or attended religious services, Michael discovered serenity, joy, and occasional feelings of transcendence that he sought to recapture throughout his life.

Michael has devoted himself to enhancing his spiritual privilege and sharing his many discoveries with others. He views writing as one of his central spiritual practices, validating Esalen's doctrine that almost any deeply focused activity can be a kind of meditation. Sometimes, while thinking or writing, he is conscious of nothing but the flow of ideas and words (Csikszentmihalyi 1991; Neitz and Spickard 1990). He views this flow as a sacred experience akin to channeling a higher power that is writing through him (Alan 2007:5).

After enthusiastically joining golf games and fraternity parties during his first year at Stanford, Michael dropped out and devoted himself to meditation, reading, and maintaining his private vow of chastity (Anderson 1983:77–78). Until his early thirties, Michael was a virgin, but he made up for the lost time in the mid-1960s, during the Institute's halcyon days of heterosexual promiscuity.

Even after he happily joined the sexual revolution, Michael devoted his days to addressing his spiritual growth and shepherding the Institute. His regular practices included meditation, reading, writing, mid- and long-distance running, and golf, leaving him little space to deepen his relationships with women. His heart belonged to one or two close comrades like George Leonard.

Toward the end of what he sometimes termed his Dionysian period, Michael impulsively married a woman who had moved to Big Sur to be near him. Their stormy union lasted less than two years (Anderson 1983:147–148, 150–151). Then in the mid-1970s, George introduced him to his second wife, Dulce Wilmott Cottle, who shared Michael's interests in meditation and spiritual and personal growth. She typed and edited drafts of *Golf in the Kingdom*, trained beside Michael at the Esalen Athletic Center, and traveled to the Soviet Union to create cultural exchanges and promote Esalen-sponsored conferences on nongovernmental diplomacy (Kripal 2007a:285, 335–336).

Because of her own substantial financial resources and social networks, Dulce could accompany Michael on his far-ranging quests to discover new human possibilities and spiritual paths throughout the world. Their partnership over the decades, like Michael's and Dick's, reflects both their shared history and their complicated financial arrangements, including family trusts and joint ownership of property in California and on Vashon Island, near Seattle.

Dulce and Michael had one son, who usually lived with his mother throughout his parents' many separations and reconciliations. Unlike David Price, Mac Murphy rarely visited the Institute during his childhood or adolescence, but, after college, he spent two years in Big Sur, charting his own paths to self-actualization and flamboyantly reenacting some of the personal excesses that defined Esalen in the 1960s.

Michael's younger brother, Dennis, once joked that occasionally Michael "became Jesus"—someone who wanted to save humanity, even if it meant paying a high personal price (Tompkins 1976:33–34). Michael deliberately sacrificed lasting intimacy with women and traditional professional success in order to devote his life to selecting, revising, and combining his spiritual beliefs and practices. He has worked steadfastly to transform himself and to lead the way to a collective evolutionary leap forward.

One of his personal and financial investments is a film adaptation of *Golf in the Kingdom* (1972), the only one of Michael's many books that became a best-seller. He had once envisioned a major motion picture with a star like Sean Connery or Clint Eastwood, but he settled for a low-budget production of about $7 million, hopeful that it would revive the Institute's visibility and interest new audiences in Aurobindo's approaches to spirituality.

Spiritual privilege made it possible for Michael to leave his mark on the world, and he believes that *Golf in the Kingdom* is central to his legacy. Recently he mused, "I often say that I gave my family inheritance to God and God gave me back *Golf in the Kingdom*" (Alan 2007:5). Even with his extraordinary resources, Michael has had to forgo financial and emotional rewards in order to create a lasting legacy that will allow others to explore alternative spirituality and personal growth psychology.

Salvation from the 1960s: Gordon Wheeler

Gordon began to explore self-actualization three decades before he first visited the Institute, but the approaches to spirituality and psychology that Esalen popularized changed his life many years before he set foot in Big Sur. Esalen's diffusion of spiritual innovations made it possible for him to select, combine, and revise his beliefs, personal commitments, and spiritual practices while living on the East Coast. In the mid-1970s, he followed Swami Muktananda to help build a Siddha Yoga community in upstate New York, and he emerged in the early 1980s to become a Gestalt psychologist and an influential critic of Fritz Perls's approaches to personal growth (Kripal 2007a:437–438).

Since the late 1990s, as Esalen's president and temporary CEO, Gordon has gradually changed the CTR and the Institute itself in terms of his commitments to Gestalt psychology, yoga, and progressive political perspectives. He resembles other baby boomers who once lived in communal religious groups and later reentered mainstream society to center their lives on repairing the world (Barker 1995; Tipton 1982). Gordon speaks most directly to and for the prosperous, college-educated boomers who are still the Institute's core constituents and workshop leaders.

Although he was born in 1944, almost two years before the baby boom officially began, Gordon identifies with the Vietnam generation, linking his own history to the social movements for peace and justice that swept through elite college campuses during the mid-1960s. He shared the abundant opportunities for education and work available to many early baby boomers, and he was able to shift his personal and professional priorities throughout his lifetime.

Although he is now a senior citizen, Gordon is still tall, slender, and dashing. A veteran of individual psychotherapy and Gestalt groups, he projects confidence in himself and in others, along with an enthusiasm for new ideas that resembles Michael's. Over many decades, Gordon has recounted parts of his biography in therapy groups, his own books and articles, and interviews; like Michael, he often edits his narratives to suit his immediate purposes. Despite Gordon's shifting emphases, however, his accounts consistently describe a trajectory from restless affluence through political activism to alternative spirituality and Gestalt psychology.

Gordon grew up in a prestigious Dallas suburb, but he felt that he never fit into his surroundings or his own family. Most other Highland Park children proudly sang Dixie, waved Confederate flags, and happily attended segregated schools in their elite enclave. The Wheelers opposed overt signs of racism, and they taught Gordon that the Civil War represented the termination of centuries of inhumanity. His parents despised the lasting Southern legacies of intolerance and discrimination. As their only son, Gordon believed that he was destined to carry on his family's liberalism and uphold the equalitarian, rational values that stemmed from the European Enlightenment (Wheeler 2000:359).

He learned that he would grow up to meet important challenges and leave his mark on America, while his two sisters did not have similar responsibilities. Despite his sense of personal destiny and many talents, however, Gordon felt like a social outsider in Highland Park because of his family's broadmindedness and his own interests in politics and religion. When his father worked long hours in his medical practice and his alcoholic mother was depressed and indisposed, he often avoided his peers and spent time with African American household servants, although the chasm between their hard lives and his family's comfort troubled him.

Gordon's father pressed his son to excel in everything so that he could someday advance humanity. He learned that greatness and goodness meant "being responsible at all times for the whole relevant world, from the body politic to the immediate family to the disadvantaged of society" (Wheeler 2000:360). Throughout his life, Gordon remembered those early lessons about maximizing his full potential in order to better humankind.

Money was not an issue for the Wheelers, and the material resources that can contribute to spiritual privilege enabled Gordon to seek emotional and spiritual growth throughout his lifetime. His parents always assumed that he would earn a good living on his own, but Gordon knew that he could also count on inherited wealth in the future. They minimized the importance of making money for its own sake. Gordon said, "No family tales glorified members who 'went out west and struck it rich'" (Wheeler 2000:360). Instead, his father steered him toward a career in teaching, science, law, or medicine, because those noble professions served humanity. Gordon was supposed to be grateful for his family's status and his own great prospects, without unwarranted pride or complaints about the social responsibilities that accompanied his many advantages. Dr. Wheeler urged his son to demonstrate good cheer, modesty, and humility at all times.

Gordon wanted to live up to his family's ideals, although he felt lonely and stressed most of the time that he lived at home. In high school, his curiosity about ethics contrasted with his friends' preoccupations with football, cars, sex, and money. While other students worshipped famous athletes, Gordon admired people with high ideals and the ability to implement them. Despite his academic and sexual successes at Highland Park High School, Gordon could barely wait to move on. He still remarks on his friends' constant sports talk and their delight in one another's failures and inadequacies. He wryly observed, "Among boys in middle childhood to adolescence, surely the modal remark is, 'He stinks'"(Wheeler and Jones 1996:98). The stereotypical American masculinity of the late 1950s bothered him at an early age, and he considered different ways to become a real man.

Gordon's parents were delighted when their son was accepted to Harvard, because it was an institution that represented both excellence and liberal commitments to the public good. He was even happier than they were. "I went to Harvard to study, because it seemed geographically and culturally the farthest place I could go." He majored in German history and literature, focusing on the Holocaust and issues of violence, aggression, and victimization.

During college, from 1962 to 1967, Gordon supported student movements to end the Vietnam War and bring social and economic justice to America. After graduation, he studied at the University of Munich, traveled in Europe, and then returned to Harvard to earn a master of arts in teaching, concentrating on early childhood studies and the relationship between healing and personal growth. Gordon tried out different political and spiritual possibilities, but he made no significant decisions for several years.

Because he was a teacher, Gordon did not have to decide whether to resist the draft and go to jail, leave the U.S., or enter military service. His education, social networks, and financial resources allowed him to avoid military service during the Vietnam War and continue to explore various personal and spiritual options.

In his early twenties, he advocated on behalf of troubled children and taught in public schools, where he was both frustrated and inspired by the emotionally and economically vulnerable students (Wheeler 1996:203–204). While working with disadvantaged children, Gordon continued to enjoy sensual pleasures, skiing in Switzerland during the winter and summering on a Vermont farm, where he drafted a tongue-in-cheek novel about a Boston psychologist-private investigator (Wheeler 1974).

He was already married with a small daughter, when he enrolled in Boston College's doctoral program in counseling psychology in order to embark on a professional career that would allow him to explore personal and spiritual growth. Gordon was inspired by the teachings of Swami Muktananda, affectionately known as Baba, whose First World Tour in 1970 had passed through Esalen, as well as Boston and other parts of the Northeast (Brooks et al. 1997:575).

In 1974, Muktananda's devotees purchased three dilapidated Catskill resort hotels near South Fallsburg, New York, where they started a modest intentional community, with crowded sleeping quarters and rough public spaces. The South Fallsburg community grew into a beautiful, twenty-first-century headquarters for SYDA, the North American Siddha Yoga Dyam [Home] (Harris 1994), but in the 1970s, it was a work in progress.

Gordon put his Gestalt training and doctoral studies on hold and moved to the Catskills with his family. He plunged into meditation, yoga, and also the hard manual labor that was necessary to build and maintain the ashram (Kripal 2007a:437–439). In South Fallsburg, Gordon participated in intense encounters where people sought to uncover their true selves, meditated close to his guru, and practiced Kundalini yoga, a powerful, sexually charged discipline that can produce ecstatic states and enhanced consciousness (Harris 1994). Muktananda urged his devotes to develop a heartfelt emotional and spiritual connection to him so that they could awaken their full cosmic energy, known as Shakti (Caldwell 2001).

After about five years at the ashram, Gordon and his family moved back to Boston, during a period of tension and transition in South Fallsburg. Muktananda had a series of heart attacks, and different factions vied for leadership while he was still alive. Moreover, there was a steady stream of allegations that Baba had sexually exploited girls as young as twelve years old (Harris 1994). Back in Boston, Gordon went to work in the public schools, divorced his wife, married a fellow psychologist, and raised four children. He returned to the Boston College program in counseling psychology and also trained at the Gestalt Institute of Cleveland, receiving his Ph.D. in 1988.

When he left the Siddha Yoga community, Gordon exchanged a clear spiritual path for a more worldly vocation that could still incorporate Baba's teachings. He shifted from devotional religiosity to Gestalt, blending spirituality and psychology in some of the ways that they mixed them together in the Gestalt awareness process at Esalen. Gordon still keeps a picture of Baba with him and acknowledges Muktananda's importance to his life.

Like Sri Aurobindo, Michael's guru, Muktananda described sparks of divinity within everyone. He advised his devotees to discover their essential identities through meditation, and he urged them to respect both their core divinity and the innate holiness that connects everyone in the world (Brooks et al. 1997:288–289; Caldwell 2001). The guru also instructed his devotees to live every day with full awareness of their immediate emotions in order to be able to improve both their own lives and the human condition (Brooks et al. 1997:351).

Gordon applies Muktananda's teachings about complete awareness to his work as a therapist and writer. He addresses other professionals, rather than ordinary readers, in his books and articles because he hopes to revitalize American psychology so that patients and therapists alike can reach their full potential and move beyond individualism (Wheeler 1996). Describing the importance of overcoming selfishness and isolation, Gordon outlined the spiritual foundation of his work:

> In religion and spiritual practice, this sense of fit is the state of deep union, or *grace*; it explains why meditation and other practices of spiritual discipline can be so effective at transforming developmental and pathological feelings of shame. "Maya," or illusion in many eastern systems of thought, after all, is the sensation that I am alone, atomized, existentially cut off from meaningful context. (Wheeler 1996:48–49)

Gordon's current commitment to Esalen extends his earlier spiritual affinities and builds on the knowledge and practices that he acquired through his devotion to Muktananda and his own interpretations of Gestalt. This accumulation of complementary religious knowledge exemplifies how individuals increase their spiritual privilege by adding other beliefs and activities that amplify rather than diminish the spiritual capital that they already have.

During his ashram years, Gordon added to his abilities to experience and understand sacred aspects of life, and he also accumulated more specialized religious knowledge. However, his sojourn in South Fallsburg also involved the tradeoffs that are common when people devote extensive time and resources to select, combine, and revise their religious beliefs and practices.

When he went to South Fallsburg, Gordon left some of his Cambridge friends, and, when he returned to the city years later, he abandoned the extended family of fellow devotees whom he saw daily. His residence in Baba's community and the subsequent reentry into the secular world cost Gordon contact with different social networks that were important to him.

He gained some resources and lost others as the foci of his spiritual privilege shifted from devotion to Muktananda to a more personal combination of beliefs and practices.

Gordon's full life included his family and his work as a therapist and writer. He also developed new social networks that provided him with personal and professional support. His friends and close colleagues shared his faith in Gestalt psychology as a vehicle for growth, healing, and spiritual development. He joined professional groups in New England and worked with founders of the small but influential Gestalt circle in Cleveland. His doctoral dissertation (1988) critiqued the radical individualism that had defined Fritz's approach to Gestalt at Esalen and clouded Paul Goodman's insights in *Growing Up Absurd* (1960), a best-selling book about malaise in American society.

While his dissertation took issue with some of the Cleveland Institute's approaches, Gordon nevertheless joined its primary faculty, and, in 1989, he became an editor of the Gestalt Institute of Cleveland Press (GIC Press). He studied and later taught in Cleveland, but Gordon spent most of his time at home in Cambridge near Harvard, working with private patients, writing and editing for the GIC Press, and negotiating distribution arrangements with publishers like Jossey-Bass and the Analytic Press. His rambling house in Cambridge was his base, and, after his second wife's death, he stayed close to home and became his children's primary caregiver.

Gordon offered his first workshop at the Institute in February 1997 and explored issues of intimacy and shame. In that and in his later Big Sur presentations for professionals, he emphasized the need to move beyond clinical settings and deal with shame and its sources in daily life.

Professional colleagues often appreciated Gordon's critique of individualistic Gestalt approaches, his emphasis on human connections, and his progressive social agenda. However, in the early 1990s, some influential theorists grew uncomfortable with his spiritual agenda and challenged Gordon's theoretical positions, historical references, and clinical interpretations (Yontef 1/1992, 2/1992). By the end of the decade, he had reached another turning point, as he reconsidered the viability of transforming Gestalt psychology in America through his work with GIC and his wider professional networks.

In the late 1990s, at a time when Gordon began to reconsider his close identification with the GIC and better understand the enmity among different Gestalt factions, he visited Esalen and also started a love affair with Nancy Kaye Lunney, one of the few women who were part of Michael's current inner circle. Nancy had lived in Big Sur since the late 1970s, when she trained as a Gestalt therapist and worked closely with Dick Price. In the early 1980s, she became Esalen's director of programming, scheduling visiting workshop leaders and organizing the Institute's catalogues (Kripal 2007a:378–379).

After Dick's death, in 1985, Nancy continued to schedule workshops, and she was Michael and the CTR's informal liaison with the Institute's operations staff and bodyworkers, although she usually operated behind the scenes. Nancy's distrust of abstractions and theorizing limited her participation in the CTR, but her focus on action and spiritual practice made her more available to other Esalen stakeholders. She was a member of Esalen's Board of Trustees for many years, and she consistently influenced major decisions and Institute policies.

Nancy introduced Gordon to Michael and his circle, as well as to key people in operations and bodywork. As Nancy and Gordon's relationship became more serious,, so did his connection to Esalen. His approach to spirituality and his modifications of Gestalt psychology meshed with the Institute's longstanding goals. Less than four years after they met, Gordon and Nancy exchanged vows at a formal wedding ceremony at a landmark Boston hotel, where George Leonard gave the bride away.

Well before his wedding, Gordon started to move his headquarters to the Institute, while he still commuted to Cambridge to see his old friends and his children. As part of the transition, he scaled back his work as a therapist, although he continued to publish and to present professional papers. He had found a new home.

For several years, the Wheelers occupied a cliffside cottage at Esalen, but, in 2003, they designed and built a house in Santa Cruz, about fifty miles north of the Institute. Six visiting Lamas from an ancient Tibetan religious lineage expelled symbolic snakes from their new property during their groundbreaking ceremony. Like other spiritually privileged Americans, the Wheelers drew on diverse sacred traditions to create personal practices, and the foundation of their house and their lives reflects changing combinations of Gestalt, Siddha Yoga, and Buddhism.

Gordon and Nancy divide their time between Santa Cruz and Esalen, driving up and down scenic Highway 1. Gordon's oldest daughter and her family relocated from Boston to Santa Cruz, and Nancy's younger daughter, her husband, and their child also live close by. Gordon strives for emotional connection and supportive contact in every area of his life, often mixing professional and personal relationships. He relies on his family and longtime colleagues to help him reshape the Institute, much as Michael once depended on his inner circle and their networks.

Gordon calls on family members and close professional associates to participate in his vision of the Institute as a twenty-first-century catalyst for personal and global transformation. His Santa Cruz son-in-law, a nationally known yoga teacher, offers Vinyasa retreats in Big Sur (Gates and Kenison 2002), and one of his sisters has presented several poetry workshops at the Institute (Wheeler 2005). He has also recruited visiting leaders who were once part of the South Fallsburg community and who reentered the secular world much later than he did (Davidson 2007:249–253).

Fellow therapists from the East and newer colleagues from the Pacific Coast help Gordon redefine Esalen. Along with presenting public workshops and directing work-study programs, a handful of his closest associates are changing the CTR through a Psychology Council and its conference series, "Evolution of Gestalt." The first CTR Gestalt conference produced a collection of essays about human connections and social transformation that Gordon and an old colleague coedited (Ullman and Wheeler 2009).

Like Michael, Gordon possesses all of the attributes that support spiritual privilege: abundant economic, cultural, spiritual, and social resources. The Wheeler family's financial assets allowed him to attend Harvard without worrying about money, and his independent means later enabled Gordon to devote his life to spiritual and personal growth. Although he does not supply the tremendous financial resources that Michael poured into the Institute, Gordon has had enough money to sustain his passions, help his children, and make generous donations to the Gestalt Institute of Cleveland and to Esalen.

Gordon's general cultural capital from his Harvard education and from his subsequent graduate work at Boston College supplemented the social graces and knowledge that he acquired in childhood because of his upper-class family and his excellent Highland Park schooling. In Cambridge and Boston, Gordon was free to explore different spiritual paths before he moved to Muktananda's American ashram, a context that amplified his specific religious knowledge and access to transcendent sacred experiences. Professional and social networks, however, were the most important elements of the spiritual privilege that carried him to the center of the Institute.

Another Gestalt professional introduced Gordon to Nancy and invited him to offer his first Esalen workshop (Kripal 2007a:438). As his relationship with Nancy unfolded and he led more Esalen workshops, Gordon got to know Michael and members of his inner circle, major donors, longtime Esalen trustees, and community residents. Within two years of his first visit, Gordon began to attend the CTR's invitational conferences, participate in movement and yoga classes with EMBA members, and join community meetings. His marriage, his move to Big Sur, his appointment as Esalen's president and temporary CEO, and his embrace of his old friends and colleagues enabled Gordon to enact his spiritual priorities and reshape the Institute.

Esalen's Child

While Gordon explored many different options during his decades of seeking, study, and spiritual practice, David Price's lasting connection to Esalen was almost inevitable. He holds a unique place in the Institute's collective memory, because he is Dick Price's only son. David embodies Esalen's lifetime impact and the ways that its broad spiritual doctrine can enrich every action.

For many years after Dick died, the old operations staff and EMBA members yearned for an inspiring leader (Carter 1997:82). They romanticized the close group that had formed around Dick in the late 1970s, and some of them hoped that his son could lead an effort to redefine Esalen as a cohesive hub for bodywork and the Gestalt awareness practice that Dick had developed.

When David returned to live at the Institute and work as its gate manager, in 1993, his reappearance fueled their desires to recapture an idealized past. Old hands cheered when David became Esalen's general manager, overseeing internal operations and guest relations. But David *never* wanted to be a charismatic figure leading the grass-roots rebellion to restore Esalen's early glory.

He came back with the hope that he could revive his father's vision of Esalen as a place for personal transformation, improve relations among various factions, and help build an organization that allowed the Institute to function efficiently and serve guests well. None of these was a simple goal.

From 1993 to 2006, David routinely demonstrated both his collaborative management style and his boundless self-confidence. The combination of frustration with constant internal crises and conflicts, his marriage to an Esalen work-study student from Poland, the birth of his son, and his developing international career as a bass player caused him to step down from management in 2003, although he continued to work at Esalen until he moved his family to Poland, in 2006.

The Institute has always been David's hometown, although he spent much of his childhood in Northern California and traveled extensively as an adult. In recent summers, David has returned to Big Sur and worked as the stage manager at one of the Monterey Jazz Festival's many venues. But, wherever

David goes , Skype, the Internet, and e-mail allow him to keep in touch with his many Esalen friends.

David does not possess either Michael's or Gordon's wealth, and he never participated in the tight social networks associated with the CTR. His privilege is grounded in considerable cultural resources that reflect both a lifetime of intimate engagement with the Institute and affinity for spiritual experience that he expanded through music and Gestalt awareness practice at Esalen.

A journalist once identified David as "the first child of the sixties" (Lattin 2003:13), and he knew both the freedom of the era and its many dysfunctions. When his mother, Eileen, was twenty-six, she turned away from her large, Roman Catholic family in New York and traveled west in order to reinvent herself. She worked as a part-time waitress in Big Sur, painted, and bonded with a number of artists and writers that frequented Nepenthe. Four years after she arrived in California, Eileen and Dick had a casual liaison, and David was born in 1963.

David and his mother shared an old house on the north end of the Esalen property with another single mother and her two children. Although Dick ignored the day-to-day responsibilities of fatherhood, he often visited them. He also saw David when Eileen dropped him off in order to pursue her own agenda for personal and spiritual growth at the Institute or up the coast in San Francisco.

A few old-timers remember keeping an eye on David while he toddled around the Esalen grounds. He enjoyed freedom to enter every door, although people often ignored David after acknowledging his presence. However, several Esalen community members were devoted to him and they became his de facto aunts and uncles, although they had no desire to become full-time, nurturing parent substitutes.

When David was five, he watched Big Sur disappear in Eileen's rearview mirror, as they drove to their new home in Northern California. Eileen had become a follower of Swami Chinmayananda, and some devotees from Napa urged her to move nearby. Their teacher, like Aurobindo and Muktananda, believed that people could transform the world when they cultivated their own divine sparks. Eileen changed her name to Nalini, worked in an art store, and continued to paint. A few years after the move, she married a fellow disciple, and they had a daughter in 1970. Nalini and her husband established a Chinmayananda West Mission in their home and assumed responsibility for editing the movement's newsletter, publishing its books, and organizing outreach.

Until his half sister, Anjali, entered public school, David felt like the only kid in Napa who ate vegetarian food or knew about yoga. Schoolmates treated him like a freak and laughed at his long hair. He enrolled in first grade with an Indian name. However, he soon insisted that he would be "David" at school and he also rejected his mother's Hindu-based spirituality. Nalini's exercise of her spiritual privilege involved heavy costs to her relationship with her son, and it also marginalized him from his schoolmates.

David felt better when he visited Big Sur, where the unconventional adults were a lot more fun than his Napa family and their friends. Although his father's apparent ambivalence still frustrated him, David now received extra attention from community members because he was one of the few children around, and he knew how to charm adults: "I think I had it better than other kids that arrived later, in that I was more of a novelty."

While David was in grade school, Nalini occasionally drove him to Big Sur, and Dick visited Napa a few times a year. As he grew older, David began to have more contact with Dick, because he could ride the Greyhound to Monterey and then drive down to Esalen with his father. After David entered seventh grade, in the mid-1970s, Big Sur began to feel like his true home, because of his increased autonomy there and his father's growing interest in him.

David stayed at Esalen during spring breaks and for at least two weeks every summer. The Institute seemed like a teenage paradise. Despite his youth, David felt that he was an honored community member. He debated philosophy, smoked pot, and hung out with men and women friends of all ages, earning adults' recognition while working beside them on maintenance and in the vegetable and flower gardens.

When he was seventeen, David passed his high school equivalency exams and moved to Esalen for the foreseeable future. Over the three years that he spent there, he accumulated more resources that allowed him to select, combine, and revise his spirituality. He added to his knowledge and experiences of the sacred through music and Gestalt awareness practice, the fusion of Zen and personal growth psychology that his father had developed two decades earlier. He also expanded his understanding of Esalen and accumulated the store of local cultural knowledge that is the hallmark of his spiritual privilege.

Dick had already become a more engaged parent when his son came to live in Big Sur (Lattin 2003:26). He had settled in with his second wife and their daughter, at the same historical moment that many other men and women at Esalen began their second or third families. Father and son shared LSD and other psychedelics, hiked in the mountains, soaked in the hot springs, and worked through their stormy relationship in one-to-one Gestalt awareness practice. Dick wanted to be David's guide and confidante instead of an authoritarian father. He had begun to re-father in ways that presaged the men's movement's recent emphasis on emotional authenticity and nurturing between older and younger generations.

During those three years at Esalen, David's central spiritual path involved Gestalt awareness practice with his father and other mentors. While living at the Institute, David picked up the bass guitar and performed with casual groups. As he played music, he occasionally felt the sublime spiritual rewards of accessing his core self and connecting to some larger, higher power. Esalen's makeshift house bands were not very good, however, and David's interest in music and its spiritual dimensions expanded dramatically after he moved to San Francisco in the early 1980s.

With Dick's blessings, David decided to study painting and drawing at the San Francisco Art Institute. However, group collaboration and the spiritual possibilities in music attracted him more. He took elective music classes at the Art Institute and sat in with local bands in bars and clubs, gradually dropping visual art for bass guitar.

After spending several years in San Francisco, David moved to Los Angeles to learn more and to work in McCabe's Guitar Shop, a famous store and small concert venue with a long list of clients that included Judy Collins, Bob Dylan, and Mick Jagger. While he was living in LA in 1985, David awakened to a phone call in the middle of the night and learned that his father had died. He returned to Big Sur to grieve with his stepmother and the rest of the community. Messages poured in from around the world, as the Institute's extended family mourned together.

Playing bass allowed David to deal with his grief and to temporarily forget about his strained relationship with Dick's widow. After staying in Big Sur for a few months, he moved to Santa Barbara to work as a sound engineer for an old family friend, Jim Messina, a well-known guitar player and songwriter. David briefly returned to Esalen, where he began to make music with a visiting artist, Babatunde Olatunji, an internationally famous Nigerian drummer and social activist, who profoundly influenced late-twentieth-century jazz and rock (Olatunji 2005).

He went back to San Francisco and then spent a year in Berlin, playing with various groups and traveling with his girlfriend. After they broke up, David returned to San Francisco and worked in another well-known string shop. He had become a talented musician and now performed in famous clubs with established jazz and blues groups. At that point in his life, David reached an enviable position of spiritual privilege, because his career and his

David Price's son, Aleksander, smiles with two musicians who toured with Babatunde
Olatunji. © Patrice Ward: www.patriceward.net

spiritual commitments merged through his music. For a time in the early
1990s, he realized the integration of mind, body, spirit, and psyche through
his vocation.

During the 1990s, after David moved back to Big Sur, Babatunde became
a central figure in his life, helping him add more spiritual depth to his music.
The great drummer even traveled to Big Sur in order to conduct a traditional
Yoruba naming ceremony for David's new son, Aleksander. Shortly afterward,
David arranged for his mentor to live at Esalen during the year and a half that
he suffered from the grave complications of diabetes that led to his death.

Over the years that he worked at Esalen, David brought new kinds of
vitality and spirituality to Big Sur through music and visual arts. Despite his
many accomplishments at the Institute, however, after Babatunde's death,
David wanted to find a new home for his family. He connected with well-
known European musicians, traveled to Poland to visit his wife's family while
he performed with an American blues band, and thought seriously about living in Europe.

At the time that David seriously began to consider moving far from Big
Sur, he also made sure that his son attended the Institute's Gazebo Preschool.

Aleksander ran barefoot in the muddy yard and freely expressed his emotions in a setting that had been inspired by Janet Lederman's Gestalt model for education from the 1960s (Lederman 1969). He learned both his mother's Polish and his father's English at home, and the move overseas somehow became a satisfying family challenge rather than a painful break.

In the years after settling close to his wife's family in Legnica, David toured Europe playing clubs and concerts and he also became a well-known Polish TV actor. While working for supplementary income as a film extra, he met an influential director, who became one of his best friends. When his friend's wife, a casting director, needed to find an American actor, she picked David for a leading role in a primetime TV series, opposite one of the country's most beloved actresses. A major Polish entertainment agent signed him. While continuing to play bass and tour, he was once again on his way to something new. He landed featured roles in several films and he has also moved behind the camera, as an assistant line producer.

His experience as a musician made David a natural for TV and movies. However, his success as an actor also reflects his abilities to access and articulate his deepest feelings, because of his Gestalt awareness practice. His cultural resources and spiritual affinity have fueled David's film career. Moreover, acting sometimes provides him with the same mystical moments that he finds in music, as he moves into a zone that connects him to something much greater than himself.

The Institute provided David with possibilities and skills to explore art, music, psychology, acting, and spirituality throughout his life. His adaptability and his willingness to revise his choices reflect self-confidence gained in his early Esalen years, when everyone recognized him and he was welcomed everywhere at the Institute. David maintains a profound faith that his emotional and spiritual authenticity will always allow him to overcome misfortune and transform himself throughout his lifetime.

Science and Spirituality

Although Albert Wong's childhood was unusual, it was far more conventional than David's. While he was growing up, Albert could not imagine a place like Esalen. Instead, he sometimes daydreamed about winning a Nobel Prize. His father, a theoretical physicist, encouraged him to surpass his own considerable accomplishments and someday discover scientific theories that explained the mysteries of the universe. Albert grew up believing in demonstrable empirical truths. "Science in those days was my religion," he said (Wong 2002:15).

By the time he reached his early twenties, however, Albert had abandoned science in order to search for keys to the cosmos and to personal fulfillment through philosophy and spirituality. After being accepted as an Esalen work-study student, in 1995, he left a prestigious doctoral program in philosophy and bought a one-way plane ticket to California. Albert's impressive list of academic credentials, fellowships, and science awards, as well as his work ethic, made him a natural candidate to become Michael's assistant for a few years, like a number of other talented young men before him. However, he did not bond with individuals from the CTR, because he focused on Gestalt awareness practice. His closest relationships at Esalen were with other work-study students and community members involved in Gestalt.

Unlike David, Gordon, or Michael, Albert possessed relatively little spiritual privilege when he arrived at the Institute at the age of twenty-five. He was the only one of the four who was truly gifted, but his extraordinary scientific talents had little connection to his quest for personal and spiritual fulfillment.

Albert came to Esalen with few economic resources or specific cultural understanding of the Institute and its many spiritual paths. Moreover, he had no close relationships with individuals in the EMBA, the Esalen community, or the CTR.

He left Big Sur five years later with far more spiritual privilege. After living and working at Esalen for an extended period of time, Albert possessed heightened sensitivity to spiritual experience, detailed understanding of the Institute's foundational doctrines and practices, membership in varied networks of fellow seekers, and possibilities for developing an economically viable vocation that was in tune with his spiritual priorities.

Albert's life history illustrates Esalen's lasting impact on individuals with the desire, persistence, and willingness to sacrifice in order to develop their spiritual privilege and transform themselves. The Institute provides a context for personal and spiritual growth for people like Albert, who possess a burning desire to discover their core sparks of divinity and who can devote almost all of their energy to selecting, combining, and revising their personal identities and spiritual commitments.

Both of Albert's parents were children when their families fled the civil war in China in the late 1940s. His father, Cheuk-Yin Wong, grew up in British Hong Kong and spoke both Chinese and English throughout his childhood. He immigrated to the United States because of an undergraduate scholarship to Princeton, and he continued there for his doctorate in theoretical physics. In 1966, at the age of twenty-six, Cheuk-Yin brought his new wife to Oak Ridge, Tennessee, a small city that the U.S. Army Corps of Engineers had built to house scientists and workers developing atomic weapons during World War II.

The cold war between America and the Soviet Union was still intense when the Wongs moved to Tennessee, and, for almost three decades, much of Cheuk-Yin's research at Oak Ridge National Laboratories was top secret. He became a distinguished senior scientist with honors that included appointment as a fellow of the American Physics Association and president of the Overseas Chinese Physics Association.

Albert's older sister was born a year after his parents settled in Oak Ridge, he followed three years later, and a younger sister came along eight years after him. All three children excelled academically, and both of his sisters later became medical doctors with research interests. Albert, however, was the star. He remembers, "For the first seventeen years of my life, I was the golden child. Fast track, high flyer."

As the only son in a Chinese American family that abided by Confucian ethics, Albert tried to demonstrate great respect for his parents and his ancestors and to shine in every undertaking. Confucianism holds that people can perfect themselves through individual and collective effort, just as Esalen's foundational doctrine encourages full personal and spiritual growth (Rainey 2010). Thus, the Wongs lived out a philosophy that was remarkably similar to Esalen's spiritual foundations, and Albert traveled to Big Sur with beliefs that meshed with the Institute's commitment to maximizing human potential.

Albert characterizes his family as a classic first-generation Chinese American household, with strong traditions and social codes binding parents and children together. His full name is Albert Jun-Wei Wong, and each of his sisters also has a Chinese middle name. Friends and colleagues know him as Albert or sometimes Al. He uses Albert when he talks or writes about Esalen, in order to differentiate himself from Chungliang "Al" Huang, a Tai Chi master and philosopher who has offered workshops and seminars at the Institute for many decades.

Albert's sensitivity to the possibility that strangers might confuse Al Wong for Al Huang illustrates his recognition of the rocky terrain that ethnic minorities in the United States inevitably travel. However, in Oak Ridge and later as an undergraduate at Princeton and Oxford, being Asian American was rarely an emotional issue for him, and he did not pay much attention to ethnic identity politics. In many ways, he was an honorary white, navigating easily in the American mainstream (Tuan 1998). At Esalen, Albert's ethnicity was never an issue for him or others. It was simply part of who he was.

He was acutely aware of stereotyping after he left Esalen, however, when he auditioned for TV and movie roles in Hollywood as part of his efforts to find a spiritually meaningful vocation. And, in 2003, he worked with a political theatre company, TeAda Productions, and presented a one-man piece, *Myth*, about immigrants and people of color in America. Albert is neither culturally marginalized nor fully assimilated; instead, he has constructed a multicultural life that includes being Asian American (Dhingra 2007).

Until he went away to college, Albert idolized his father and wanted to be just like him. As a teenager, he basked in Cheuk-Yin's approval when he won national science prizes and scholarships. Nevertheless, recognition for excellence in physics at Princeton, like his Kusaka Memorial Prize, became less meaningful after he moved away from home. He began to experience an intense contradiction between his current life and his true hopes and dreams. In his senior year at Princeton, Albert privately defined himself as a spiritual seeker, and he believed that he had reached an important turning point (Lofland 1977). As he questioned the scientific career that he had envisioned since childhood and weighed his father's disapproval, Albert was frightened: "I started wavering from the true path of the good son. It was difficult."

After he won a Marshall scholarship to study philosophy at Oxford, Albert was relieved that his father dismissed his new interest as an immature phase that would soon pass. Cheuk-Yin remained fairly calm, because Harvard Medical School had agreed to hold Albert's place for a year. However, he grew more troubled when his son tried to explain that a life dedicated to science could never fulfill him spiritually or emotionally: "I didn't think that following in his footsteps or just heading on up the escalator was going to be right for me."

Albert began to count the costs of his stellar achievements. He resented his parents because he had sacrificed close friendships, fun, and much more in order to please them. In turn, his father was furious because Albert refused to discuss his disillusionment with science or his doubts about a medical career. Father and son each felt betrayed by the other.

At Oxford, Albert investigated spirituality more systematically. He read Martin Buber's *I and Thou*, and he suddenly realized that he had discovered a whole new world, where emotions, relationships, and connection to some higher power really mattered (Wood 1969). A few other Oxford philosophy students and faculty members also sought personal authenticity, and they shared his concerns about making the world a better place for everyone. Albert felt at home reading philosophy in England, and he hoped that academic philosophy and ethics would become his vocation.

He earned his second undergraduate degree at Oxford and left to attend graduate school in philosophy in the United States. After he returned to America, Albert kept in touch with his family, but he still refused to discuss his career plans. Their relationship deteriorated even more as he began to consider leaving graduate school altogether, because it failed to offer him an ethical basis on which to lead a meaningful life. At the time that he started to think seriously about his exit from academia, he read about Esalen in *Revisioning Philosophy* (Ogilvy 1991), a book that was edited by a member of Michael's inner circle.

Soon after he first read about the Institute, Albert applied to the work-study program, and, as usual for him, he was accepted. He quit graduate school with a terminal master's degree and moved to Big Sur. After learning about his decision, no one in Albert's horrified family spoke to him for almost a year.

He started out washing dishes in the main Esalen the dining room, toiling in the kind of menial position that is often assigned to new work-study students. After he was promoted to the extended work study student program, Albert screened visitors at the gate. Then, about a year after he arrived, he successfully applied for a staff position that involved organizing Friends of Esalen, editing the donors' newsletter, and developing the Institute's first systematic fund-raising database. Albert rose from the extended student ranks with unusual speed because he was one of the few Esalen residents familiar with computer programming, and his skills meshed with the Institute's new fund-raising priorities. Although he worked long hours and volunteered for other duties, Albert continued to participate wholeheartedly in Gestalt awareness practice workshops, ecstatic dance groups, and meditations.

Over his five years in Big Sur, he came to terms with many of his old relationships through Gestalt awareness practice, and, by the time Albert left the Institute, he felt more positively toward his family. At the beginning of his sojourn in Big Sur, however, things went very badly.

His father, mother, and sisters surprised Albert with a visit after he had been there for a year. They remarked on the Institute's gorgeous location and Albert's apparent happiness, but they still had no idea why he had walked away from his promising scientific career. Two years later, his father visited alone and tried to convince Albert that the Institute was academically disreputable, silly, cultish, and unworthy of his participation. Somehow after that awkward encounter, they started communicating again.

In 2000, Albert left Big Sur, a few months after he attended a small family gathering in China, where he first met his Hong Kong grandmother. He accepted a position in Los Angeles as an assistant to Jeremy Tarcher, a long-time Esalen trustee and a successful publisher. Tarcher had just started a small think tank for research on psychedelics and the expansion of human potential. The project never got off the ground, and, in a year, Albert had to look for another job. However, despite Albert's temporary unemployment, his father was relieved that his son had returned to the outside world, and they began to phone each other regularly.

After he reached LA and began work for Tarcher, Albert enrolled in acting and movement classes. Like David Price, he discovered that acting put him in touch with his core self and also provided a spiritual dimension that connected him with something vast and transcendent. His Esalen experiences with dance, psychodrama, and Gestalt were invaluable. Albert soon landed parts in commercials, music videos, daytime TV shows, and small independent films.

He cobbled together a living through acting jobs and teaching as an adjunct professor in the Theater Arts Department at Santa Monica College. Despite Albert's outstanding student evaluations, however, state budget cuts did away with new tenure-track jobs at all community colleges in the Los Angeles area. Long-term job security at Santa Monica College was out of his reach.

For almost eight years after leaving Tarcher's start-up, Albert auditioned, performed, and taught one or two classes a term at Santa Monica College. In order to survive financially, he also tutored science students from an elite private high school, taught an SMC outreach class at a low-income high school, and developed a psychodrama class at a small private college that offers psychology degrees. For the most part, he lived alone, although he had several intense romantic relationships with women. In order to stay in Los Angeles, he had to cope with brutal hours, a sense of fragmentation, and exhausting freeway commutes to his different jobs.

Albert started the website i/Thou (www.ithou.org) early in 2006. It is a social networking site for people who worked or studied at Esalen or who feel strong connections to the Institute because of its outreach. Members can chat, share pictures and news, send healing messages, and meditate online.

In 2008, he applied to one of the few mainstream clinical psychology graduate programs that might welcome someone interested in Gestalt approaches. It was also close to Oak Ridge, and Albert hoped that the proximity could make it easier to improve his relationship with his parents. Although Albert was almost forty years old, the department gambled on an unconventional student and offered him a fellowship. He started the doctoral program in clinical psychology at the University of Tennessee, where his faculty mentor supports his interest in Gestalt, although his own research focuses on hypnosis (Nash 2005). Albert can easily drive from Knoxville to Oak Ridge and visit his bemused parents, who are delighted that he has returned home to Tennessee and to academia.

Albert hopes to blend meditation, mindfulness, and bodywork in his clinical practice, and he is also interested in doing research about the ways that social media, like his website, can contribute to psychotherapy. In his new graduate-student career, he builds on the specific cultural and spiritual knowledge that Esalen gave him, his personal experiences with sacred meanings, and his wide networks of social contacts. If he becomes a successful clinician, Albert can earn a good living while helping his clients learn how to access their personal authenticity and expand their spiritual privilege. Like the other three men whose lives we have just explored, he will have discovered a vocation that provides him with personal and spiritual fulfillment.

Entitlement and Empowerment

As we noted earlier, each of the four men represents a different generation of individuals who have discovered new options in every area of their lives because Esalen democratized spiritual privilege. Michael devoted his life and his fortune to enable every American to maximize his or her human potential in mind, body, spirit, and psyche. Gordon explored Siddha Yoga and later became a therapist because Esalen had introduced Asian spirituality and Gestalt psychology to established academics, practitioners, and eager seekers in urban centers and college communities across America. David came of age in Big Sur and grew up with the knowledge that personal transformation was a lifelong possibility. Albert arrived at the Institute with less privilege than the other three, but Esalen allowed him to discover his spiritual priorities and the vocation that meshed with them.

Michael, Gordon, David, and Albert gladly sacrificed a great deal in order to embark on their quests for self-actualization. However they also found many rewards. Over time, they discovered personal and spiritual authenticity, and they acquired social contacts and skills that allowed them to change their lives. They took risks in order to fully comprehend and experience something sacred within and outside themselves.

When they were children, each one of them learned that that he was somehow different and special, with a unique destiny and an obligation to somehow make a difference in the world. Most of the time, they were all sure that their innate abilities would allow them to overcome every obstacle to their goals of maximizing their full human potential (Coles 1977:403–409).

Esalen's diffusion of alternative spirituality and personal growth psychology has allowed committed seekers and more casual samplers to add to their spiritual privilege in many different contexts. In the twenty-first century, the soul rush reaches women, as much as if not more than men. However, it started with men like Michael and his comrades. When Esalen began, the options to exercise spiritual privilege reached men first, because they enjoyed far more social freedom and economic flexibility than most women (McGee 2005:13–18). Men like Michael, Gordon, David, and Albert continue to embody the Institute's doctrines and practices, but Esalen's message beckons many other kinds of spiritual seekers.

Gender at Esalen

Men's continued centrality to Esalen reflects the ways that spiritual privilege combined with their gender advantage to enable the members of the founding generation to shape the Institute for themselves and other men like them. Michael, Dick, and their comrades made internal policies, built external social networks, and developed broad outreach in conformity with their personal standpoints. Those contributions attracted younger men like Gordon, David, and Albert.

When Michael and Dick founded the Institute, their attention to their own and other men's priorities was both inevitable and almost accidental. Men continue to chart the course because of the historical priorities that frame social arrangements and personal relationships in Big Sur. The CTR's conferences and research initiatives still reflect the founding generation's priorities. And, throughout Big Sur, a handful of widely known, enduring narratives verify men's centrality to Esalen and its mission.

Women are now central figures in other places that are part of the marketplace for alternative spirituality and personal growth. For example, Gurumayi succeeded Muktananda, Gordon's guru, as the international leader of Siddha Yoga, and Deborah Szekeley, who advised Michael and Dick about starting Esalen, founded the prestigious Golden Door spa chain.

Esalen influenced a number of leaders at the forefront of feminist spirituality in the 1970s. Anne Kent Rush belonged to the massage crew before she left Big Sur to work in the Bay Area feminist movement, writing best-selling books about women's personal growth and body issues (Mander and Rush 1976; Rush 1974, 1976). Dr. Rachel Naomi Remen, the internationally known author of *Kitchen Table Wisdom* (1976) and a key figure in the holistic health movement, participated in a number of Esalen's invitational seminars. Neither of them, however, became part of the inner circle or strongly identified with the Institute.

Rush and Remen were among the women who tried to redefine American spirituality in ways that reflected feminine priorities, just as Esalen's founders had emphasized their own concerns in the Institute's early agenda. However, Esalen indirectly contributed to the growth of feminist spirituality by opening up a range of choices that women could reinterpret in terms of their own priorities. Beginning in the mid-1970s, feminist spirituality addressed an expanding audience of women interested in reaching their full human potential, and, since that decade, more and more women have gained economic empowerment and other attributes associated with spiritual privilege (Davidson 2007; Gilbert 2006).

American women now enjoy far more opportunities to select, combine, and revise their religious commitments than they did when Esalen began. There are more options that mesh with their priorities and they have greater economic resources and more extensive social networks to explore possibilities for self-actualization (McGee 2005). Nevertheless, despite the development and spread of spiritualities that explicitly address women's aspirations, men's concerns still shape the Institute's and the CTR's broad agenda.

Although Gordon has worked to make Esalen more sensitive to gender questions in every area, men's advantage is still a subtle, complicated dimension of spiritual privilege at the Institute and in many other religious contexts, as well (McGuire 2008:159–184). In general, being an American man adds extra weight to other key resources that are part of spiritual privilege: wealth, advanced education, and access to political power. Gender subtly influences the shifting combinations of personal attributes and structural opportunities that make it possible for people to commit time and effort to personal transformation and spiritual fulfillment.

Following Gordon's lead, other CTR members and regular workshop leaders have started to think about gender and spirituality more critically. Esalen was one of the first places in America to encourage men's emotional awareness and expression of strong feelings and people at the Institute now try to create new definitions of masculinity and femininity. However, the old framework still supports gender inequality.

Stories About Men

The story about Michael and Dick's fateful road trip was one of three narratives that symbolically defined the Institute as a men's club. Like the creation story, two later narratives took on lives of their own and further underscored the founders' bravery and willingness to defy conventions. One was about an evening raid on gay trespassers that clarified the Institute's real and symbolic boundaries, and the other described rule breaking at a gala Hollywood dinner.

The three central stories cement men's primacy in Esalen's past, present, and future. They supported Esalen's unspoken commitment to men's spirituality, affirmed the founding circle's importance, and emphasized the Institute's cultural significance. For decades, these three stories have contributed to the Institute's organizational culture and men's solidarity within the CTR (Griswold 1994:124–126), and they are still part of contemporary folklore about Esalen (Kripal 2007a:96–97, 208–209).

The creation narrative, the description of drawing sexual and spatial boundaries, and the story about humiliating a famous movie star all illuminate ways that Esalen's inner circle accepted and affirmed their gender advantage. The three tales encouraged public recognition of the founders' substantial spiritual privilege and also supported their mission to democratize it.

Familiarity with the narratives adds to anyone's spiritual privilege at Esalen, because the tales are important markers of insiders' knowledge about the Institute's culture. When people refer to the stories, they differentiate themselves as informed participants, rather than casual visitors. While the creation narrative that we considered earlier is the one that the general public knows best, all three have helped position Esalen within the spiritual marketplace.

Securing Boundaries on the Night of the Dobermans

The narrative that defined Esalen's real and symbolic boundaries describes an incident that took place soon after Michael and Dick returned from their road trip and claimed the Murphy family's resort as a place for themselves and people with similar goals. One evening late in 1961, they gathered a handful of friends to drive away a rowdy group of gay men who routinely partied late at night in the hot-springs tubs (Anderson 1983:51–52; Kripal 2007a:96–97). Shortly afterward, Michael and Dick began to call their story "The Night of the Dobermans," because of three gentle but fierce-looking dogs that accompanied them on their mission.

When they took over the lease on the Murphy family's motel, the two founders paid workers to encircle the hot-springs bathing area with a high metal fence that protected their property's chief asset and marked its physical boundaries. They installed a gate, which they planned to close at 8:00 every evening (Anderson 1983:50). This innovation surprised and disconcerted many Big Sur residents and regular visitors.

Free access to the hot springs at all hours had been routine for years, and, since the late 1930s, people from up and down the coast had gathered together in the tubs. Beatniks, bohemians, Hell's Angels, weary workers, men and women, gays and straights all visited the hot springs occasionally. Although they were symbolically important, the new fence and curfew did little to restrict nighttime visitors' activities. Most Big Sur regulars ignored the recent designation of the springs as private property, and bathers easily climbed the fence.

On the evening that the story took place, a group of young men, some of them paying guests at the Murphy family's motel cabins, refused to obey the evening curfew and get out of the tubs. The two founders perceived the relatively small group as a significant challenge to their new authority, and they strongly believed that it was necessary for them to confront the trespassers and act bravely to identify the springs as a private enclave that would be a meeting place for people who shared their interests in spirituality and personal growth.

Michael and Dick gathered about a dozen friends and neighbors to storm the hot springs and evict the trespassers, but, when they arrived, they discovered no opposition. The three Dobermans that accompanied them continued to bark and snarl forebodingly, while the founders' contingent searched for the intruders, who had vanished almost as soon as they heard the band of human and canine enforcers scrambling down the path.

After their supporters disbanded and took the dogs home, Dick and Michael strolled up their steep driveway toward Highway 1, enjoying the quiet, beautiful night. In the bright moonlight, they came upon a young man and woman embracing. The benign intruders explained that Big Sur seemed so magical that they had been moved to stop and walk a bit. Michael interpreted the affectionate couple as a good omen, another instance of synchronicity, when serene (heterosexual) lovers displaced offensive (gay) trespassers. He believed that it was an auspicious portent of a loving and peaceful future for the new retreat (Anderson 1983:52).

On the Night of the Dobermans, Dick and Michael signified that their resort was no longer open to all comers. Big Sur Hot Springs belonged to them and to members of their social networks. They successfully claimed the land and made it a haven for spiritual explorers instead of unattractive hedonists. In reality, drugs, drink, and reasonably discrete sex have never disappeared from the hot springs, but those transgressions are usually framed in the broad context of personal growth, rather than pure pleasure. And, over the decades, most of the welcome visitors to the springs have been affluent, attractive heterosexuals.

Michael and Dick were willing to fight to further their goal of creating a peaceful spiritual retreat. The fusion of physical daring, emotional courage, and some higher purpose became a consistent theme in their own and Esalen's definitions of masculinity. By driving out the gay trespassers, Michael and Dick planted the flag of heterosexuality and underscored their own heroic masculinity (Bird 1996).

Men were supposed to value the maximization of human potential and, if necessary, to defend that ideal through bravery and a willingness to defy conventional social norms. Therefore, the narrative about the Night of the Dobermans has remained central to the Institute's self-definition and its emphasis on personal heroism.

Michael's admiration for the couple reflected the fundamental unspoken assumption of heterosexuality that still prevails at Esalen. The heterosexual bias shaped the founding circle's unrestrained activities in the 1960s and early 1970s, when the early "sexual revolution" embraced opposite-sex promiscuity and marginalized gays and lesbians.

During that period, affluent, educated young Americans openly discussed and explored heterosexual sex and masturbation. They viewed liberated sexuality as central to emerging values that supported personal authenticity and broke through emotional repression (Allyn 2000). The broad cultural shift that supported heterosexual freedom also affirmed Esalen's tolerance for *almost* any kind of personal experimentation that could lead to personal and spiritual actualization.

The Institute has tailored some workshops for gays and lesbians since the late 1960s, but its informal culture supports the consistent, invisible heterosexual principle that was part of the early sexual revolution and that is still generally associated with true masculinity in America (Kimmel 1994). Despite the presence of well-known individuals like the poet Allen Ginsberg and Betty Berzon, a pioneering gay and lesbian psychologist, almost everyone at Esalen assumed that their peers were heterosexual at heart unless they clearly indicated otherwise (Kripal 2007a:462).

Over the decades, the founders' model for sexuality and romance remained staunchly heterosexual, but, as they aged, their sexual activities and ideals veered away from casual experimentation to relatively long-term commitments. By the time they reached their fifties, Michael, Dick, George, and other inner circle members defined long-term relationships as the appropriate finales for their youthful sexual exuberance (Leonard 1983). They came to view steadfast erotic love as a means to make commitments to all humanity and repair the world, imbuing monogamy with profound spiritual dimensions (Leonard 1983:214–218).

Contemporary work-study students and seminarians in their twenties and early thirties generally renounce the joys of commitment, and they are usually unconcerned with fervent monogamy or anything approaching it. Younger Esalen generations are equally, if not more, sexually adventurous and promiscuous than earlier cohorts, although, as they age, they may also become more interested in sexual fidelity. They view the founding generation's once groundbreaking sexual openness as a fairly conventional option amid a wealth of other possibilities that have emerged in recent decades.

Since the 1990s, a wide range of personal sexual choices have been accepted at Esalen, so long as they do not infringe on others' freedom to choose. Gay, lesbian, and transgender visitors comfortably acknowledge their sexuality, soak naked in the hot springs, and enroll in diverse Esalen workshops, not just those related to lesbian, gay, or transgender issues. While heterosexual assumptions still frame most discourse at the Institute, Esalen offers space for varied sexualities and for activities that range from celibacy to abandoned promiscuity.

The story about the Night of the Dobermans demarcated the Institute's initial physical and moral boundaries and underscored the founders' commitment to emotional and spiritual growth, rather than mere narcissistic pleasure seeking. Gender identities are no longer so constrained, but the goal of expanding human potential has remained unchanged since the Night of the Dobermans.

The Gestalt Guru and the Movie Star

The third narrative is about rule breaking that facilitates personal and social transformation. It endorses outrageous behavior to advance human potential, and it uncritically supports men's dominance at Esalen and in the wider society.

In Big Sur and elsewhere, men from the founding generation sometimes flouted many kinds of social conventions and demonstrated their superiority to widely accepted norms. They chose when and where to follow rules, because they believed that they had the special knowledge, abilities, and means to change themselves and also to make history.

The story of the Gestalt guru and the movie star illustrates the arrogance that can accompany spiritual privilege and also demonstrates how Esalen's founding circle took its gender advantage for granted. This narrative is about insiders' activities at a glamorous party where they were honored guests.

Michael, George, and Fritz accepted their famous hostess's invitation because they wanted to convince Hollywood celebrities to support the Institute, without appearing as if they were desperate missionaries.

In 1966, an Esalen contingent attended a star-studded party in order to educate the movie industry about the benefits of spiritual privilege and to encourage other guests to cultivate their full potential. Michael and his comrades wanted to bring their vision of personal and spiritual growth to some of America's best-loved movie personalities. They also hoped to tactfully communicate the fact that Esalen's history-changing mission made them more important than mere actors and actresses, however famous. No one anticipated that Fritz would take a vulnerable movie queen, Natalie Wood, over his knee and spank her in front of a circle of bemused guests.

Men from the Institute's founding generation and those who later became part of the Center for Theory and Research still repeat this narrative. They treat the story as a delightful joke on self-important celebrities that demonstrates the Institute's lasting cultural significance (Kripal 2007a:208–209).

Fritz's reputation as a star therapist made him an ideal member of the delegation to the Hollywood party, along with Michael, George, and some other well-known men associated with Esalen. They were the Institute's aristocrats, just as Jennifer Jones, their hostess, was Hollywood royalty. Jones had won the Academy Award for best actress for her role in *Song of Bernadette* (1943), and, soon afterward, she divorced her first husband to marry David O. Selznick, the mercurial producer of *Gone with the Wind*. A few years before Selznick died, in 1965, Michael became her confidante because of their mutual interests in psychology and alternative spirituality.

Jones rarely left home during the year after her husband's death, but she kept in touch with Michael and her other friends in Big Sur. She hoped that her first major party after her recent reclusiveness would honor the Institute and introduce Hollywood elites to its approaches to healing and personal expansion. The dinner party promised to extend Esalen's visibility into new social networks and to increase public awareness by associating it with major celebrities.

She initially envisioned a small informal event, but the party grew into an extravagant production, lit by glowing Chinese lanterns outside and candles inside. Michael and Jennifer constructed a guest list of eighty names, mixing Esalen representatives with the film industry's established old guard, including Jason Robards Jr. and newcomers like Dennis Hopper (Leonard 1988:251–256). Almost all of the guests were rich, therapeutically savvy, and very interested in combining psychotherapy and spirituality. Moreover,

Fritz was always a powerful presence at the Institute. © Gene Portugal: www.pamwalatka.
com

many of them had already explored new ways to understand and augment their spiritual privilege. Among those present were Rock Hudson, a Scientology devotee; Shirley McLain, an outspoken advocate for trance channeling; and James Coburn, who would soon become a follower of the Indian guru Bhagwan Shree Rajneesh.

George introduced Esalen's general goals in a brief speech over predinner drinks, neither inviting his audience to come to Big Sur en masse nor requesting donations. He feared that celebrities would be so attracted to Esalen that "they'd take it over" (Leonard 1988:251). He also worried that an overwhelming Hollywood presence in Big Sur could diminish the Institute's serious commitment to develop theory and practice, although, for many decades to come, he frequently promoted Esalen's fame by dropping movie stars' names (Leonard 1988:255).

After the low-key introduction, guests adjourned to a flower-filled solarium for the sumptuous candlelit dinner. When the meal ended, the hostess led her company to another room to view and discuss *Journey into the Self*, a black-and-white documentary of a rather dull therapy group that was led by a well-known humanistic psychologist, Carl Rogers. Bored guests drifted away, and, when the film ended and Rogers offered to lead an encounter group, only one person was interested in joining.

The real action was out by the swimming pool, where the flamboyant Fritz had organized a Gestalt therapy demonstration for about a dozen people. It was a relatively small, informal replication of the large Gestalt workshops, where he examined immediate behavior to increase participants' awareness of their motivations and actions. Individuals volunteered to sit facing Fritz so that he could be their guide as they explored their current conflicts and questions about their self-identities.

Resembling an ancient turtle dressed up in black tie, Fritz cajoled and coerced his growing audience as he sought volunteers willing to place themselves in his hands. Natalie Wood was the first to assume the patient's hot seat. She was a top box-office draw at the time, and her visible support for Esalen could add dramatically to its public prominence. A former child actress who had become an even bigger star as an adult, Wood bridged old Hollywood and the new, restless generation of the 1960s. She was known both for her mainstream leading roles in popular hits like *West Side Story* and for her edgy performance in *Rebel without a Cause* (Lambert 2004).

According to one observer, Wood looked sparkling and desirable, as she sat across from Fritz and adorably skipped out of his verbal traps. The

Gestalt guru tried to get her to admit that she was acting out a flippant role, but she refused to change her style. Fritz confronted her, "You're nothing but a little spoiled brat who always wants her own way" (Leonard 1988:254). Suddenly, Fritz seized Wood and spanked her. She did not cry, but she immediately left the party. Afterward, a lesser star took the vacated hot seat, but, when Fritz also accused her of "absolute phoniness," she walked away before there was another spanking (Leonard 1988:254).

None of the Esalen insiders' accounts of the dinner party, verbal or written, ever dealt with Fritz's use of physical force or his utter disregard for Natalie Wood's feelings or well-known emotional fragility. The Esalen representatives at the party regarded the Gestalt guru's behavior as typical of his eccentricities and nothing more. They accurately assumed that his outrageous behavior might tempt Jones, Wood, and other dinner guests like Dennis Hopper to visit the Institute someday, because of the intense experience and personal expansion that the makeshift Gestalt group had previewed.

Other movie people learned about the spanking within a week. And, true to Michael and George's predictions, Esalen began to intrigue some A-list celebrities who did not attend the dinner, like Candice Bergen and Ali McGraw. They considered the spanking as nothing more than a rock on the bumpy path to self-actualization, and they were eager to visit Big Sur with friends who had actually been to Jones's soiree and observed the incident between Fritz and Wood.

Despite or possibly because of the Gestalt demonstrations, the party created a number of lasting connections between Hollywood and Big Sur. Jennifer Jones became Fritz's patient, and she gave him a white embroidered Russian shirt that was one of his prized possessions (Perls 1969; no pagination). Natalie Wood visited Esalen in 1970, with no obvious hard feelings, in order to prepare for her role in *Bob & Carol & Ted & Alice* (Lambert 2004:78–82). Jennifer Jones's event, according to Esalen's emissaries, marked the moment when the culture of human potential trumped the cult of celebrity, and Fritz's shameful behavior showed the film colony about the immediacy and importance of the human potential movement.

Because of widespread cultural assumptions about men's prerogatives in the mid-1960s, no core members of the founding generation publicly criticized Fritz's contemptuous behavior at the party or his frequent outbursts at Esalen. Natalie was one of many women whom Fritz manhandled. In his book *In and Out of the Garbage Pail* (1969), Fritz rationalized his routine practice of spanking women on the hot seat:

And there are thousands of patients like her [a woman in an Esalen Gestalt group] in the States. Provoking and tantalizing, bitching, and irritating their husbands and never getting their spanking. . . . A Polish saying is: "My husband lost interest in me. He never beats me anymore." (no pagination)

In Fritz's view, physically punishing assertive women as if they were wayward children brought them to their senses and made it possible for them to deal with their illusions about personal empowerment. Although he questioned the possibility of an inner divinity within each individual, Fritz believed in a true self that could be touched and restored. Michael called Fritz a closet mystic who experienced his own versions of satori (Kripal 2007a:164). The Gestalt guru asserted that any means, including violence and sexual exploitation, were justifiable if they contributed to a woman's full feminine development.

Justifications for emotional and physical abuse were by no means limited to Fritz and Esalen. During the 1960s and 1970s, therapists and spiritual teachers often promised to heal women in exchange for complete submission to their demands. Physical violence and emotional abuse were common to the guru culture of the era (Jacobs 1989:91–103, 124–131).

When Jennifer Jones introduced the human potential stars to her friends, the Institute cadre condescended to them. They were certain that Esalen's luminaries would someday outshine Hollywood celebrities throughout the world. Fritz enjoyed considerable leeway because he was one of the Institute's major attractions. The night that he spanked the Natalie Wood, he staked additional claims for Esalen's social importance and for men's domination of the human potential movement.

The narratives about the Hollywood party and the Night of the Dobermans, as well as the tale of Esalen's creation, illustrate how men developed stories to affirm their centrality at the Institute and in the wider American culture. Over decades, the founders' pursuit of spiritual growth has involved fun, self-discovery, and interpersonal validation within a close-knit circle of comrades (Kimmel 2004:218–219). The foundational stories and their ongoing importance represent one way that Esalen's first generation has reached out and spread the Institute's mission to younger men and to women who might be able to appreciate Esalen's extraordinary early history.

Heroes

The narratives about the Institute's birth, the Night of Dobermans, and the Hollywood party describe individuals in Esalen's early inner circle as masculine men who were willing to take physical and emotional risks to affirm and share their ideals. At Esalen in the 1960s, Michael, Dick, and their friends created the kind of social space where men commonly hang out together and fashion their masculine identities in relation to other men like themselves (Bird 1996; Martin 2001). The inner circle developed and enacted definitions of masculinity that established spiritual seekership as a rational, admirable concern for every twentieth-century man.

At the time that Michael and Dick founded Esalen, Americans rarely questioned men's prerogatives, and men completely dominated American spiritual and intellectual life. Mainstream liberal or conservative faiths had no major women leaders, and there were few women academics or public intellectuals. Esalen simply mirrored its host society.

The founders always welcomed women like Nancy Lunney-Wheeler, the long-time program director, because she possessed spiritual affinities, cultural resources, social networks, and financial means that resembled their own. However, they never fully included any women, however privileged, in their boisterous masculine camaraderie. Most of the women who were closely associated with Esalen's early inner circle entered as girlfriends or wives; otherwise, like Nancy, they stayed on its margins for decades.

Michael, Dick, and their comrades venerated a handful of accomplished older women whose writing and practice inspired massage and bodywork at the Institute. Ida Rolf (1978) and Charlotte Selver (1979) had national reputations when they came to Big Sur, and they distanced themselves from the sexual promiscuity and interpersonal games that defined life at Esalen during its first decade.

Another woman, Janet Lederman (1969), founded the Gazebo Preschool and codirected the Institute in the late 1970s. She augmented her personal power by never entering Esalen's competitive heterosexual arena, since she was a lesbian. While these three women, as well as a few others like Nancy, influenced specific spheres at the Institute, they rarely shaped the goals and doctrines that characterized Esalen and secured its preeminent position in the spiritual marketplace.

There were many informal sexual rules that marginalized women in Big Sur during the 1960s and early 1970s. At the same time that Fritz held sway in his Gestalt programs, other men played out their personal sexual fantasies in workshops, encounter groups, and casual interactions (Miller 1971). One member of the Institute's early inner circle interviewed a highly qualified applicant for the select Esalen fellows program and told her, "If you are a resident fellow, you must be sexually open. If you come here, expect to put out"

(Doyle 1981). After being admitted to the program, she was able to cope with the predatory environment and turned away unwelcome overtures. Nevertheless, men's domination and women's submission at the Institute continued to disconcert even this strong woman:

> The psychological environment there was fraught with mountain men. If they didn't have guns on their hip, they should have. They were very macho! If they didn't have codpieces in their pants, they should have. The other side was willowy maidens given to moss in their hair and doe-like glances. (Doyle 1981)

In the 1960s and 1970s, most Esalen men found its ethos of heterosexual experimentation entrancing, even if some women refused to cooperate with them. Men could pursue spiritual experience and emotional growth with masculine bravado, gainsaying what one current Esalen resident described as fears of being "fake men."

Esalen was a new, exciting context for masculine spirituality. Its founding generation added spirituality and self-knowledge to traditional masculine attributes of heterosexuality, physical prowess, bravado, certainty, and personal empowerment. The Institute's ideal of emotionally available and spiritually sensitive men contrasted dramatically with established social norms in an era when the majority of mainstream Americans had equated religiousness and spirituality with emasculation (Miller and Stark 2002).

Stoic cowboys or silent astronauts embodied masculinity in the popular imagination (Connell 1995). In the late 1960s, however, media that were directed toward sophisticated audiences began to describe different kinds of heroes who exemplified Esalen's expanded definitions of masculinity (Litwak 1967).

Despite the widely shared definitions that separated spirituality and masculinity, the Institute's founding circle successfully redefined middle- and upper-class men's spirituality for themselves and for other men who joined the human potential movement. Earlier American revitalization movements had failed to make lasting connections between manliness and religious commitment because they offered men neither the bravado nor the sexual rewards that the Institute linked to self-actualization. Unlike Esalen, the earlier revitalizations were embedded in American Protestantism, and they did not build on popular the definitions of masculinity that included sexuality and boisterous enjoyment of food, drink, and drugs.

Nevertheless, some of earlier revitalization movements partially incorporated the rewards that Esalen offered decades later. In the late nineteenth century, muscular Christianity emphasized sports and physical accomplishment in many of the same ways that Esalen did (Putney 2001). And, in the early twentieth century, Billy Sunday, a former Major League outfielder and famed revivalist, crusaded against feminized Christianity and evangelized men to pursue aggressive, assertive religiosity (Martin 2002). Despite advocating for men to become more religious, however, these Protestant movements never supported the worldly pleasures or the possibilities for personal fulfillment that Esalen offered. The Institute moved beyond conventional revivalism to define masculine spirituality as something that could not be contained within the boundaries of established faiths.

The three central Esalen narratives' emphasis on personal heroism as part of spiritual wholeness allowed men to focus on the sacred without becoming feminized. Practices leading to spiritual and emotional transformation at Esalen embraced a number of activities traditionally associated with American masculinity: flamboyant heterosexuality, sports, and also meaningful, fulfilling work.

Men at Esalen work hard in order to realize their full human potential and implement their visions of a better world. Self-actualization that requires manly focus and commitment is viewed as a greater reward by far than money or external recognition (Leonard 1991). At Esalen and elsewhere, men who have been directly or indirectly influenced by the Institute's doctrines sometimes labor to exhaustion in the service of their broad spiritual goals (Leonard and Murphy 1995). They run marathons, climb mountains, or build houses for hurricane victims in order to affirm their religious priorities. The Institute has always supported a work ethic that contradicts some lasting popular stereotypes of Big Sur as a haven for effete spiritual dilettantes who wallow in outrageous activities (Wolfe 1976).

Sport, sex, and public service emerged as key early themes at Esalen, although there was no explicit focus on definitions of masculinity. However, well before an American men's identity movement began in the late 1970s, Esalen's workshops and groups addressed men's yearning to discover their core selves and connections to the cosmos by means of challenging personal quests that involved self-examination, confrontation with their inner demons, and revision of their life stories (Abell 1976).

Michael and his colleagues wrote and spoke publicly to audiences of men about ways that they could enrich their lives and actively transform society. The founding generation's public testimony and efforts to exemplify their own ideals helped spread new definitions of masculine spirituality to middle-class men, who embraced the men's movement in the late 1970s and 1980s (Ehrenreich 1983).

From the mid-1970s through the 1990s, many Esalen workshops and seminars helped men become heroes of their own lives, as they reworked their autobiographies and mapped their personal journeys. This approach reflected Joseph Campbell's (1949) claim that ancient mythology made it possible for everyone to discover a unique spiritual and emotional identity. Men could find archetypes that enabled them to explore the labyrinths of contemporary society in order to fully know themselves.

Campbell and Sam Keen (1991) became heroic men's movement figures long after they first visited Big Sur. From the late 1960s on, both of them worked individually, but they also collaborated as workshop and seminar leaders. Like Michael and his comrades, they urged people to identify with mythological heroes and to dedicate themselves to lifelong personal quests (Faludi 1999:179).

Esalen was a launching pad for the ideas that fueled the men's movement in the same ways that it catalyzed the human potential movement and other cultural uprisings that enabled Americans to define and refine their personal identities. During the two decades when the men's movement surged, Campbell's and Keen's earlier Esalen seminars and workshops became models for other leaders' programs at the Institute and at retreat centers explicitly associated with the men's movement.

The two men's-movement champions shared the same kinds of spiritual privilege as the Institute's founding circle. Campbell was a retired academic philosopher and mystical writer, and Sam Keen was an Ivy League Ph.D. and *Psychology Today* contributing editor. Bill Moyers's 1988 PBS series, *The Power of Myth*, featured Campbell's interpretations of the force of heroic tales across all cultures, and, three years later, Moyers spotlighted Keen in a related set of programs, *Your Mythic Journey*.

Campbell died in 1987, shortly before PBS aired his interviews and made him a celebrity. The 1988 May-October *Esalen Catalogue* memorialized him and his wisdom, with tributes by Keen, George Lucas, and other well-known men. Michael acknowledged Campbell as "a radiant presence" (Murphy 1988:11).

However, throughout Campbell's lifetime and afterwards, Michael and his comrades never dealt with his patronizing attitudes toward women or his casual, virulent anti-Semitism, which involved frequent comments and occasional diatribes (Gill 1989). The inner circle generally ignored those failings, as they had Fritz's, because they believed that Campbell's contributions overshadowed his misdeeds. No one in power at the Institute wanted to detract from the important ongoing conversations about heroes and archetypes by bringing up issues that they believed had far less importance (Kripal 2007a:190–192).

The inner circle's tolerance for obvious prejudice was part of a broad pattern that made it possible for influential, spiritually privileged men to make their own rules at Esalen and perpetuate different kinds of discrimination that, at the time, seemed only to add to their masculine power and authority. There was little censure of anyone, man or woman, who maximized personal possibilities, contributed significantly to the advancement of human potential, and generated positive publicity for Esalen. Although the Institute's current leaders, such as Gordon, address gender inequalities and racism in many contexts, they have never come to terms with Esalen's historic legacies of exploitation and occasional bigotry.

Other men, not women, were the only ones who could have legitimately questioned men who misused power at the Institute, because they alone validated one another's full masculinity at Esalen. In the same ways, only men have had the power to fully define maleness within the larger society. While considering the social contexts for affirming masculinity in America, the sociologist Michael Kimmel (1994) described the essence of the Institute's workshops that celebrated men as heroes of their own lives: "We test ourselves, perform heroic feats, take enormous risks, all because we want other men to grant us our manhood" (129).

Revising Masculinity

Esalen men never built a highway to a new American masculinity. Instead, they provided a compass that pointed toward a number of innovative routes toward being a man. In the 1960s, the inner circle acted from a shared standpoint, without intentionally considering gender issues. Later, some CTR members thought about masculinity more purposefully. Shifts in the wider culture and recognition of the contributions of the second wave of American feminism led to critiques of men's bad behavior and exploitation of women in American society as a whole and also at Esalen (Leonard 1983). Later revisionists at the Institute took note, and they encouraged men to examine masculinity as a set of relationships with their inner selves, other men, women, and future generations (Wheeler 2000).

Despite their continued appreciation of heroism, in the 1980s, men at Esalen explored slightly different meanings of gender and masculinity in workshops and seminars. Sam Keen, who had been Campbell's close, apparently uncritical comrade, stressed interpersonal respect and social equality as elements of heroism. Influenced by the progressive politics of the late 1970s, his work engaged issues of social justice and diversity. As new leaders like Keen emerged at the Institute and in the wider society, the old ones faded away, along with much of their overt prejudice.

Keen's best-seller, *Fire in the Belly: On Being a Man* (1991), became required reading for participants in the late-twentieth-century men's movement. As men pursued self-knowledge and spiritual awareness, Keen argued, they needed to create private ethics and practices of strength, potency, and virility that affirmed fairness. Keen challenged men to discover their true hearts and personal callings by selecting, combining, and revising their personal practices and religious beliefs. He called for American men to enact and enhance their spiritual privilege by embracing fundamental values of equality and decency and moved beyond Campbell's emphasis on individual heroism and virility to endorse feminism and progressive social values as hallmarks of manhood.

At the height of the men's movement, in the 1980s and early 1990s, Keen and other influential workshop leaders offered upper- and middle-class men new possibilities to define masculinity in terms of equality, helping them adapt to an era when they felt besieged by feminism on one side and shrinking job opportunities on the other (Faludi 1999). Toward the end of the twentieth century, however, an emphasis on men's connections to other men, as fathers and friends, crept into conversations about politically progressive personal quests,

This recent approach to masculinity at Esalen reflects a slow cultural shift among educated men that is influenced by an informal movement for alternative masculinity (Matlack, Houten, and Bean 2010). This perspective calls for full equality between women and men, while recognizing the possibility of differences in masculine and feminine approaches to social relationships (Connell and Messerschmidt 2005).

Gordon first brought alternative masculinity to Esalen by means of his Gestalt workshops and seminars where participants explored their current gender roles in relation to personal identity and interpersonal connections. Like Keen, he urged men to work toward progressive change, calling on them to create a society that affirmed their genuine emotional and material appreciation of one another, of women, and of children (Wheeler and Jones 1996).

As both a therapist and a theorist, Gordon scrutinizes men's desperate need to break away from vicious, competitive power struggles and their attempts to demonstrate their power over one another. By tearing down other men, they temporarily ward off their feelings of worthlessness and demonstrate their masculinity. Gordon asserts that the relentless competition to prove their masculinity often humiliates men, whether they win or lose their endless contests with one another. Feelings of shame lead men to be selfish, lonely, and isolated from meaningful contact with others (Wheeler 1996:36–37).

Men will continue to re-create the worst aspects of a shaming society in their own lives, Gordon argues, unless they come to terms with their systematic mortification and develop lasting bonds with other men so that they can nurture and support one another through re-fathering. Gordon defines re-fathering as men's positive emotional connection to younger men, peers, and also to elders. Re-fathering involves men of different ages, biologically related or not, working together to develop a supportive context for their ongoing relationships.

Gordon has tried to implement this approach in his own life. Similarly, much earlier at Esalen, when the concepts of re-fathering and alternative masculinity had not been articulated, Dick Price brought an alternative masculinity to his relationship with his son David, as they developed new bonds during the late 1970s.

According to Gordon, supportive fathering and re-fathering can build nurturing communities of men who can work together for a better, more equal society. His perspective on alternative masculinities has informed a number of Esalen's recent offerings, including a June 2010 workshop, "Fathers and Sons: Celebrating Fathers' Day in the Tradition of the Old Ways," which was led by several generations of men from the same family. The workshop provided young men and their fathers or older mentors with experiences like wilderness hikes, storytelling around a campfire, and conversations about the meanings of manhood, much like those that David experienced as a son and Gordon developed as a father to his adult children.

When he was asked what advice he would offer youths trying to discover how to become happy, productive adults, Gordon responded, "Believe me, older men need to give to younger men just as much as younger men need mentoring and re-fathering" (Wheeler 2010). He argues that emotional contact and interpersonal connection can start to fill the emotional void left by fathers who were physically absent or emotionally tuned out from their children. Moreover, extensive, long-term re-fathering allows older and younger men to reveal their vulnerability to one another. As men of different generations meet to create and revise their personal stories, they can change themselves and join together to change society.

The Institute currently offers a number of workshops about alternative masculinity and re-fathering, while it still schedules offerings that deal with ethical quests, personal mythology, and mastery. As in many other areas of personal and spiritual growth, the Institute has not adopted a single approach to becoming a self-actualized man. The new focus on alternative masculinity, however, represents a sea change from Esalen's earlier emphases on hypermasculinity, lone heroes, or even ethical individual quests. Its recent popularity marks a massive transition from Esalen's historically uncritical acceptance of men's power.

Despite these recent challenges, the founding generation's assumptions and narratives about gender continue to influence the Institute, particularly the CTR. During Esalen's formative years, the men at its core created a unique American spirituality that changed their lives and appealed to other men like them. Over the years, they slowly revised some of their assumptions and reached out to offer their discoveries to other men and to women who appreciated the extraordinary possibilities that the Institute promises everyone privileged enough to select, revise, and combine their spiritual beliefs and practices.

For many years, women have made up the majority of Esalen's visitors, and they also predominate as clients in almost all personal and spiritual growth venues in the United States (Cornwall 2009; Miller and Stark 2002). However, the Institute continues to draw disproportionate numbers of men to its workshops about quests, sports, and alternative masculinity.

A Bay Area man who has been both Esalen's friend and a critic for five decades wondered about the CTR and asked me a question that uncovered the foundational link between spirituality and masculinity at the Institute: "Why did these guys need to invent their own religion when there are so many great traditional practices out there?" My answer: They wanted to transform themselves *on their own terms*, without questioning the benefits of masculinity or examining their overall spiritual privilege. Instead, they assumed that everyone, both men and women, would someday join the soul rush and maximize their human potentials at Esalen and throughout America.

Esalen's Legacies

When Michael and Dick founded Esalen early in the 1960s, they sought guidance and support from spiritually privileged elites and intellectuals. Michael soon reached far beyond his friends and acquaintances in California, however, to create relationships with other privileged seekers on the West and East Coasts.

Michael's genial personality, cultural and spiritual knowledge, and economic resources attracted moneyed supporters, public intellectuals, and politicians to Big Sur, where they met and became casual friends with Esalen insiders and with one another in the 1960s and early 1970s. The Institute was a gathering place and site for exchanges that led to a few close alliances and also generated many loose social networks that would later benefit their members (McAdam, McCarthy, and Zald 1996).

Esalen was never an independent social movement. Instead, it was a magnet for strategic actors from various grass-roots and professional groups that focused on expanding different aspects of human potential. Key members of diverse organizations that were engaged in transforming American psychology and spirituality sometimes met for the first time in Big Sur. They discovered common values and new possibilities for action when they participated in seminars and workshops or talked informally over meals and in the hot springs.

After they departed, the visitors often formed temporary coalitions to advance their shared goals. Relatively brief alliances and mutual support contributed to both Esalen's enduring social impact and to the independent accomplishments of different movements for social change in the 1960s and early 1970s (Burt 2005).

The human potential activists rarely became lifetime friends with the founding circle or with other notable individuals who passed through Big Sur. However, acquaintances, not close friends, are the people that are most likely to help others enter different social networks, start new careers, or get projects off the ground (Granovetter 1973). During the Institute's first decade, dozens of privileged visitors who were central to different movements for maximizing human potential developed loose personal ties with new acquaintances. Their alliances created Esalen's enduring influence on psychology, spirituality, education, and bodywork.

The effective leaders and committed rank and file who visited the Institute usually identified with fairly narrow perspectives such as Gestalt psychology or sensory awareness. But, like successful political activists, advocates for specific approaches to maximizing human potential bonded with one another because of their shared values (McAdam and Paulsen 1993). Because of its founders' commitment to diverse approaches, Esalen became a unique crucible for mobilizing support for alternative spirituality and psychology across different perspectives.

Faculty and students from Brandeis, Harvard, Stanford, the University of California at Berkeley, and UCLA traveled to Big Sur and met one another in small invitational seminars, lectures, or workshops, where they could share ideas and also participate in intense experiences. In the 1960s, the human potential trade route started in New York City around the New School for Social Research and Columbia University and jogged up to the Boston area's university communities. It bypassed most of Middle America before going through Berkeley, San Francisco, and Palo Alto, as it ran down the Pacific Coast to Esalen, where the East Coast branch connected to the route running up from West Los Angeles through Santa Barbara. About a half-dozen key communities on the Esalen route each housed thousands of people who were engaged in exploring new approaches to personal and social transformation, and most of them were eager to connect with their counterparts from other places.

High-profile figures like the father of humanistic psychology, Abraham Maslow, or Episcopal bishop James Pike, who later left the Church to head the Center for Democratic Institutions in Santa Barbara, visited Esalen and publicly supported the Institute. Michael made friends with these and other less eminent but nevertheless influential men who wanted to make lasting changes to American society through diverse movements for personal and spiritual transformation. Core members of explicitly political groups, however, rarely marched under Esalen's banners of personal and spiritual growth.

Only a few well-known political activists publicly identified themselves with Institute. The folksinger Joan Baez lived nearby in Big Sur in the 1960s, and she became lifelong friends with some of the people at Esalen (Anderson 1983:102–103; Didion [1968] 1990:42–60). Another high-profile political figure, Daniel Ellsberg (2003), the man who gave the *New York Times* explosive documentation about America's covert military actions in Southeast Asia, visited Esalen a number of times over the years (Anderson 1983:291). Most people identified with the New Left, however, derided Esalen's goal of expanding human possibilities as bourgeois and individualistic (Rakstis 1971).

Despite their many political differences, activists across the spectrum of progressive movements for social or personal change all believed that American society was fundamentally flawed. Whether they wanted to incite revolution or simply transform individuals, participants in varied progressive movements demanded new kinds of self-knowledge and more honest interpersonal relationships.

Human potential advocates and quasi-revolutionaries sometimes supported one another's outreach because of their shared desire to stimulate critical thinking throughout America. Dissident theology students from the Pacific School of Religion, in Berkeley, for example, succinctly presented the New Left's and the personal growth advocates' shared vision of inevitable personal, political, and social growth when they prophesized: "What we confront—willingly or not we are thrust into it—is a time of disintegration of a dying civilization and the emergence of a new one" (Goodman 1971:215).

Political activists and human potential advocates often agreed about inevitable changes that could bring about new, better kinds of relationships among friends and lovers. Core members of movements for racial equality, peace in Vietnam, and student empowerment on college campuses also resembled human potential advocates and spiritual seekers in terms of their families' many economic and cultural resources (McAdam and Paulsen 1993; Whalen and Flacks 1990). Personal affluence allowed them to take temporary risks and abandon college or careers, and their money also helped fund their causes. In many ways, the New Left activists' ability to select, combine, and revise their political values mirrored the flexibility that characterized spiritually privileged seekers.

During the late 1960s, most successful human potential activists and spiritual entrepreneurs had good incomes or other financial resources that helped support their personal quests. Without substantial gifts from wealthy individuals and nonprofit foundations, however, their larger projects might have faded away. Generous benefactors backed the alternative spirituality and human potential movements' short-term victories and enabled them to have a lasting impact through enduring organizations. Over the decades, a number of generous donors helped support Esalen and also supported other institutions that shared its mission to expand every aspect of human functioning—mind, body, psyche, and spirit.

The singer Joan Baez has had a long connection with Esalen and she has known her friend, David Price, since he was a baby. ©Patrice Ward: www.patriceward.net

Esalen's Angel

External financial support helped alternative spirituality and human potential psychology become culturally legitimate, just as wealthy individuals and nonprofit foundations made it possible for movements for racial equality to build lasting social traction (Shiao 2005). Universities usually welcomed innovative research and teaching in new areas such as ethnic or woman's studies or humanistic psychology, as long as it came with significant new funding. Moreover, when emerging paradigms also engaged the hearts of students and faculty in the 1960s and 1970s, they were even more likely to receive a warm welcome from academia.

From the nineteenth century onward, wealthy Americans had funded academic research and other projects about alternative spirituality (Menand 2001). For example, Thomas Welton Stanford, the founder's brother, bequeathed Stanford University a substantial legacy to support research on psychic phenomena (Radin 2004:13–15). However, academic interest in this area dwindled and most students were uninterested, so the University gradually redefined Stanford's intent by broadening the meaning of "psychic" to include dreams, methodology, and various conventional fields of psychology.

Other prestigious schools, including Harvard and the University of Pennsylvania, also accepted donations for research on alternative spirituality and later used the money for other things. Mindful of the ways that mainstream universities could subvert their purposes, wealthy Americans who were interested in research and teaching about spirituality carefully specified projects or endowed independent institutions that were committed to exploring the expansion of full human potential and a better understanding of the sparks of divinity within everyone.

Academic work that was informed by alternative spirituality interested two twentieth-century billionaires who subsidized hundreds of projects that connected spirituality, science, and social advancement. John Templeton, who developed global mutual funds, and Laurance Rockefeller, an heir to one of America's great fortunes, promoted inclusive religiosity and spiritual innovation through their extensive philanthropy. Rockefeller and his Fund for the Enhancement of Human Spirit supplied vital resources for the Institute and projects directly related to it, while Templeton supported different venues, although he occasionally funded specific projects and individuals associated with Esalen.

Laurance Rockefeller once informed Michael that there were three living Americans who might be able to transform American culture: the comedian Woody Allen, California governor Jerry Brown, a longstanding friend of the Institute, and Michael himself (Kripal 2007a:421). From the early 1970s until his death, in 2004, Rockefeller donated millions of dollars to Esalen and three related organizations that promote inclusive spirituality and synthesize Asian and Western traditions: the San Francisco Zen Center, the Lindisfarne Association, and the California Institute for Integral Studies.

Because of his mother's interest in Zen Buddhism, Rockefeller, an exemplar of spiritual privilege, explored religion and philosophy as a teenager. His curiosity about alternative spirituality and transcendent experience expanded after he became an undergraduate philosophy major at Princeton (Winks and Babitt 1997:52). Throughout his life, Rockefeller supported endeavors that he believed could reconcile science with the supernatural and demonstrate that God is an ephemeral, albeit powerful essence that permeates all human existence (Kaufman 2004; Stark 2001:99–113).

Investments in profitable start-ups like Eastern Airlines, Intel, and Apple helped Rockefeller multiply his inheritance and made him a billionaire (Kaufman 2004). He was a high-profile advocate for environmentalism and wilderness preservation and donated hundreds of millions of dollars for conservation and environmental research (Winks and Babitt 1997). However,

Rockefeller usually downplayed his controversial financial gifts to projects involving alternative spirituality. For example, he rarely discussed his substantial grants in support of Harvard professor John E. Mack's research on earthlings' encounters with interplanetary aliens or the money that he later supplied for Mack's legal defense against allegations of professional misconduct.

Several years before Mack received his first Rockefeller grants, he attended a small invitational symposium in Big Sur that Michael organized in 1987 (Grof 2003). While he never entered the Institute's inner circle, Mack continued to participate in Esalen's loose social networks, and some of those contacts helped him tap Rockefeller's largesse, just as casual social connections that developed at the Institute have helped many other spiritual entrepreneurs.

However, good friends, rather than acquaintances, introduced Michael to Rockefeller in the 1960s, and Michael soon became the billionaire's trusted adviser for different projects to advance personal and spiritual potential. Rockefeller donated millions of dollars to Esalen for renovations and new buildings, invitational conferences, and Michael's book about extraordinary human functioning, *The Future of the Body* (Murphy 1992:xii). With Rockefeller's support, Michael transferred his personal archive of more than ten thousand documents and case histories about extraordinary human abilities to the Stanford Medical School Library, unintentionally carrying forward Thomas Welton Stanford's early vision of elite universities as sites for research and teaching about the supernatural.

Rockefeller also gave millions of dollars to the San Francisco Zen Center from 1971 through 1984, during the years when Richard Baker, one of Michael's closest friends, served as abbot. In the late 1960s, Baker became a nationally known figure when he spearheaded fund-raising for the first American Zen training monastery at Tassajara, another inland hot-springs retreat just over the Santa Lucia Mountains that backed the Institute (Downing 2001:104–107). A few years later, after Baker became abbot in charge of the San Francisco Center and Tassajara, Rockefeller provided money for the Zen Center to buy Green Gulch Farm on a beautiful site twenty miles north of San Francisco. New outreach possibilities for Americanized Zen developed through the Green Gulch residential community for families that practiced Zen while they worked at organic farming (Downing 2001:178–183).

During the 1970s, the Zen Center's Bay Area business empire expanded to include an organic produce market, partially stocked by Green Gulch; the Alaya Stitchery, which made and sold futons and natural-fiber clothing;

a small bookstore; a bakery; and an award-winning vegetarian restaurant that overlooked San Francisco Bay (Downing 2001:32). All but one business closed within a decade, and most of them only survived for a brief time because of creative bookkeeping and virtually free labor from Zen Center students. Rockefeller did not fund the projects directly, but his generosity to the Zen Center fueled Baker's ability to take it in many directions and to demonstrate that Zen could be practiced by anyone in almost any context.

Greens Restaurant was the only Zen Center enterprise that lasted. It has remained financially viable for more than thirty years because of its magnificent site, its beautiful, Japanese-inspired interior, and the cuisine that still features produce from Green Gulch (Madison and Brown 1987).

Michael sympathized with the abbot's strategy of using commerce to alert Americans to Zen and its potential relevance for everyone's daily life. He observed, "Richard had put an ancient and rich tradition into the center of the Bay Area scene" (Downing 2001:107). The two friends enthusiastically promoted each other's efforts to spread spiritual privilege, and Rockefeller supported their aspirations.

Baker's startups were less about making money than increasing public awareness and democratizing access to Zen (Tipton 1982). Therefore, publicity and fund-raising marked the auspicious beginning of each new venture. Early in 1967, for example, San Francisco's Avalon Ballroom was the site of a huge benefit where the Grateful Dead and Janis Joplin raised money for the Tassajara monastery and retreat center (Downing 2001:107).

Hundreds of people attended the concert and even more made small donations afterwards, but much of the money to build Tassajara came from three spiritually privileged elites who were interested in Zen: the founder of Xerox and the Zen Center's first six-figure donor; the CEO of Fidelity Mutual Investments; and a well-connected, wealthy East Coast socialite. All three eventually gave the Zen Center and Tassajara hundreds of thousands of dollars, but Rockefeller's largesse soon eclipsed the sum of all of their generosity.

During the 1970s and early 1980s, Baker and Michael traveled together to the Netherlands and the Soviet Union, brainstormed about new projects at the high table at Greens Restaurant, and telephoned one another almost every week (Downing 2001:33, 301). And they eagerly collaborated on different projects, such as the Zen Hospice in San Francisco and the CTR conference on extraterrestrial life.

Michael praised the wide-ranging networks of intellectuals, politicians, spiritual leaders, and celebrities that his friend brought together in the 1970s and 1980s, when he hosted private events or dinners in his quarters at the Zen Center and, later, at Greens. Michael remembered, "Because of Dick, everyone was meeting everyone else. Zen Center was the great connector" (Downing 2001:210).

By everyone, Michael meant people like California governor Jerry Brown, the celebrity restaurateur Alice Waters, the actor Peter Coyote, and other luminaries who were interested in transforming themselves and also repairing the world.

Rank-and-file Zen Center students never joined their lively conversations, and they silently served Baker's guests at his home and at his restaurant table. Unless people were very talented or wealthy, they never became part of Baker's or Michael's inner circles, and they rarely met Rockefeller or other major donors.

Long after Zen students had forced Richard Baker out because of his various transgressions, including his love of luxuries, Michael defended his friend. He drew parallels between dissidents at the Zen Center and his own critics at the Institute, imagining an envious rebel's thoughts:

> I want to practice with Baker-Roshi. I start to practice. My parents told me I had to be somebody. But right now, I'm just working here, changing sheets. Forgetting that when I came here, it was my choice, I didn't have to come. Meanwhile, there's Baker over there with the Governor and some friends. (Downing 2001:224)

Many of the abbot's other friends, including Laurance Rockefeller, shared Michael's perceptions about inevitable social and personal inequalities and hierarchies within spiritual organizations. Everyone had different abilities that defined his or her limits to personal and spiritual growth (Leonard and Murphy 1995:2–3). However, the leaders also believed that the doctrines and practices that they advocated would allow all people to move beyond their immediate limitations (Leonard and Murphy 1995).

Baker left the Bay Area in 1984 and established a short-lived center in Santa Fe. He then moved to Colorado as founding abbot of Crestone Mountain Zen Center, an isolated retreat high in the Sangre de Cristo Mountains (Downing 2001:286, 341). At Crestone, Baker continued to spread the message of maximizing human and spiritual possibilities, and he still maintained his close ties to Michael and Esalen.

Laurance Rockefeller funded Crestone Mountain Zen Center through the Lindisfarne Foundation, a nonprofit organization that began in 1972 with the purpose of investigating the spiritual foundations that are shared by all religions. Esalen inspired its founder, William Thompson, a former MIT professor, although he never wanted to build an enterprise as large, inclusive, or lively as the Institute (Thompson 1998).

Another wealthy Zen Center supporter had introduced Thompson to Rockefeller and the billionaire provided Lindisfarne with significant donations from the 1970s through the 1990s. Lindisfarne has now dwindled from an ambitious residential retreat and think tank to a loose association of fellows who meet annually. Since Rockefeller stepped back, the Fetzer Institute, founded by a Michigan media entrepreneur, provides most of Lindisfarne's funding.

Without cash infusions from major donors, Fetzer, Lindisfarne, and other small foundations dedicated to maximizing human potential can rarely sustain projects like the Crestone Mountain Zen Center or Esalen. They can, however, spread spiritual privilege by formalizing networks of individuals, such as the Lindisfarne Foundation fellows, who encourage and publicize one another's efforts to expand human possibilities and discover the ways that supernatural forces influence life on Earth. These groups bring together compatible spiritual entrepreneurs who affirm the invisible sparks that connect everyone and create loose social networks of spiritual elites like the select groups that dined at Richard Baker's table at Greens.

Although Rockefeller donated funds to the Institute for decades, the California Institute for Integral Studies in San Francisco, or CIIS, not the Institute, represents his greatest single contribution to Esalen's enduring influence. CIIS offers accredited undergraduate and graduate programs that are directly shaped by Aurobindo's integral philosophy and Esalen's emphasis on the full range of personal and spiritual growth.

Education for Spiritual Privilege

The symbolic road to Esalen passed through no more than a than a dozen communities before it reached Big Sur in the 1960s, but, fifty years later, the enlarged highway has developed branches that cover every corner of the United States. Because of the soul rush that Esalen started, possibilities for personal and spiritual transformation are now available in every college town. People take classes in meditation or humanistic psychology in Grand Forks, North Dakota; Provo, Utah; and Oxford, Mississippi—places that the Institute's founders could barely imagine.

Throughout the United States, adjunct professors at community colleges and mainstream universities teach one or two popular courses that emphasize the full development of human potential, providing experiences that range from psychodrama to meditation. And their higher-status tenured colleagues in university departments in the social sciences and humanities often discuss some of Esalen's approaches to philosophy, psychology, spirituality, and holistic health. However, despite inspiring individual teachers and a few mainstream graduate programs, Esalen never changed higher education in the fundamental ways that Michael and George had hoped (Leonard 1968).

Esalen's vision of education, based on the integration of emotion, body, mind, and spirit, however, is the foundation for two unconventional universities that seek wide recognition and academic legitimation. Both Naropa University and the California Institute of Integral Studies (CIIS) focus their research and teaching on alternative spirituality and personal expansion. Both schools are dedicated to developing theory, research, and community action in order to expand every aspect of human potential.

The two institutions emerged in the early 1970s, during the period when Esalen was central to drawing together and popularizing many approaches to alternative spirituality and humanistic psychology. Naropa and CIIS are recent additions to the array of religious colleges and universities that add vitality to the spiritual marketplace in America and produce clergy and lifetime adherents (Riley 2004).

Naropa, a Buddhist university in Boulder, Colorado, maintains loose ties to the Institute through individual faculty and associates who lead workshops or attend invited conferences in Big Sur. At the beginning and end of every class meeting, Naropa students and professors bow to each other's inner divinity. Their bows are part of the university's broad Buddhist orientation, which is sometimes called nonsectarian Buddhism. However, when it began, in 1974, Naropa was tied to a specific brand of Tibetan Buddhism and a controversial Tibetan teacher whose American followers had built and funded it.

After difficulties with its first regional accreditation in the late 1980s, Naropa's administration severed formal ties with the founder's religious lineage and sought a broader base of support. The Allen Ginsberg Library and the Jack Kerouac School of Disembodied Poetics had already endeared the institution to a wide range of American Buddhists, and a number of wealthy donors stepped forward. Naropa has received its most consistent financial support from the estate of Frederick Lenz, a software entrepreneur who took the name Rama and became a flamboyant spiritual teacher of Zen, Tibetan Buddhism, and his own brand of mysticism (Laxner 1993).

Naropa has never enjoyed the academic cachet that characterizes the California Institute for Integral Studies (CIIS). Unlike Naropa, CIIS maintains direct connections with members of the CTR that go back to a time before Esalen was founded. Soon after World War II, Michael's mentor, Frederic Spiegelberg, helped establish the Academy of Asian Studies, which eventually became CIIS.

Spiegelberg's lofty intellectual goals and respected academic supporters helped him attract funding from a wealthy San Francisco businessman who made it possible to invite Haridas Chaudhuri, a Bengali professor of philosophy and a disciple of Sri Aurobindo, to serve as the Academy's key academic resource (Chaudhuri and Spiegelberg 1960). Aurobindo's belief that all true religions venerate the same invisible supernatural force was foundational to both the Academy and, later, Esalen.

In the early 1950s, Spiegelberg and Chaudhuri inaugurated their project by offering classes that were informed by Hindu, Buddhist, and Western philosophy (Chaudhuri and Spiegelberg 1960; Kripal 2007a:59). Within a year, however, their principal donor lost most of his fortune and the Academy nearly ran out of funds. Spiegelberg rejoined the Stanford faculty, while Chaudhuri remained at the Academy, scaled it back, and renamed it the Cultural Integration Fellowship. It was a place where students meditated and studied Aurobindo's integral philosophy and lived at East-West House, the place where Michael and Dick first met (Anderson 1983:33).

In 1974, Laurance Rockefeller donated money so that the California Academy of Asian Studies could split off from the Cultural Integration Fellowship and offer advanced classes in philosophy and religious studies. The small, unaccredited graduate school changed its name to the California Institute of Integral Studies, and, in the early 1980s, two members of Michael's inner circle founded new academic programs there. In 1981, the Western Association of Schools and Colleges, an organization that also credentials Stanford and the University of California system, accredited the newly named CIIS.

A decade later, Michael encouraged Rockefeller to donate an additional $5 million to expand CIIS and raise its academic stature. The gift funded additional faculty positions and also facilitated the Institute's relocation to its present site in downtown San Francisco, which CIIS purchased for $17 million in 2007 (California Institute of Integral Studies 2007:5–7). As it grew in size and academic standing, CIIS legitimated Esalen's spiritual orientation as a reasonable foundation for higher education.

CIIS has educated thousands of professionals who offer new possibilities for personal and spiritual growth to their clients and colleagues, carrying Esalen's message to an even wider public. Contemporary CIIS students usually hope to be therapists, teachers, or academics, working in professions that reflect their spiritual priorities. These careers pay relatively well, and they justify the steep tuition and fees of almost $25,000 a year (as of 2010).

CIIS occupies a nondescript urban office building that was constructed just before World War I. Once inside, however, one finds ever-present signs of alternative spirituality. Students shop for books and class materials at the InnerLight Bookstore, eat vegan meals at the Conscious Café, and attend big lectures and public events in Namaste Hall. They can also sit in a quiet meditation room or the small rooftop Zen Garden. These amenities reflect CIIS's foundational commitments to diverse religious traditions. The Laurance S. Rockefeller Library of well over forty thousand books is the Institute's centerpiece, and it symbolizes the mandate to combine alternative spirituality with academic ideals.

At CIIS, a two-year undergraduate program accelerates students' entry into graduate options that feature a variety of M.A. specializations in psychology and a relatively new clinical psychology doctoral program that leads to a Psy.D. The Psy.D. degree is attractive to prospective graduate students, because the America Psychological Association's provisional accreditation is a mark of the university's growing academic and professional standing.

CIIS also offers masters and doctoral degrees in fields like philosophy, cosmology, and consciousness; transformative studies; and women's spirituality. However, each year, the esoteric academic programs attract a smaller share of students than do the different concentrations in professional psychology. The school's future growth and financial stability depend on tuition from its psychology programs.

In order to encourage more interest in fields that do not necessarily lead to careers, Michael recently donated money to CIIS for Esalen Scholarships for graduate students' research in arcane areas that link spirituality, science, and Aurobindo's theory of evolutionary human potential. The scholarships support studies of life after death, supernormal abilities, and observable bodily transformation and uphold Esalen's legacy more explicitly than the psychology programs.

CIIS expands interest in personal and spiritual fulfillment because it offers implicit doctrines of evolving human potential and inclusive spirituality to ever wider circles of mental health and educational professionals and their clients. While dozens of small autonomous graduate institutes emphasize humanistic psychology and bring inclusive spirituality into their courses of study and their students' careers, CIIS is probably the only institution in this group that has moved beyond marginality. Its ties to Esalen and its noteworthy external financial support have allowed it to grow and become more academically respected.

The InnerLight Bookstore at CIIS stocks course materials and a variety of books and magazines about spirituality and transpersonal psychology. © Nicole Sheikh

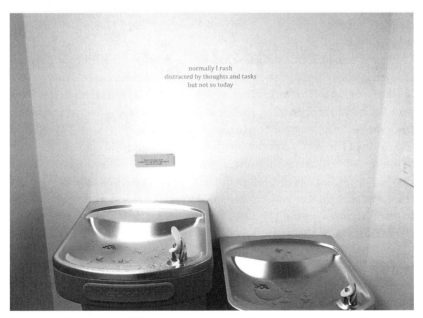

normally I rush
distracted by thoughts and tasks
but not so today

Signs posted throughout CIIS remind people to attend to their spiritual priorities. © Nicole Sheikh

Humanistic Psychology, Spirituality, and Esalen

Humanistic psychology has become an accepted approach in educational and clinical settings, and with each passing decade, it carries Esalen's message farther into mainstream culture. The field of humanistic psychology incorporates Esalen's vision of almost endless possibilities for personal fulfillment and encourages emotional and spiritual growth, rather than mere adjustment to social norms.

For a few years in the early 1960s, the key academics and professionals who pioneered humanistic psychology strongly identified with the Institute. However, by 1970, when Abe Maslow died, his public and private connections to Esalen had deteriorated dramatically, and most humanistic psychologists avoided Big Sur (Anderson 1983:1–6, 134–136).

In the 1960s, Michael and his inner circle lionized Maslow and other well-known psychologists and social critics whose popular books and scholarly articles provided new directions for theory and research about maximizing human potential. At Michael's invitation, Maslow, whose gentle demeanor sometimes masked his steely ambition, made presentations in Big Sur. The two men became close friends, drawing their networks together to develop mutually advantageous projects, such as the Association for Humanistic Psychology and the short-lived branch of Esalen in San Francisco (Anderson 1983:149–150).

Even after he became disheartened by the flamboyant leaders and rowdy followers who shaped day-to-day life at the Institute in the mid-1960s, Maslow maintained his warm friendship with Michael. He continued to support Michael's conception of Esalen as a place for innovative research and theory that had a secondary experiential component.

Less than five years after the Institute began, Maslow was among the first to inform Michael that it had started to lose its intellectual moorings. He discussed the possibilities of Esalen's sinking in a sea of intense experiences and emotions unless there was greater intellectual rigor and personal restraint in workshops (Anderson 1983:293–294). In a notable aside, the worried psychologist quipped that if Satan himself had showed up in Big Sur, Michael would have invited him to lead a seminar (Kripal 2007a:99).

A disastrous weekend early in 1966 became a turning point in Esalen's strained relationship with Maslow and the whole field of humanistic psychology (Anderson 1983:134–136). Maslow asked Michael to select a small group of accomplished, empathic participants to join a proposed seminar about self-actualization. He convened the seminar in order to explore the language and styles of communication that stimulated personal growth and better interpersonal relationships. A somewhat larger group of handpicked observers also received invitations to attend.

Fritz Perls was one of the observers. From the first session onward, he frequently interrupted Maslow and the group in order to embarrass the psychologist and to disparage academic research and theory about self-actualization. At every opportunity, Fritz promoted his own version of Gestalt and its emphasis on absolute honesty and attention to the connections between physicality and emotion. During the first meeting, for example, Fritz suggested that everyone in the room dance in order to relieve the general discomfort with his acrimony toward Maslow. Then he swept up an astonished existential psychologist and proceeded to waltz around the seminar with him (Anderson 1983:135–136).

During the last group session, Maslow quietly told Fritz that he was childish, and his remark provoked the weekend's final confrontation. After the humanistic psychologist called him out, Fritz crawled over to his chair, hugged Maslow's knees, and kept up a piercing infantile wail (Anderson 1983:136; Sutich 1976:151–152).

At the wrap-up the next day, Maslow reminded the remaining participants that academics' good will was important for Esalen's public image and that it could only continue through mutual respect. Very few people in the room seemed to agree with him. However, Maslow was not particularly discouraged, because the Institute had already dropped far down on his list of priorities.

After Maslow helped found the six-thousand-member Association of Humanistic Psychology in the early 1960s, he worked tirelessly for recognition of a humanistic psychology division within the high-status American Psychological Association. He cultivated contacts inside the organization, reached out to the academic networks that he had developed when he was professor and chair of psychology at Brandeis University, and sought endorsements from public intellectuals like Erich Fromm, whose popular psychology book *The Art of Loving* (1956) was a relatively recent best-seller.

The American Psychological Association elected Maslow president in 1968, and, two years later, humanistic psychology became Division 32 of the APA. Maslow's professional associates shaped the seven departments in conventional American universities that still feature humanistic approaches in their twenty-first-century master's and doctoral programs in education, counseling, or clinical psychology. Three are at public universities: California State Universities at Northridge and Sonoma and the University of West

Georgia. The other four are at liberal Catholic institutions: Duquesne University, the University of Dallas, Immaculata University, and Seattle University.

Maslow's contemporaries and their students also helped found dozens of private institutions with concentrations in humanistic psychology. Many were short lived, following the same course as the small organizations dedicated to personal and spiritual growth that sprung up in Esalen's wake and then died within a decade. However, a few independent humanistic psychology graduate schools, like Saybrook University in San Francisco, have survived for decades.

Saybrook began in 1971 as the Humanistic Psychology Institute, and many of its early faculty and graduates retained their personal ties with people at Esalen, despite Maslow's critiques of the Institute. These longstanding relationships led Saybrook to bestow honorary doctorates of humane letters on Michael and George in 2002.

Saybrook and other small independent graduate schools that focus on humanistic psychology deliver distance education to working adults. Students take almost all of their classes online, with occasional interaction at weekend workshops. There are few of the weekly classroom offerings or opportunities for informal student life that characterize mainstream universities with humanistic psychology concentrations, Naropa, or CIIS. In San Francisco, many Saybrook students gravitate to CIIS to attend public lectures, sit in on classes, or just hang out.

Spirituality is embedded in humanistic psychology programs because of transpersonal psychology, an approach that identifies mystical experience as essential to personal development (Lajoie and Shapiro 1992). The pathbreaking psychologists Carl Jung (1972) and William James ([1903] 1961) emphasized the importance of religious feelings and otherworldly forces. In the late twentieth century, Esalen elaborated on their theories and explicitly combined spirituality and psychology to directly influence the development of a clearly defined transpersonal orientation (Sutich 1976).

Psycho-spirituality informed Esalen seminars in the early 1960s, Gestalt awareness practice in the 1970s, and workshops about spiritual emergencies in the 1980s (Grof and Grof 1989; Kripal 2007a:266–267). The links between spirituality and personal fulfillment are embedded in the Institute's foundational doctrine, and they continue to ground many of its workshops and programs.

Many mainstream psychologists adamantly oppose connecting spirituality and psychology, despite pressure from advocates for transpersonal approaches. The American Psychological Association never recognized spirituality as part of academic research or clinical psychology. During the 1980s, influential APA members questioned whether religious exploration was appropriate for the behavioral and social sciences, and the association did not certify transpersonal psychology as an independent division within its ranks. However, most members of the Humanistic Psychology Division of the APA acknowledge transpersonal approaches, and spirituality is embedded in humanistic orientations.

Psychotherapy and education are important to the diffusion of spiritual privilege, but almost all Americans have also become more aware of their spiritual options because they read popular books, watch TV, and surf the Web. As media consumers, they question their general assumptions about the meaning of life and its aftermath long before they enroll in classes or seek psychotherapy.

American media have opened many gateways to spiritual seekership in recent decades. However, the trend began at the Institute. Its energetic outreach to middle-class Americans made it unique in the 1960s. Michael and George cultivated the press and the entertainment industry in order to spread the good news about Big Sur and all it had to offer (Leonard 1988).

While the Esalen no longer dominates the field of personal growth retreats or shapes media perceptions about spirituality, people with historic relationships to the Institute continue to diffuse its doctrines about personal and spiritual possibilities in every corner of contemporary culture. At times, Esalen's subterranean cultural power can surprise. For example, few people—insiders or outsiders alike—are aware of the Institute's direct influence on the best-seller *Tuesdays with Morrie* (Albom 1997).

Tuesdays with Esalen

Almost twenty million Americans bought *Tuesdays with Morrie*, and the book's Facebook page has attracted over a quarter of a million fans to date. The wise old professor at the center of the book was wasting away from Lou Gehrig's disease when a former student came to visit him. Over the course of thirteen Tuesday afternoons, they talked about personal and spiritual fulfillment. Throughout their conversations, Morrie Schwartz, the fading seventy-year-old sage, communicated Esalen's fundamental doctrines although he never mentioned the Institute.

Morrie spoke about the sparks of divinity within everyone and believed that everything on Earth was invisibly connected in some essential way. He borrowed from all religions to construct a personal spirituality that included Judaism, Buddhism, and Christianity, as does Esalen's "religion of no religion" (Albom 1997:81–82; Kripal 2007a:8–11). Moreover, throughout his painful illness, Morrie expressed his optimism about inevitable, if slow, human expansion and social progress.

For more than thirty years, Morrie taught social psychology in the Department of Sociology at Brandeis University near Boston. He befriended Abraham Maslow and also collaborated with other professors who wanted to transform America so that everyone could fulfill his or her full human potential. He believed, "The most important thing in life is to learn how to give love, and to let it come in" (Albom 1997:52).

Morrie organized many undergraduate classes as sensitivity training groups, where participants voiced their feelings about one another and the group as a whole (Back 1972:214–215). On the first day of social psychology classes, Morrie entered the room, sat down, remained silent, and, after about fifteen minutes, asked his students, "What's happening here?" (Albom 1997:53). Then he gently facilitated a dialogue about expectations, the social role of silence, and the importance of voicing feelings.

Morrie took a leave of absence from Brandeis in 1971 in order to found Greenhouse Growth Center with two good friends, Philip Slater, from Brandeis, and Jacqueline Larcombe Doyle, from Esalen. Each led encounter groups and personal growth workshops for poor and working-class clients in the Boston area. They wanted to add an immediate political dimension to Esalen's agenda and to spread opportunities for self-actualization far beyond the middle class. The three founders envisaged their nonprofit organization as an early model for other growth centers that would differ from the Institute because their daily operations would emphasize ideals of social equality and progressive social change.

When Greenhouse closed its doors, Morrie, Philip, and Jacqueline took separate roads, but they all continued to extend Esalen's influence. In different ways, each offered students, clients, other professionals, and the general public options for selecting, combining, and revising personal spirituality.

Morrie continued to mentor his students and colleagues at Brandeis. He went back to the sociology department and taught for another twenty-five years, until he was too ill to stand up in front of his classes.

When Philip Slater resigned from the Brandeis faculty, in 1971, in order to devote himself to the Greenhouse collective, his best-selling book *The Pursuit of Loneliness* (1970) had already made him a well-known, relatively affluent public intellectual. After the collective collapsed, he joined the first generation of faculty at the University of California at Santa Cruz and then resigned in order to act on stage, write plays, and publish more books about America's ills and possibilities. Philip continued to write, act, and teach online classes in transformative studies at CIIS when he was well into his eighties.

Jacqueline Doyle, Greenhouse's other founder, had spent three years in Big Sur before moving to the Boston area. She came to Esalen in 1967, after one of her former graduate school professors, Will Schutz, invited her to join him and help lead encounter groups. A year later, she became a peripheral member of Michael's inner circle, because they had a brief romantic affair that turned into a semiplatonic friendship (Doyle 1981).

In 1970, with Michael's support, Jacqueline orchestrated a trip to London for some of the Institute's best known figures: Michael, George, Will Schutz, and Alan Watts. They hoped to export Esalen's many paths to personal and spiritual fulfillment and perhaps to start a branch of the Institute in London (Anderson 1983:219–220; Doyle 1981). After a month, most of the group returned to California, while Michael and two close friends traveled to Italy to meet with the founder of Psychosynthesis, a small social movement that integrated spiritual experience with self-actualization (Assigioli 1973).

Jacqueline stayed in England, introducing new constituencies to humanistic psychology and Esalen's integration of mind, body, spirit, and psyche through encounter groups and public lectures. She asked the Esalen Board of Trustees to appoint her to a formal position and to guarantee her salary, but it refused. When Michael wrote to say that he would not facilitate her request because he did not want to anger his board, she was irate (Doyle 1981). Jacqueline left England and Esalen to work with Slater and Schwartz on Greenhouse, hoping to combine her therapeutic skills and her progressive feminist politics (Doyle 1981).

After Greenhouse closed, she went back to California to practice as a psychotherapist in Marin County and teach classes at Saybrook. Jacqueline became an influential advocate for blending spirituality and humanistic psychology through transpersonal approaches (Doyle 1973; May, Krippner, and Doyle 1994). In the 1980s, she was elected president of the Association for Humanistic Psychology and became a Saybrook Trustee.

The three Greenhouse founders' professional histories illustrate how many leaders in the wide-ranging human potential movement refined and spread options for personal and spiritual growth. During the 1960s and 1970s, Esalen had a pronounced impact on leading professionals, social critics, and spiritual innovators who learned from one another, provided mutual support for some projects, and also developed their own priorities (Oliver and Myers 2003). Social critics like Schwartz, Slater, and Doyle were part of the broad human potential movement that embraced the Institute's foundational doctrine. They tried to wake up Americans to the fact that there was something wrong with their lives and offered many paths to facilitate personal transformation that could generate social change.

In the Air

During the 1960s and early 1970s, people who came to Esalen or identified with its aims from afar believed that everyone, regardless of class, race or gender, should be able to exercise his or her own spiritual privilege. And, over the past half -century, the Institute has directly affected thousands of people who shared the benefits of spiritual privilege with many more thousands. The beliefs and practices that Esalen brought together and diffused now seem to be part of the air that Americans breathe.

A popular article from Oprah Winfrey's website demonstrates how alternative spirituality is embedded in the contemporary pursuit of health and personal fulfillment. It is about a woman who was divorced, unemployed, clinically obese, and often too depressed to get out of bed in the morning. With support from her friends and family, she transformed her life by completing a sixty-day course of Birkram Yoga (Sanders and Barnes-Browne 2010:33).

Narratives like this run through media descriptions of self-help and wellness resources. Stories encourage consumers to try new practices and to explore different approaches to spirituality in order to lead better, more meaningful lives. This continues the spread of spiritual privilege that Esalen began fifty years ago, when it was the first organization to awake ordinary Americans to many new options for personal and spiritual growth. Since the 1960s, the long-term impact of thousands of media accounts about integrating spirit, body, mind, and psyche have exercised as much overall cultural impact as formal institutions like the California Institute for Integral Studies, Saybrook, or Esalen itself.

A number of contemporary authors, editors, and publishers are linked to Esalen or with individuals close to the Institute. For example, Jeremy Tarcher, a successful publisher and Albert's boss for a brief time, served as an Esalen trustee for many years, and his story illustrates how a few key actors can lay the groundwork for the continued diffusion of Esalen's message.

Tarcher grew up in a wealthy Manhattan family. After college, in the 1950s, he studied Vedanta philosophy and meditation in India (Armstrong 1976; Krantz 2000). After writing and producing television shows with his wife, the puppeteer Shari Lewis, he started JP Tarcher, an independent publisher. He first succeeded with books like the comedian Joan Rivers's *Having a Baby Can Be a Scream* (1974). Tarcher then defined his market niche in personal growth and spirituality with the best-selling *Drawing on the Right Side of the Brain* (Edwards 1979). He became one of the first publishers to cultivate mass markets for books about yoga, tarot cards, meditation, alternative religions, and human potential psychology.

Tarcher negotiated a relationship for distribution with St. Martin's Press in New York City shortly after he began his venture. Putnam/Penguin purchased JP Tarcher in the early 1990s, but Tarcher remained as its president until 1996. Tarcher/Penguin continues to publish books that focus on spirituality and personal growth and also reissues earlier Tarcher imprints, including George and Michael's *The Life We Are Given* (1995).

In the 1970s, Jeremy Tarcher became friends with George and Michael and published their books (Leonard 1978; Murphy 1977). He personally reached out to members of Michael's inner circle, encouraged them, and introduced them to other publishers. Once more, the loose social networks that developed at Big Sur had far-reaching effects on American spirituality.

The Internet diffuses Esalen's influence beyond the groups that conventional media have reached. It is likely that books will always be important to the Institute's core constituents and other spiritually privileged individuals, especially those trying to separate themselves temporarily from information technology. However, the historic shift from print to the World Wide Web has enabled spiritual entrepreneurs to reach out to seasoned seekers and to new recruits in unprecedented ways (Dawson and Cowan 2004).

The rise of the Internet and the surrounding software industry has also created jobs where talented, spiritually privileged individuals can maximize control over their workplaces and schedules. They transfer their professional skills to produce spiritually oriented Web sites such as i/Thou.org, Albert Wong's Esalen website, and The Self Knowledge Symposium (SKS), a general resource for college students seeking new spiritual possibilities. The founder of SKS asserted:

> The rise of the Internet and its surrounding software industry had given birth to a wide class of wandering *ronin* (literally master-less samurai), techno-warriors, intelligent freelancers whose skills in Web design, programming, graphics, or networking were in high demand. (Buehler 2002:128)

The Webmaster found that his expertise enabled him to join new social networks of likeminded seekers, augment his religious knowledge, and increase his affinities for supernatural meanings and explanations.

Dozens of writers, therapists, and bodyworkers associated with Esalen maintain personal websites and Facebook pages that reach spiritual consumers interested in massage, psychotherapy, yoga, or similar pursuits. An official Esalen site posts stories about Big Sur, recent Esalen catalogues, and space to register and pay online for upcoming workshops and other programs. In addition, the Institute's Facebook page has more than four thousand friends, including a number of individuals who first visited Big Sur less than five years ago.

While Esalen's official website and Facebook page both address seekers who may not be very familiar with the Institute, Albert Wong directs i/Thou. org toward people with established ties to Esalen. Many of them first visited Big Sur in its heyday, and slightly more than half of the site's almost eight hundred members lived, worked, or studied there. A core group of about two dozen people regularly post comments and meditate together online, but most online community members are far less involved.

Even casual i/Thou members, however, occasionally share photos and receive news about events in Big Sur. A short video that is one of the site's most compelling features captures the views and sounds from the sulfur baths so that people can reconnect with their visceral memories of Esalen in two-minute reveries.

All three websites reinforce the Institute's ongoing influence on alternative spirituality and humanistic psychology. Esalen has touched millions of Americans through direct and indirect institutional legacies and its wide networks continue to expand.

Conclusion

New Beginnings

Esalen has encouraged people to maximize their full potential for over fifty years. Because its founding generation popularized an amazing array of options for personal and spiritual growth in the 1960s and 1970s, there are now virtually unlimited ways for Americans to select, combine, and revise their individualized spirituality. The Institute enlivened and expanded the religious marketplace and diffused spiritual privilege. Nevertheless, in spite of its extraordinary impact, Esalen's future is uncertain.

By the late 1970s, the Institute had lost much of its public visibility and noticeable cultural significance. Esalen no longer had a unique, clearly defined identity because many mainstream Americans acknowledged beliefs and practices that had once been unavailable to them (Finke and Stark 1992:237–295).

When encounter groups, Gestalt, yoga, and other approaches for maximizing human potential became fashionable, they often floated free from both Esalen and their original spiritual moorings. Seekers often desired instant gratification and sifted through numerous options, looking for practical magic that would produce immediate results. As they sought experiential rewards, Americans still exercised some spiritual privilege because they selected, combined, and revised their beliefs and practices, even though they had few incentives for fundamentally changing their behavior or systematically exploring varied doctrines and philosophies.

Esalen was the original model for dozens of contemporary retreats, growth centers, and spas that now compete with it for clients. Moreover, hundreds of educational programs and thousands of independent psychotherapists, bodyworkers, and spiritual teachers crowd the niche that the Institute shaped and briefly monopolized. They all offer paths to self-actualization that were available only to elites and intellectuals until Esalen diffused spiritual privilege. Temporary gratification is easily available in the twenty-first century, while only a few alternative institutions like the California Institute of Integral Studies and Esalen itself explicitly link lifelong personal dedication and hard work to the realization of full human potential.

George and Michael encouraged people to sample innovative spirituality and other options for personal growth because they believed that a momentary spiritual experience could inaugurate a lifetime of daily practice that included disciplined participation, study, and service to others: "Taking the all-important first step with a sincere heart can be a sort of enlightenment. It presages an evolutionary adventure, and offers inner peace" (Leonard and Murphy 1995:39–40). However, a step in one or another direction is often all Americans take, because they do not connect personal or spiritual expansion with long-term commitment or sacrifice (McGee 2005).

The Institute's foundational doctrines about individual sparks of divinity, benevolent supernatural forces, public service, and evolutionary human potential have not been adopted as enthusiastically as the varied practices that Esalen introduced to Americans. While Michael recognizes that temporary rewards may usher in decades of spiritual passion and dedication, he also worries that casual consumers of mystical moments often settle for immediate emotional highs or physical benefits and never link those rewards to lasting commitment (Leonard and Murphy 1995:3–18). He referred to Americans' fascination with brief transcendent moments as typical fixes that were "fast, easy, and cheap," and he equated the fleeting rewards of a sacred moment or sudden emotional insight with the temporary satisfaction offered by fast food or street drugs (Badiner and Gray 2002:82–83).

Michael's critique of instant spiritual gratification once more revealed his assumptions that the full exercise of spiritual privilege and the pursuit of human potential were universal rights and also collective obligations. Nevertheless, Michael—and everyone else who is part of Esalen—recognizes the power of immediate rewards to motivate people to cultivate greater affinities for spiritual experience and to explore more possibilities for self-actualization.

Choices and Challenges

By introducing countless options, Esalen appeared to spark virtually unlimited demand for alternative spirituality and human potential psychology. However, by the 1980s, there were so many doctrines and practices promising personal and spiritual growth that people frequently found it difficult and frustrating to decide what to sample and whether to fully commit themselves to one or another spiritual path (Schwartz 2004:18–22). They moved quickly from things like trance dancing to meditation to affirmations and then moved on to other things.

When hundreds of novice seekers no longer rushed to Big Sur after the mid-1970s, some members of Esalen's founding generation feared that the market for alternative spirituality and humanistic psychology was saturated because there were so many possibilities. However, Americans' desires for personal growth and self-transformation are rarely satisfied. Rather than give up when they are disappointed with their choices, they often try something new. Pervasive hopes for personal transformation and unflagging enthusiasm for additional ways to select, combine, and revise doctrines and practices create an endless demand for new ways to exercise and accumulate spiritual privilege (Schwartz 2004:170–179).

Seasoned seminarians and middle-aged beginners still travel to Big Sur to try out different techniques and to explore the latest paths to fulfillment. However, the Institute struggles to attract younger, more diverse clients, who are usually drawn to present-day venues that offer newer approaches to self-actualization.

Some people at the Institute wonder whether Internet spirituality might further diminish Esalen's attraction for Americans born after the mid-1960s. It introduces innovations and ways of worship that allow people to develop social networks and to expand their religious affinities and knowledge about the sacred without traveling or even having direct contact with others (Howard 2011). However, the Web rarely, if ever, produces the emotional and physical sensations that are key rewards of alternative spirituality. Esalen has always championed embodied spirituality that engages every sense and cannot be replicated by merely watching or reading.

The Web will support and probably even enlarge the demand for face-to-face interaction that defines the Esalen experience. Sitting at a screen is very different from journeying to a sacred space, and people may want more immediate experiences once they become interested in a particular practice. Collective rituals, physical expression, and mystical moments have always been part of spirituality and humanistic psychology in Big Sur. The different websites that feature the Institute and connect its supporters to one another allow them to cement their allegiances, but secondary access cannot substitute for visiting Esalen or exploring spirituality with like-minded seekers

Recession and Revitalization

Even during the twenty-first century's great recession, varied doctrines and practices that are associated with spiritual privilege enlivened the religious marketplace and attracted both new and experienced seekers. Although Esalen developed during a period of unprecedented economic abundance, once the Institute democratized spiritual privilege, Americans' appetites for new practices and doctrines did not diminish during hard times. In fact, persistent economic instability may motivate even more people to select, combine, and revise their spirituality because investments in spiritual and personal growth can be relatively inexpensive alternatives to spending time or money on other things.

Doctrines of unlimited human potential offer hope and comfort in hard times—they promise that life will be better someday, and they also empower people to act, rather than withdraw. Moreover, there are immediate experiential rewards from many practices, particularly when they involve groups of like-minded seekers. Even participants in transitory informal groups can provide one another with solace and encouragement to overcome difficulties (Leonard and Murphy 1995:185–192).

A number of spiritual practices on the web require only commitments of time. Others, such as sojourns at retreat centers, cost far more in terms of both money and time. Esalen is once again unique, because, unlike most of its direct competitors, it partially compensates for unequal economic resources by means of work-study programs and community-based groups like George and Michael's Integral Transformative Practice (Leonard and Murphy 1995).

Some social critics (Ehrenreich 2009) argue that optimism about everyone's ability to develop his or her full potential makes it difficult for Americans to confront economic inequality. According to this critical perspective, spiritual privilege provides no viable solutions and instead defines hardship as an individual issue, rather than a social problem.

However, many alternative spiritual doctrines and practices offer strategies, however implausible, to deal with and possibly overcome material hardships. For example, a book that focuses on accumulating spiritual privilege for worldly ends, *The Secret* (Byrne 2006), has sold almost twenty million copies worldwide. Its message is a simple one: thoughts exert an immense physical power, and it is possible for everyone to create his or her own materially and emotionally abundant life. In other words, frequent, concentrated affirmations of personal goals enable believers to reach their highest potentials.

While material rewards and full personal and spiritual fulfillment may remain out of reach, affirmations sometimes provide unexpected benefits because they allow people to substitute hope for desperation and depression. Variations on the theme of co-creating an ideal life all encourage faith in benign supernatural forces that will respond to affirmations for personal happiness and abundance. The media mogul and cultural icon Oprah Winfrey offered her audience testimony about the ways that unaffiliated spiritual seekers and liberal Christians can easily practice affirmations and combine them with other religious orientations:

> I was raised a Christian. I still am a Christian. The Number One question that I had was: "How does all of this metaphysical thinking, this new way of taking responsibility for my life and co-creating my life with the Creator, how does that mesh with everything that I've been taught?"
> And what I realized is that exactly what they're saying—is that it reinforces. Because, above all else, God gave us free will. (Sanneh 2010:88)

Oprah presented a personal theological justification for countless revisions of her own practice, and she implicitly urged all Americans to expand their spiritual privilege, whatever their financial or emotional challenges.

The Secret (Byrne 2006) offers few original ideas. Like Esalen's foundational doctrine, it draws from a number of different sources and simply frames them in new ways. Other practices of imagining, affirming, and obtaining fulfillment can be traced back to late-nineteenth-century America, when many religious innovators enthused about the powers of positive thinking (Satter 2001). During that epoch, the popular philosopher Ralph Waldo Trine embraced the same inclusive religiosity as Oprah and Esalen, arguing that all true religions could accommodate compatible doctrines and new practices like affirmations (Kripal 2007b; Trine 1897). It is not surprising that Michael and George made affirmations part of Integral Transformative Practice, when they asked participants to write out and regularly chant, "I am balanced, vital, and healthy" (Leonard and Murphy 1995:22–23, 65–72).

Long before nineteenth-century religious leaders exalted the powers of positive thinking or Michael and his comrades encouraged Americans to develop their full human potential, the U.S. Constitution provided safeguards that enabled citizens to select, combine, and revise their religious beliefs and practices. Alternative spiritual practices like affirmations and institutions like Esalen could develop only because of safeguards that separated church and state and protected the free exercise of religion. Those provisions reflected the religious pluralism that flourished in the colonies before the American Revolution, and they have sustained a vibrant, competitive religious marketplace from that time onward (Stark 2005:207–220). The Institute was able to embrace and popularize any doctrine that did not insist that there was only one true God because the Constitution implicitly supports varied paths to self-actualization (Kripal 2007a:7–11).

Americans' willingness to explore unfamiliar options for spiritual fulfillment also reflects pervasive ideals of new beginnings and starting over that are found in both mainstream religious traditions and secular culture. For several centuries, American evangelical Protestants have emphasized salvation and transformation through accepting Jesus as a personal savior (Mead 1963). During the Second Great Awakening in the mid-nineteenth century, people flocked to new faiths like Methodism because they promised redemption and offered direct experience and transcendent moments that dramatically contrasted with worship in most established faiths (Finke and Stark 1992:85–87). Their doctrines declared that people could change at any point in their lives, and, if they fell back, they could recommit themselves to Christ again and again.

Variations on religious faith in unlimited new beginnings is also found in secular justifications for physical reinvention by means of diet, exercise, and cosmetic surgery or emotional transformation through psychotherapy and pharmaceuticals (McGee 2005). Possibilities for new beginnings drew people to Esalen in the 1960s, and similar desires to start over make the Institute attractive today.

Beginning Again in Big Sur

Michael and Dick founded Esalen because they believed in new beginnings. Innovative spirituality and humanistic psychology offered possibilities for starting over and constructing new lives. And the Institute's remarkable site was a wonderful place to embark on voyages of self-transformation.

The staggering beauty of the crashing surf and the looming cliffs that surround Esalen create a sacred space (Cox 1965). All of the buildings that have been constructed since the 1930s blend into the landscape, and their simplicity underscores the Institute's consistent message that luxury is not what one buys or owns but is instead the opportunity to exercise and accumulate spiritual privilege.

Most visitors and work-study students leave Big Sur with heightened spiritual affinities and knowledge about themselves. Opportunities for personal exploration and sacred moments unfold in every corner of Esalen. Powerful emotions and surprising feelings of personal expansion suddenly overwhelm people while they bake bread together, gaze at moonbeams on the ocean, enjoy an Esalen massage, or take part in Gestalt awareness practice. These intense experiences often allow people to feel that they have ignited new sparks of inner divinity. They are motivated to create better lives for themselves and others (Litwak 1967).

People who work at the Institute or stay for more than a few months are grateful that they can continually dip into doctrines and practices that promise them more new beginnings and provide opportunities for them to enact spiritual privilege. In small and large ways, they consistently revise, combine, and change their religious beliefs and practices.

At Esalen, opportunities for spiritual experience and personal growth are never confined to scheduled activities. I overheard casual conversations among staff in the main kitchen that morphed into informal encounter groups. A discussion in the hot springs led two new work-study students to try ecstatic dance and, later, to adopt it as their primary spiritual practice. These incidents are among many that illustrate the Institute's most significant assumption about sojourners to Big Sur: Whatever their differences, everyone who journeys to Esalen shares the purpose of maximizing their full potential and living their best lives, while supporting others with similar goals.

The Institute sometimes catalyzes unanticipated connections that may last a weekend or continue for a lifetime. Over the course of this research, I met one or both members of eight couples whose ages ranged from thirty-five to eighty. They described how they had found the loves of their lives at the Institute. Half of them had been work-study students or staff members, like David Price, who fell in love and married an old acquaintance after they got to know one another while working at the Institute. Others told me about brief interactions with strangers that led to lasting relationships after they departed from Big Sur. One couple got together at a weekend yoga retreat in the early 1990s, and they return to the Institute every year to mark the anniversary of their first contact. I saw a pair of late-middle-aged seminarians lock eyes over a brown rice casserole and introduce themselves. They invited me to their wedding less than a year later.

More commonly, loose, supportive social networks develop through the CTR and its conferences, in the EMBA, and in other parts of the Institute. People add to their spiritual privilege by making acquaintances that may someday boost their careers or introduce them to fresh spiritual practices

(Granovetter 1973). Conversations about real estate investments, descriptions of good graduate schools, or invitations to interesting urban Zen groups are examples of the casual connections that add to participants' general cultural knowledge and can augment their spiritual privilege in the future.

Workshops that offer continuing education units (CEUs) are especially likely to generate loose social networks and provide specific resources for professional advancement. Between July and December 2010, Esalen listed more than a hundred different workshops that provided credits to social workers, therapists, nurses, and therapeutic bodyworkers. Opportunities for professionals to earn CEUs at the Institute began with a small number of massage and personal growth programs in the early 1980s and have expanded over the decades. Meditation and Gestalt awareness practice are among the offerings that explicitly integrate spirituality into professional development, while workshops about personal growth and holistic medicine incorporate elements of religious doctrine and practice more subtly.

The Institute's long history, remarkable setting, and intellectual foundations set it apart from other spas and spiritual retreats, but, like the others, it must meet growing financial obligations. Revenue from workshops and professional credit programs alone cannot support its current level of operations or Michael's unwavering desire to advance evolutionary human potential through the CTR.

Michael celebrated his eightieth birthday in 2010, and the terms of his planned bequests to Esalen are not yet public. The Institute's other major benefactor, Laurance Rockefeller, died in 2004, and so far no one has stepped up to take his place. A handful of very generous donors have helped, but none of them provides consistent extensive financial support.

Esalen's long-term financial survival requires an explicit definition of its mission that identifies priorities and generates trust among members of the CTR, the EMBA, and the guest relations/operations staff. Open discussions of the Institute's future will necessarily involve questions about leadership, legitimacy, and what will happen after Michael is no longer there.

Michael and his comrades have made statements about age, such as "Sixty is the new forty, and eighty is the new sixty." But they are well aware that nothing lasts forever. Although the Institute's foundational spiritual doctrine never considered aging or death in detail, those issues are now unavoidable. George's passing in 2010 spurred a great deal of private speculation, but there have been few public discussions about what will happen when all of Esalen's founding generation disappears.

Some key staff and EMBA members have begun to retire and move away from Big Sur or at least to cut down their working hours. The next decade may usher in Esalen's new beginning or its slow demise, depending on whether there is a well-considered plan for succession and internal governance (Stark 1996). And questions of governance lead back to the relationships and power differences between the CTR and the rest of Esalen.

In ancient Greece, like modern Esalen, the cultivation of the self was every full citizen's responsibility and privilege. In Greece, however, only men who owned property were full citizens. Self-mastery and growth were impossibilities for women and slaves, because they were subject to the whims of privileged men (McGee 2005:139–140). While Esalen offers the rights and obligations of spiritual privilege to everyone, Michael and his comrades have always had the final say about the Institute's organization, short-term priorities, and long-term goals. They continued to have the last word when they once again shared the three central Esalen narratives that celebrated brave men and their exploits while coming together for Michael's eightieth birthday (Ogilvy 2010).

To create possibilities for a true new beginning, Michael and his inner circle might review the public history and narratives that they have repeated for decades, revisiting and reinterpreting the Institute's history in the same ways that workshop participants often examine their lives. In both cases, the goal is to discover new truths that provide additional meaning and value for the present. A process of reworking the three central stories could engage many different Esalen constituencies within and outside Big Sur.

A different creation narrative that is as colorful as the one about Michael and Dick's road trip describes the birth of the Institute's current signature practice, Esalen massage. Bodyworkers tell stories about the small group of close friends who spontaneously created a spiritually centered massage that engaged giver and receiver in a mutual quest for personal truths.

A number of different tales challenge the themes in the Night of the Dobermans and provide alternative views of Esalen's boundaries. They are stories about connection, rather than separation. Various narratives describe magic in the trees and mountains and important messages from animals, like the whales that migrate along the coast or the cougars that roam the woods.

There is no counternarrative that is the equivalent of the description of self-promotion and domination at the Hollywood party, because celebrities and public recognition interested few members of the Institute's early massage crew or operations staff. However, stories that describe courage through life passages like birth or death powerfully illuminate values about human divinity that are part of the Institute's foundational doctrine.

Full awareness and appreciation of the ways that everyday life is also extraordinary are embedded in almost every spiritual practice at Esalen. Stories about ordinary miracles, such as bringing massage into being and connecting with nature in various ways, can complement the old narratives and underscore issues that are at least as important to the Institute as celebrations of heroic men.

The people who are deeply committed to Esalen are seldom loyal to a specific set of teachings or a single divinity. Their god is an invisible essence that is part of everyone and everything, and it is almost impossible for them to establish a direct exchange relationship or constant loyalty with something so amorphous (Stark 2001:10–17). Instead, they are devoted to networks of their sister and brother seekers, to the Institute itself, and to the endless process of exploring and accumulating spiritual privilege.

Some people in Big Sur fear that Esalen could become like the Shaker movement, the tiny religious community that has been on the verge of extinction for many years because of dedication to sexual abstinence (Stein 1992). Celibacy is definitely not a problem in Big Sur, but related issues about future generations are very important to the Institute's future. Full recognition of women's vital contributions and outreach to younger generations are objectives that could engage everyone at Esalen and attract new support.

Despite the Institute's disappointing attempts to attract people under forty, some women and men in their twenties and thirties still long to experience Esalen. Young adults from the United States and Western Europe want to explore alternative spirituality and options for personal growth at the Institute because they have heard about its early contributions and they have read about it on Facebook or Albert Wong's i/Thou website.

A few months ago, an aspiring actor who worked at a Southern California Starbucks overheard me talking with a friend about Esalen's future. He stopped everything and held up the line of waiting customers to let us know that he had been saving money for months in order to attend his first workshop and that he was driving up to Big Sur in a few days. I asked him why he was so excited, and he replied, "I'm sure that it's the only place where I can find my spiritual path, and I can't wait to try the hot springs."

The Institute's younger supporters, clients, and workers resemble him. They implicitly understand spiritual privilege, and they appreciate the ways that Esalen provides unique opportunities to embark on personal quests in the company of other spiritual seekers. Few want to create a new society or struggle for progressive social change, but they share the founding generation's passions for self-knowledge and spiritual fulfillment.

Most people familiar with the Institute wonder about its future. Many hope that a revitalized Esalen will once again transform American spirituality. This is unlikely. But it will continue to change individual lives in small and large ways, through immediate contacts and through its many legacies to the soul rush.

Appendix 1

Experiential Exercises: When Words Fail

Esalen's signature approaches to personal and spiritual expansion engage all five human senses: sight, touch, hearing, smell, and taste. Big Sur has always been known as a site for extraordinary experiences that can open doors to emotional and spiritual growth.

The rewards from powerful spiritual or emotional experiences draw people to Big Sur time after time so that they can select, combine, and revise their spirituality and intimate relationships.

The following are simple, structured exercises that capture some experiences that I discovered at the Institute. It was impossible to locate their original sources, because different versions appear in many different places and because, over the years, people have modified them in various ways. I tried these out and later shared them with students in classes about the sociology of religion and alternative religious movements.

The seven exercises supplement different chapters and illustrate one or more of these concepts: the power of groups, the spiritual dimensions of awareness, effects of altered breathing, and the ways that nonverbal communication is central to human experience and growth.

Most of the exercises work best in small groups, but they can also be carried out alone or in classes of fifty or more. Writing about an exercise afterwards is a good way to consider what happened, and a brief write-up can add value to later reflections. Many workshop leaders at the Institute encourage everyone from novices to Institute elders to keep journals about what they experienced.

Exercise for the Introduction

Stepping into Esalen means moving outside daily routines, because people go to Big Sur with the intention of exploring new feelings and ways to create personal spirituality. Compared with city life, it is very quiet, and the loudest outdoor sounds may be birds, distant drums, or migrating whales. Even before the silence is noticeable, the scents that waft over Esalen's steep driveway mark a passage into a spiritual space. The smell of California eucalyptus trees is one of the first things that welcomes people to the Institute.

Eucalyptus oil distills one of Esalen's central scents, and it can be purchased at health food stores or alternative markets. Holistic healers and aromatherapists say that the oil refreshes, helps overcome sluggishness, and improves concentration. Some believe that it can cool the heat of anger after conflict.

At home, add a few drops to the floor of a bath or shower in a closed bathroom, get in, and breathe deeply. Afterwards, lie down in a warm room, relax, and let your imagination wander for five minutes.

In a class or other group setting, be quiet and closes your eyes in a dim room as saucers filled with a few drops of eucalyptus oil in hot water are set down nearby or a bottle of the oil is passed around. After deeply breathing in the scent for a few minutes, take a deep breath in and out, close your eyes and let your imagination wander.

Think about what feelings and ideas this experience produced and write about what, if anything, happened. Did you experience unfamiliar feelings or perceptions during and after the eucalyptus exercise?

Exercise for Chapter 1

It is surprisingly easy to participate in a psychodrama group and collectively create a different reality. This exercise can be done in a small group or in a larger class, and it demonstrates the emotional power of groups. In some ways this resembles Fritz's large Gestalt workshops, because the people in the audience are often as moved as those who enacted scenes from their lives.

Leaders who guide people in this exercise say that its powerful effects demonstrate ways that invisible spiritual connections create altered realities. They assert that participants may access their supernatural sparks by suspending routines and dialoguing with their true inner selves.

Begin to work on this exercise several days before meeting to enact it. Everyone needs to try it out alone, in private, or with one or two supportive friends. Ask yourself whether you would be willing to do the exercise in front of a relatively large number of people.

The group exercise begins with discussions among six to eight people. For about five minutes, participants talk with one another about why they would or would not like to enact personal dramas while relative strangers look on. At the end of the five minutes, two volunteers agree to try the exercise in front of everyone else. Extra credit and/or lots of encouragement help motivate volunteers.

One actor at a time will have a brief conversation of about three minutes each with money, power, sex, time, and death, as if they were real people. Each one of the five forces in life occupies a separate chair, and these objects represent them: money, a hammer for power, underwear (male and/or female) for sex, a watch or a clock for time, and emptiness on the death chair.

The person on stage talks out loud with each representation about what she or he knows about them, what he or she likes, and what he or she fears. The actor can chat with the symbolic presences, ask them questions and respond to their answers, or just rant.

When the actor finishes, she or he takes a few minutes to talk about what if anything was surprising abut the exercise. Then there is a group discussion about what people learned as they watched or what they learned when they did the exercise in a more private setting.

After the discussion, participants and observers all write down what they thought and felt about the five elements of life. What differences were there in the private and public contexts? Was there a spiritual element that they could sense?

Exercise for Chapter 2

Sri Aurobindo's philosophy frames the Institute's foundational doctrine. Aurobindo's integral yoga and many other Asian spiritual approaches offer ways to greet the morning. Even when they are done late in the day or during the evening, these practices seem to calm and energize people. A number of different Western adaptations of Asian spiritualities have similar practices.

Sit upright on a chair or the floor with a very straight back and your legs in a comfortable position. Then take a long deep breath through your nose and take in as much air as possible, filling from the bottom of the torso upward.

Do not think about anything except breathing, and, if any thoughts intrude, brush them from your mind. While doing this, imagine how your breath is traveling, and then hold it when it fills your body completely. Slowly release breath from the torso upward by exhaling a little bit at a time until there is no more air left inside. Do this eight times, Some people at Esalen believe that this breathing exercise allows participants to connect with their personal sparks of divinity.

After the last cleansing breath, participants can talk about how they felt before and after the exercise. How did it affect your mood and physical sensations? If something was different for you, could the changes be interpreted as some spiritual connection?

Exercise for Chapter 3

Spiritual privilege allows people to better appreciate ordinary activities. This brief active meditation deals with attention, awareness, and sincere gratitude. It can be done alone or in large or small groups.

Breathe in deeply through your nose and out through your mouth several times, and slowly focus on the immediate moment. Sit comfortably, and help yourself to one chocolate candy or an alternative, although really good chocolate is best.

Eat very slowly and try to experience the smell and texture of the chocolate. Imagine the farmer who grew the cocoa, the people who made the candy, and all of the others whose dedication helped make the delicious moment possible. Silently thank them, and also thank people who helped you be here and who are also responsible for your enjoying something sweet. Bring your hands together in a prayerful gesture, and offer thanks for the wonderful gift of taste.

Sometimes, people who practice this eating meditation are amazed at how much better food tastes when they take the time to notice and appreciate the many people and the everyday miracles of life that brought food to their lips. Do you believe that a single sweet that is eaten with sincere appreciation offers more joy and happiness than a whole box of morsels swallowed without this kind of awareness? Would eating like this regularly, though not all the time, change your life in any way?

Exercise for Chapter 4

All four of the men profiled in this book as exemplars of Esalen experienced moments when they felt at one with the universe. Supernatural forces touched Michael on the golf course. Gordon felt rushes of connection in Gestalt groups in Boston. Mystical moments sometimes overwhelmed David while he played bass guitar. Albert experienced an epiphany during his senior year at Harvard.

These kinds of sacred experiences unfold in any situation when individuals are completely aware of the immediate moment. In Gestalt awareness practice and other Esalen approaches based on Zen concepts of mindfulness, all of someone's life is about the immediate moment, not the future or the past.

This exercise is the only one that should be explored alone or possibly with a silent partner. It is about mindfulness that facilitates mystical moments while someone is driving a car or walking. Driving is preferable, but the exercise can be adapted to walking. The practice should last for about fifteen minutes, and absolute silence is important. Each mile that you drive and every step that you take should engage only the present, without consideration of any past or future destination.

Before beginning to move, take three cleansing breaths through the nose, and slowly exhale each one. Appreciate the car seat that supports you or the shoes that connect you to the pavement. Be sure to thank the seat belt in the car as you fasten it.

When there is a red light or a stop sign, smile at it and give thanks, because it helps return you to the present moment. The sign or red light is like a Zen bell of awareness, helping the driver or walker develop awareness of the immediate experience.

Breathe deeply, smile, and concentrate on the act of driving or walking, rather than on the rush of traffic or any extraneous sounds. Focus on precautions that keep everyone safe. Be grateful for opportunities to help others avoid difficulties, and note other people and cars that are around. The key to mindfulness is concentrating on the act of driving or walking in the present moment and nothing else.

Later, you can discuss whether participating in this practice might have been difficult in some ways and easy in others. Did the practice change the meaning of something ordinary, like driving or walking? Did time go faster or more slowly during the exercise? How could this mindfulness change responses in other contexts? Did this have any mystical elements?

Exercise for Chapter 5

The Institute's three central narratives ignore the women and men who created Esalen massage when they gathered around the hot springs in the early 1960s and spontaneously developed techniques that connected the mutual sparks of divinity within the giver and the receiver. Esalen massage was meant for humans, but occasionally grateful dogs and cats became part of the process. A member of Michael's inner circle in the 1960s described the happiness cats and dogs displayed after they received an Esalen-style massage that involved wordless mutual communication: "They jumped off, purring or barking with pleasure."

Contemporary EMBA members and staff who discuss massage for pets believe that it cements lasting connections and trust between animals and their human caregivers. This massage illustrates the assumption that everything and everyone on Earth is interconnected. It is best shared between you and one pet, away from other animals, because a room full of cats, dogs, or other furry pets like gerbils might not be at all calm.

Do not use oil or cream during the massage. Touch should be very soft at first, and then it may grow harder, as long as the massage is consistent and focused. Knead the animal's spine and the two furrows on either side of it, and massage this area for a relatively long time. Another important place is the base of the skull, where animals sometimes hold their tensions, just like humans.

As the massage continues, breathe deeply and try to align your breathing with the animal's. The pet may have trouble when you stop, so do so slowly and gently. Be prepared for future silent requests for massages from your partner in this exercise.

This exercise is rarely suited for a class or a group, but pet massage demonstrates the range of options for personal and spiritual growth that are available at the Institute. How did you feel and how the did the animal seem to feel? Was there any unique mutual communication in the process? Was there any spiritual experience? Will you do it again?

Exercise for Chapter 6

Esalen's approaches to personal and spiritual growth have become part of the wider culture. As we learned in chapter 6, Morrie Schwartz (Albom 1997), often began his first class of the term at Brandeis University with a sensitivity training exercise that resembled the beginning of encounter groups. This is a variation that should be offered before students in a class have time to read about the exercise.

It deals with expectations, structure, and control in a classroom situation. At some point early in the term, the professor announces an exam and passes out paper. Students have half an hour to write their own question and answer it, and the score counts toward their final grade. The professor lets students

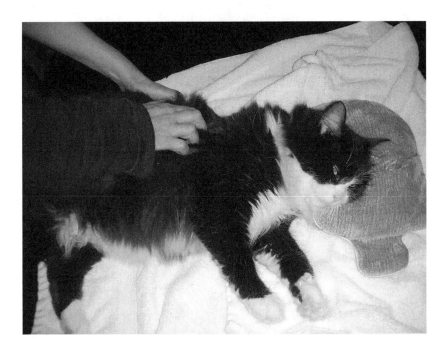

Bruzzer and his human connect at a deep level during pet massage. © Henry Goldman

know what general subject they must address by writing a word or phrase like "synchronicity," and then students structure the task for themselves.

This surprise and lack of direction can sometimes confuse and upset people. Afterwards, discuss the group's reactions to the unstructured exam. What did they learn about themselves and groups from this ambiguous experience?

None of these exercises can completely duplicate what happens at Esalen, but they offer some opportunities to explore some of the experiences that are part of spiritual privilege.

Appendix 2

The Walter Truett Anderson Collection

From 1979 until early 1982, Walter Truett Anderson conducted interviews for his book about Esalen, *The Upstart Spring* (1983). His conversations with key figures from the Institute's first two decades are crucial to scholarship on the Institute and its relationship to the larger human potential movement. The list of interviews below is from the Humanistic Psychology Archives of Special Collections at the Donald C. Davidson Library at the University of California at Santa Barbara. It is included as an appendix to amplify citations throughout this book and encourage further research.

The Anderson Collection contains a number of other resources, but the interviews represent a unique contribution to historical scholarship about Esalen and its relationship to the larger human potential movement. The original cassette tapes were reformatted as CD listening copies.

Anderson is a critical but very sympathetic observer whose initial attraction to Esalen soon diminished because of the excesses in the 60s and early 70s and its slow disintegration in the 80s. He is a journalist, political scientist, and futurist. Anderson has a lifelong commitment to humanistic and transpersonal psychology, and he currently serves on the editorial board of the *Journal of Humanistic Psychology*. His sources reflect his own relationship with Esalen and the social networks that were part of his personal spiritual privilege.

Interviews in the Walter Truett Anderson Collection

A1795/CS Bateson, Gregory, and Paul Herbert, April 3, 1979.
A1796/CS Bugental, James, and Don Michael. No date.
A1797/CS Carter, Seymour. No date.
A1798/CS Cobbs, Price, and Ron Brown, 1981.
A1799/CS Doyle, Jackie, March 19, 1981.

A1800/CS Farson, Richard. No date.

A1801/CS Fosters, The. No date.

A1802/CS Greening, Tom. No date.

A1803/CS Haigh, Gerard. No date.

A1804/CS Heider, John, and Ed Maupin [currently unlistenable].

A1805/CS Herbert, Paul [side 2 is Anderson's "random thoughts"], September 6, 1979.

A1806/CS Huxley, Aldous [interview and lecture; no Bateson as originally labeled— side 2 is telephone interviews re: California water], June 2, 1979.

A1807/CS Keen, Sam .No date.

A1808/CS Lederman, Janet [currently unlistenable].

A1809/CS Leonard, George, November 14, 1980.

A1810/CS Leonard, George, December 9, 1980.

A1811/CS Leonard, Needleman, Krassner, and Marin. No date.

A1812/CS Levy, John, February (December?) 19, 1980.

A1813/CS May, Rollo, November 18, 1980.

A1814/CS Moore, Fred. No date.

A1815/CS Murphy, Michael and George Leonard [Leonard (side 2) identity questionable], December 5 and 9, 1980.

A1816/CS Murphy, Michael, March 26, 1981.

A1817/CS Murphy, Michael, October 12, 1982.

A1818/CS Murphy, Michael, December 8, 1982.

A1819/CS Murphy, Michael, September 24, 1981.

A1820/CS Murphy, Michael ,May 21, 1981.

A1821/CS Murphy, Michael, May 21, 1981.

A1822/CS Murphy, Michael, October 4, 1977.

A1823/CS Murphy, Michael, March 9, 1979.

A1824/CS Murphy, Michael, September 12, 1977.

A1825/CS Murphy, Michael, September 20, 1979.

A1826/CS Murphy, Michael, April 5, 1977.

A1827/CS Murphy, Michael, March 9, 1979.

A1828/CS Narejano, Claudio, March 20, 1981.

A1829/CS Narejano, Claudio, March 20, 1981.

A1830/CS Price, Dick, Belvedere [1982?].

A1831/CS Price, Dick, and Emil White, December 19, 1976.

A1832/CS Price, Dick [currently unlistenable], April 20, 1981.

A1833/CS Price, Dick, June 14, 1981.

A1834/CS Dick Price, and Al Druckner [currently unlistenable], April 20, 1981.

A1835/CS Price, Dick, December 21, 1982.

A1836/CS Schultz, Will, August 24, 1981.

A1837/CS Schultz, Will, August 24, 1981.

A1838/CS Schultz, Will, December 4, 1980.

A1839/CS Schultz, Will, December 4, 1980.

A1840/CS Schultz, Will [currently unlistenable], April 20–21, 1981.

A1841/CS Silverman, Julian, and Dick Price [currently unlistenable], April 21, 1981.

A1842/CS Silverman, Julian. No date.

References

Abell, Richard G. *Own Your Own Life*. New York: Bantam Books, 1976.

Alan. "God Is Waking Up in Us: Encountering Michael Murphy." *Auroville Today* (April 2007):1–8.

Albanese, Catherine L. *Corresponding Motion: Transcendental Religion and the New America*. Philadelphia: Temple University Press, 1977.

Albanese, Catherine. *Nature Religion in America: From the Algonkian Indians to the New Age*. Chicago: University of Chicago Press, 1990.

Albom, Mitch. *Tuesdays with Morrie: An Old Man, a Young Man, and Life's Greatest Lesson*. New York: Doubleday, 1997.

Allyn, David. *Make Love, Not War: The Sexual Revolution: An Unfettered History*. Boston: Little, Brown, 2000.

Anderson, [Walter Truett] Collection. Audio Interviews. Humanistic Psychology Archive, Department of Special Collections, Donald C. Davidson Library, University of California at Santa Barbara, 1976–86.

Anderson, Walter Truett. *The Upstart Spring: Esalen and the American Awakening*. Reading, MA: Addison-Wesley, 1983.

Armstrong, Lois. "Master Puppeteer Shari Lewis and Publisher Jeremy Tarcher: It's Not a Match for Dummies." *People* 5(4/1976):58–59.

Assigioli, Roberto. *The Act of Will*. New York: Esalen/Viking Press, 1973.

Back, Kurt W. *Beyond Words: The Story of Sensitivity Training and the Encounter Movement*. New York: Russell Sage Foundation, 1972.

Bader, Christopher, and the BISR Study Group. *Selected Findings from the Baylor Religion Survey*. Waco, TX: Baylor Institute for Studies of Religion, 2006.

Badiner, Allan Hunt, and Alex Gray, eds. *Zig Zag Zen: Buddhism and Psychedelics*. San Francisco: Chronicle Books, 2002.

Baltzell, E. Digby. *The Protestant Establishment: Aristocracy and Caste in America*. New York: Vintage Books, 1964.

Barker, Eileen V. "Plus Ca Change. . . ." *Social Compass* 42(2/1995):165–80.

Bart, Pauline. "Myth of the Value-Free Psychotherapy." Pp. 356–61 in *Toward Social Change: For Those Who Will*, edited by Robert Buckhout and 81 concerned Berkeley students. New York: Harper and Row, 1971.

Becker, Howard. *Tricks of the Trade: How to Think About Your Research While You're Doing It*. Chicago: University of Chicago Press, 1998.

Bellah, Robert N, Richard Masden, William M. Sullivan, Ann Swidler, and Steven Tipton. *Habits of the Heart: Individualism and Commitment in American Life*. Berkeley: University of California Press, 1985.

Bird, Sharon. 1996. "Welcome to the Men's Club: Homosociality and the Maintenance of Hegemonic Masculinity." *Gender and Society* 10(2):120–32.

Bloch, Marc. *The Historian's Craft*. New York: Vintage Books, 1953.

Bourdieu, Pierre. *The Social Structures of the Economy*. New York: Polity Press, 2005.

Brooks, David. *Bobos in Paradise: The New Upper Class and How They Got There*. New York: Simon and Schuster, 2001.

Brooks, Douglas, Renfrew, Swami Durgananda, Paul E. Muller-Ortega, William Mahoney, Constantina Rhodes-Bailly, and S. P. Sabharathnam. *Meditation Revolution: A History and Theology of the Siddha Yoga Lineage*. South Fallsburg, NY: Agama Press, 1997.

Brown, Michael F. *The Channeling Zone: American Spirituality in an Anxious Age*. Cambridge: Harvard University Press, 1997.

Brown, Nick. *The Spiritual Tourist: A Personal Odyssey Through the Outer Reaches of Belief*. New York: Bloomsbury, 1998.

Bruggemann, Walter. *The Theology of the Book of Jeremiah*. New York: Cambridge University Press, 2007.

Buehler, Georg. "Finding a Livelihood for the Modern Spiritual Life." Pp. 119–30 in *Radical Spirit: Spiritual Writings from the Voices of Tomorrow*, edited by Steven Dinan. Novato, CA: New World Library, 2002.

Bugenthal, James, and Don Michael. Audio Tape A 1796/CS. Walter Truett Anderson, HPA Mss 2, Department of Special Collections, Donald C. Davidson Library, University of California at Santa Barbara, 1980.

Burt, Ronald S. *Brokerage and Closure: An Introduction to Social Capital*. New York: Oxford University Press, 2005.

Byrne, Rhonda. *The Secret*. New York: Atria Books, 2006.

Caldwell, Sarah. "The Heart of the Secret: A Personal and Spiritual Encounter with Shakti Tantrism in Siddah" Yoga. *Nova Religio* 5(1/2001):9–51.

California Institute of Integral Studies (CIIS). "Educational Effectiveness Report of the California College of Integral Studies Submitted to the Western Association of Schools and Colleges." November. Unpublished Report. San Francisco, CA: California Institute of Integral Studies, 2007.

Campbell, Joseph. *The Hero with a Thousand Faces*. New York: Bollingen Series/Pantheon Books, 1949.

Carter, Richard John. "Re-Invention and Paradox: The Esalen Institute in the 1990s." Master's thesis, Department of Organization Behavior, School of Management, Swinburne University of Technology, Victoria, Australia, 1997.

Cascio, Charlie. *The Esalen Cookbook*. Layton, UT: Gibbs Smith, 2006.

Chambliss, Daniel F., and Richard K. Schutt. *Making Sense of the Social World: Methods of Investigation*. Los Angeles: Pine Forge Press, 2010.

Chaudhuri, Haridas, and Frederic Spiegelberg, eds. *The Integral Philosophy of Sri Aurobindo: A Comparative Symposium*. London: Allen and Unwin, 1960.

Childs, Peter. *Modernism*. New York: Routledge, 2007.

Chopra, Deepak. *The Seven Spiritual Laws of Success*. New York: New World Publishing/ Amber Allen, 1994.

Cobbs, Price, and Ron Brown. 1981. Audiotapes A and B 1798/CS. Walter Truett Anderson collection, HPA Mss 2, Department of Special Collections, Donald C. Davidson Library, University of California at Santa Barbara, 1981.

Coles, Robert. *Privileged Ones: The Well-Off and the Rich in America*. Boston: Little, Brown, 1977.

Collins, Randall. *A Sociology of Philosophies: A Global Theory of Intellectual Change*. Cambridge: Harvard University Press, 1998.

Connell, Raewyn. *Masculinities*. 2d ed. Berkeley: University of California Press, 1995.

Connell, Raewyn, and James W. Messerschmidt. "Hegemonic Masculinity: Rethinking the Concept." *Gender and Society* 19(2005):829–59.

Considine, Bob. *Toots*. New York: Meredith Publishers, 1969.

Cornwall, Marie. "Reifying Sex Differences Isn't the Answer: Gendering Processes, Risk, and Religiosity." *Journal for the Scientific Study of Religion* 48(2/2009):252–55.

Cox, Harvey Gallagher. *The Secular City: Secularization and Urbanization in Theological Perspective*. New York: Collier Books, 1965.

Cox, Harvey Gallagher. *The Way East: The Promise and Peril of the New Orientalism*. New York: Simon and Schuster, 1977.

Coyote, Peter. *Sleeping Where I Fall: A Chronicle*. Washington, DC: Counterpoint Press, 1998.

Csikszentmihalyi, Mihaly. *Flow: The Psychology of Optimal Experience*. New York: Harper Perennial, 1991.

Dalai Lama. *Worlds in Harmony: Dialogues on Compassionate Action*. New York: Parallax Press, 1992.

Davidson, Sara. *Leap! What Will We Do with the Rest of Our Lives? Reflections from the Boom Generation*. New York: Random House, 2007.

Davis, Mike. *City of Quartz: Excavating the Future in Los Angeles*. New York: Vintage, 1992.

Dawson, Lorne, and Douglas Cowan, eds. *Religion Online: Finding Faith on the Internet*. New York: Routledge, 2004.

Dhingra, Pawan. *Managing Multicultural Lives: Asian American Professionals and the Challenge of Multiple Identities*. Stanford: Stanford University Press, 2007.

Didion, Joan. *Slouching Toward Bethlehem*. New York: Farrar, Straus and Giroux, [1968] 1990.

Dinan, Steven. *Radical Spirit: Spiritual Writings from the Voices of Tomorrow*. Novato, CA: New World Library, 2002.

Domhoff, G. William. 1974. *The Bohemian Grove and Other Retreats: A Study in Ruling Class Cohesiveness*. New York: Harper and Row.

Downing, Michael. *Shoes Outside the Door: Desire, Devotion, and Excess at the San Francisco Zen Center*. Washington, DC: Counterpoint Press, 2001.

Doyle, Jackie. Audio Tape A 1799/CS. Walter Truett Anderson, HPA Mss 2, Department of Special Collections, Donald C. Davidson Library, University of California at Santa Barbara, 1981.

Doyle, Jacqueline, ed. *Interaction: Readings in Human Potential*. Lexington, MA: D.C. Heath, 1973.

Durkheim, Emile. *The Elementary Forms of Religious Life*. London: Allen and Unwin, 1915.

Economist. "Where California Bubbled Up." *Economist*, December 19, 2007, pp. 74–76.

Edwards, Betty. *Drawing on the Right Side of the Brain*. Los Angeles: Jeremy P. Tarcher, 1979.

Ehrenreich, Barbara. *Bright-Sided: How the Relentless Promotion of Positive Thinking Has Undermined America*. New York: Metropolitan Books, 2009.

Ehrenreich, Barbara. *The Hearts of Men. American Dreams and the Flight from Commitment*. New York: Doubleday Books, 1983.

Ellison, Christopher G., and Linda K. George. "Religious Involvement, Social Ties, and Support in a Southeastern Community." *Journal for the Scientific Study of Religion* 33(1994):46–61.

Ellsberg, Daniel. *Secrets: A Memoir of Vietnam and the Pentagon Papers*. New York: Penguin Books, 2003.

Esalen Institute. "Articles of Incorporation." Monterey County, State of California, 1963.

Esalen Institute. *Esalen Catalogue*. Big Sur, CA: Esalen Institute, May-October 1988.

Esalen Institute. *Esalen Catalogue*. Big Sur, CA: Esalen Institute, May-October 1991.

Esalen Institute. "George Leonard In Memorium," 2010. www.esalen.org/tributes/george-leonard.html (retrieved February 1, 2010).

Esalen Institute Collection. Papers. HPA Mss 8. Humanistic Psychology Archives. Humanistic Psychology Archive, Department of Special Collections, Donald C. Davidson Library, University of California at Santa Barbara, 1970.

Faludi, Susan. *Stiffed: The Betrayal of the American Man*. New York: William Morrow, 1999.

Finke, Roger, and Laurence Iannaccone. "Supply-Side Explanations for Religious Change." *Annals of the American Academy of Political and Social Science* 527(1993):27–39.

Finke, Roger, and Rodney Stark. *The Churching of America, 1776–1990: Winners and Losers in Our Religious Economy*. New Brunswick: Rutgers University Press, 1992.

FitzGerald, Frances. *Cities on a Hill: A Journey Through Contemporary American Cultures*. New York: Simon and Schuster, 1986.

Fromm, Erich. *The Art of Loving*. New York: Harper and Row, 1956.

Gagarin, Nicholas. "Big Sur, California: Tripping Out at Esalen." *Harvard Crimson*, February 10, 1969, pp.4–8.

Gates, Rolf, and Katrina Kenison. *Meditations from the Mat: Daily Reflections on the Path of Yoga*. New York: Anchor Books, 2002.

Gay, Peter. *Freud: A Life for Our Time*. New York: Norton, 2006.

Ghose, Aurobindo. *The Future Evolution of Men: The Divine Life Upon Earth*. London: Allen and Unwin, 1963.

Gilbert, Elizabeth. *Eat, Pray, Love: One Woman's Search for Everything Across Italy, India, and Indonesia*. New York: Viking, 2006.

Gill, Brendan. "The Faces of Joseph Campbell." *New York Review of Books* 17(1989):16–19.

Glock, Charles Y., and Robert Bellah, eds. *The New Religious Consciousness*. Berkeley: University of California Press, 1976.

Goffman, Erving. *Stigma: Notes on the Management of Spoiled Identity*. Englewood Cliffs, NJ: Prentice-Hall, 1963.

Goldman, Marion S. *Passionate Journeys: Why Successful Women Joined a Cult*. Ann Arbor: University of Michigan Press, 1999.

Goodman, Paul. *Growing Up Absurd*. New York: Random House, 1960.

Goodman, Paul. "From New Reformation." Pp.211–16 in *Toward Social Change: For Those Who Will*, edited by Robert Buckhout and 81 concerned Berkeley students. New York: Harper and Row, 1971.

Granovetter, Mark. "The Strength of Weak Ties." *American Journal of Sociology* 78(6/1973):1360–80.

Griswold, Wendy. *Cultures and Societies in a Changing World.* Thousand Oaks, CA: Pine Forge Press, 1994.

Grof, Stanislav. "Reflections on Breathwork and Alien Encounter Experiences: Stan Grof's Recollections," 2003. www.johnmackinstitute.org/ejournal/article.asp?id=293 (retrieved September 1, 2010).

Grof, Stanislav, and Christina Grof, eds. *Spiritual Emergency: When Personal Transformation Becomes a Crisis.* New York: Jeremy P. Tarcher/Putnam, 1989.

Gunther, Bernard. *What to Do Till the Messiah Comes.* New York: Macmillan, 1971.

Halbwachs, Maurice. *On Collective Memory.* Translated by Lewis A. Coser. Chicago: University of Chicago Press, 1992.

Hannegraff, Wouter. *New Age Religion and Western Culture: Esotericism in the Mirror of Secular Thought.* Albany: State University of New York Press, 1998.

Harris, Lis. "Annals of Religion: O GURU, GURU, GURU." *The New Yorker,* November 14, 1994, pp. 92–122.

Heider, John. "The Human Potential Papers 1966–1996." Lawrence, KS. Unpublished manuscript, 1996.

Houston, Jean. *Mystical Dogs: Animals as Guides to Our Inner Life.* New York: New World Library, 2004.

Howard, Jane. *Please Touch: A Guided Tour of the Human Potential Movement.* New York: Dell, 1970.

Howard, Robert Glenn. *Digital Jesus: The Making of a New Christian Fundamentalist Community on the Internet.* New York: New York University Press, 2011.

Huxley, Aldous. *Brave New World.* London: Chatto and Windus, 1932.

Iannaccone, Laurence. "Risk, Rationality, and Religious Portfolios." *Economic Inquiry* 33(1995):285–95.

Isherwood, Christopher. *My Guru and His Disciple.* New York: Farrar, Strauss and Giroux, 1980.

Jacobs, Janet Liebman. *Divine Disenchantment: Deconversion from New Religions.* Bloomington: Indiana University Press,1989.

James, William. *The Varieties of Religious Experience.* New York: Modern Library, [1903] 1961.

Johnson, Benton. "On Founders and Followers: Some Factors in the Development of New Religious Movements." *Sociological Analysis* (Supplement/1992):S1–S13.

Johnson, Diane. "Sex, Drugs, and Hot Tubs." *New York Times Book Review,* May 6, 2007, pp. 6–9.

Johnson, Don Hanlon. *Body Spirit and Democracy.* Berkeley, CA: North Atlantic Books Somatic Resources, 1994.

Jung, Carl G. *Synchronicity: an Acausal Connecting Principal.* London: Routledge and Kegan Paul, 1972.

Kaufman, Michael T. "Laurance Rockefeller, Passionate Conservationist and Investor, Is Dead at 94." *New York Times,* July 12, 2004, p. A18.

Keen, Sam. *Fire in the Belly: On Being a Man.* New York: Bantam, 1991.

Keniston, Kenneth. *The Young Radicals: Notes on Committed Youth.* New York: Harcourt, Brace, and World, 1968.

Kerouac, Jack. *Big Sur.* New York: Farrar, Strauss and Giroux, 1962.

Kimmel, Michael S. "Masculinity as Homophobia: Fear, Shame, and Silence in the Construction of Gender Identity." Pp. 119–41 in *Theorizing Masculinities,* edited by Harry Brod and Michael Kaufman. Thousand Oaks, CA: Sage, 1994.

Kimmel, Michael S. *The Gendered Society*. 2d ed. New York: Oxford University Press, 2004.

Knight, J. Z. *A State of Mind: My Story/Ramtha: The Adventure Begins*. Yelm, WA: JZK Publishing, 2004.

Kopkind, Andrew. "Mystic Politics: Refugees from the New Left." *Ramparts* 12(1973), pp. 26–38.

Kramer, Jane. *Allen Ginsberg in America*. New York: Fromm International Publishing, [1969] 1997.

Krantz, Judith. *Sex and Shopping: The Confessions of a Nice Jewish Girl*. New York: St. Martin's Press, 2000.

Kripal, Jeffery J. *Esalen: America and the Religion of No Religion*. Chicago: University of Chicago Press, 2007a.

Kripal, Jeffrey J. "Esalen and the Religion of No Religion." *Chronicle Review: The Chronicle of Higher Education*, April 13, 2007b, pp. B6–8.

Kripal, Jeffery J., and Glenn W. Shuck, eds. *On the Edge of the Future: Esalen and the Evolution of American Culture*. Bloomington: Indiana University Press, 2005.

Kroeber, Alfred Louis. *Handbook of the Indians of California*. Seattle, WA: Kessinger Publishing, [1925] 2007.

Lajoie, Denise, and Sam Shapiro. "Definitions of Transpersonal Psychology: The First Twenty-Five Years." *Journal of Transpersonal Psychology* 24(1/1992):79–98.

Lambert, Gavin. *Natalie Wood: A Life*. New York: Alfred A. Knopf, 2004.

Larsen, Elena. "Cyberfaith: How Americans Pursue Religion Online." Pp. 17–20 in *Religion Online: Finding Faith on the Internet*, edited by Lorne L. Dawson and Douglas E. Cowan. New York: Routledge, 2004.

Lasch, Christopher. *The Culture of Narcissism: American Life in an Age of Diminishing Expectations*. New York: W.W. Norton, 1978.

Lattin, Don. *Following Our Bliss: How the Spiritual Ideals of the Sixties Shape Our Lives Today*. San Francisco: Harper San Francisco, 2003.

Laxner, Mark E. *Take Me for a Ride: Coming of Age in a Destructive Cult*. College Park, MD: Outer Rim Press, 1993.

Leary, Timothy. *Flashbacks*. Los Angeles: Jeremy P. Tarcher, 1983.

Lederman, Janet. *Anger and the Rocking Chair*. New York: McGraw-Hill, 1969.

Leonard, George. "Where the California Game Is Taking Us." *Look*, June 28, 1966, pp. 108–16.

Leonard, George. *Education and Ecstasy*. New York: Delacorte Press, 1968.

Leonard, George. *The Transformation: A Guide to the Inevitable Changes in Humankind*. Los Angeles: Jeremy P. Tarcher, 1978.

Leonard, George. *The End of Sex: Erotic Love After the Sexual Revolution*. Boston: Houghton Mifflin, 1983.

Leonard, George. *Walking on the Edge of the World: A Memoir of the Sixties and Beyond*. Boston: Houghton Mifflin, 1988.

Leonard, George. *Mastery: The Keys to Success and Long-Term Fulfillment*. New York: Dutton Books, 1991.

Leonard, George, and Michael Murphy. *The Life We Are Given: A Long-Term Program for Realizing the Potential of Body, Mind, Heart, and Soul*. New York: G. P. Putnam's Sons, 1995.

Lester, Robert C. "Buddhism: The Path to Nirvana." Pp. 847–971 in *Religious Traditions of the World*, edited by H. Byron Earhart. San Francisco: Harper San Francisco, 1993.

Levi-Strauss, Claude. *The Savage Mind*. Chicago: University of Chicago Press, 1962.

Lewontin, Richard. *The Triple Helix: Gene, Organism, and Environment*. Cambridge: Harvard University Press, 2001.

Litwak, Leo. "The Esalen Foundation: Joy is the Prize." *New York Times Magazine*, December 31, 1967, pp. 119–24.

Lofland, John. *Doomsday Cult: A Study of Conversion, Proselytization, and Maintenance of Faith*. Enlarged Edition. New York: Irvington, 1977.

Madison, Deborah, with Edward Espe Brown. *The Greens Cookbook: Extraordinary Cuisine from the Celebrated Restaurant*. New York: Bantam, 1987.

Mander, Anica Vesel, and Anne Kent Rush. *Feminism as Psychotherapy*. New York: Random House/Bookworks, 1974.

Markoff, John. *What the Dormouse Said: How the '60s Counterculture Shaped the Personal Computer Industry*. New York: Viking, 2005.

Marsh, Stefanie. "At Esalen Hugging Is Where the Esoteric Journey Begins." *The Week: The Best of the British and Foreign Media*, April 12, 2008, pp. 44–45.

Martin, Patricia Yancey. "Mobilizing Masculinities: Women's Experiences." *Organization* 8(4/2001):587–618.

Martin, Robert F. *Hero of the Heartland: Billy Sunday and the Transformation of American Society*. Bloomington: Indiana University Press, 2002.

Maslow, Abraham. *Toward a Psychology of Being*. New York: Van Nostrand, 1961.

Maslow, Abraham. *The Farther Reaches of Human Nature*. New York: Viking/Esalen, 1971.

Masson, Jeffrey Moussaieff. *My Father's Guru: A Journey Through Spirituality and Dissillusion*. New York: Addison-Wesley, 1993.

Matlack, Tom, James Houten, and Larry Bean, eds. *The Good Men Project: Real Stories from the Front Lines of Modern Manhood*. Boston: The Good Man Foundation, 2010.

May, Rollo, Stanley Krippner, and Jacqueline Larcombe Doyle. "The Role of Transpersonal Psychology in Psychology as a Whole: A Discussion." Pp. 192–201 in *The Humanistic Movement: Recovering the Person in Psychology*, edited by Frederick J. Wertz. Lake Worth, FL: Gardner Press, 1994.

McAdam, Doug, John McCarthy, and Mayer Zald, eds. *Comparative Perspectives on Social Movements: Political Opportunities, Mobilizing Structures, and Cultural Framings*. New York: Cambridge University Press, 1996.

McAdam, Doug, and Ronelle Paulsen. "Specifying the Relationship Between Social Ties and Activism." *American Journal of Sociology* 99(3/1993):640–57.

McGee, Micki. *Self-Help, Inc.: Makeover Culture in American Life*. New York: Oxford University Press, 2005.

McGuire, Meredith. *Lived Religion: Faith and Practice in Everyday Life*. New York: Oxford University Press, 2008.

Mead, Sidney Earl. *The Lively Experiment: The Shaping of Christianity in America*. New York: Harper and Row, 1963.

Melton, J. Gordon. "Another Look at New Religions." *Annals of the American Academy of Political and Social Science* 527(1/1993):97–112.

Menand, Louis. *The Metaphysical Club: A Story of Ideas in America*. New York: Farrar, Straus and Giroux, 2001.

Miller, Alan S., and Rodney Stark. "Gender and Religiousness: Can Socialization Explanations Be Saved?" *American Journal of Sociology* 107(2002):1399–1423.

Miller, Alice. *The Drama of the Gifted Child: The Search for the True Self.* New York: Basic Books, 1981.

Miller, Donald E. *City of the Century: The Epic of Chicago and the Making of America.* New York: Simon and Schuster, 2003.

Miller, Henry. *Big Sur and the Oranges of Hieronymus Bosch.* New York: New Directions, 1957.

Miller, Stuart. *Hot Springs: The True Adventures of the First New York Jewish Literary Intellectual in the Human Potential Movement.* New York: Viking/Esalen, 1971.

Miller, Sukie, with Suzanne Lipsett. *After Death: Mapping the Journey.* New York: Simon and Schuster, 1997.

Miller, Timothy. "Notes on the Prehistory of the Human Potential Movement: The Vedanta Society and Gerald Heard's Trabuco College." Pp. 80–89 in *On the Edge of the Future: Esalen and the Evolution of American Culture*, edited by Jeffery J. Kripal and Glenn W. Shuck. Bloomington: Indiana University Press, 2005.

Mills, C. Wright. *The Power Elite.* New York: Oxford University Press, 1956.

Moreno, Jacob Levy. *Who Shall Survive?* Beacon, NY: Beacon House, 1953.

Murphy, Gardner. *Human Potentialities.* New York: Basic Books, 1958.

Murphy, Michael. *Golf in the Kingdom.* New York: Viking/Esalen, 1972.

Murphy, Michael. "Sport as Yoga." *Esalen Catalogue* XII(1974):7.

Murphy, Michael. *Jacob Atabet: a Speculative Fiction.* Los Angeles: Jeremy P. Tarcher, 1977.

Murphy, Michael. Audio tape A 1821/CS. . Walter Truett Anderson, HPA Mss 2, Department of Special Collections, Donald C. Davidson Library, University of California at Santa Barbara, 1977-82.

Murphy, Michael. "A Radiant Presence." *Esalen Catalogue* (May–October 1988):11.

Murphy, Michael. "Afterward." Pp. 305–12 in *On the Edge of the Future: Esalen and the Evolution of American Culture,* edited by Jeffery J. Kripal and Glenn W. Shuck. Bloomington: Indiana University Press, 2005.

Murphy, Michael. *The Future of the Body: Explorations into the Further Evolution of Human Nature.* Los Angeles: Jeremy P. Tarcher, 1992.

Murphy, Michael. *The Kingdom of Shivas Irons.* New York: Broadway Books, 1997.

Nash, Michael. R. "The Importance of Being Earnest When Crafting Definitions: Science and Scientism Are Not the Same Things." *International Journal of Clinical and Experimental Hypnosis* 53(3/2005):265–80.

Neitz, Mary Jo. "Queering the Dragonfest: Changing Sexualities in a Post Patriarchal Religion." *Sociology of Religion* 61(2002):369–91.

Neitz, Mary Jo, and James Spickard. "Steps Toward a Sociology of Religious Experience: The Theories of Mihaly Csikszentmihalyi and Alfred Schutz." *Sociological Analysis* 51(1/1990):15–33.

Newman, Andy. "It's Not Easy Picking a Path to Enlightenment." *New York Times,* July 3 2008, pp. E-2.

Ogilvy, James, ed. *Michael Murphy and the Human Potential Movement.* Berkeley, CA: Minuteman Press, 2010.

Ogilvy, James, ed. *Revisioning Philosophy.* SUNY Series in Philosophy. Albany: State University of New York Press,1991.

Olatunji, Babatunde, Robert Atkinson, and Eric Charry. 2005. *The Beat of My Drum, An Autobiography*. Philadelphia: Temple University Press.

Oliver, Pamela E., and Daniel J. Myers. "The Coevolution of Social Movements." *Mobilization* 8(2003):1–25.

Orsi, Robert. *Between Heaven and Earth: The Religious Worlds That People Make and the Scholars Who Study Them*. Princeton: Princeton University Press, 2005.

Pascoe, Peggy. *What Comes Naturally: Miscegenation Law and the Making of Race in America*. New York: Oxford University Press, 2009.

Perls, Frederick S. *In and Out of the Garbage Pail*. Lafayette, CA: Real People Press, 1969

Price, Christine. *Food for the Senses: Recipes and Artwork from the Esalen Community*. Big Sur, CA: Christine Price Publishing, 1980.

Price, Dick. Audio Tape A 11835/CS. Walter Truett AndersonHPA Mss 2, Department of Special Collections, Donald C. Davidson Library, University of California Santa Barbara, 1982.

Price, Dick. Unpublished interview with Wade Hudson, 1985.

Putney, Clifford. *Muscular Christianity: Manhood and Sports in Protestant America: 1880–1920*. Cambridge: Harvard University Press, 2001.

Radin, Dean. "What's Ahead ?" Pp. 9–21 in *Parapsychology in the Twenty-First Century*, edited by Michael A. Thalbourne and Lance Storm. Jefferson, NC: McFarland and Company, 2004.

Rainey, Lee Dian. *Confucius and Confucianism: The Essentials*. Chichester, UK: John Wiley and Sons, 2010.

Rakstis, Ted. J. "Sensitivity Training: Fad, Fraud, or New Frontier?" Pp. 309–13 in *Toward Social Change: For Those Who Will*, edited by Robert Buckhout and 81 concerned Berkeley students. New York: Harper and Row, 1971.

Remen, Rachel Naomi. *Kitchen Table Wisdom: Stories That Heal*. New York: Riverhead Publishers/Penguin Group, 1976.

Riley, Naomi Schaeffer. *God on the Quad: How Religious Colleges and the Missionary Generation Are Changing America*. New York: St. Martin's Press, 2004.

Rivers, Joan. *Having a Baby Can Be a Scream*. Los Angeles: Jeremy P. Tarcher, 1974.

Rolf, Ida. *Rolfing: The Integration of Human Structures*. New York: Harper and Row, 1978.

Roof, Wade Clark. *A Generation of Seekers: The Spiritual Journeys of the Baby Boom Generation*. San Francisco: Harper San Francisco, 1993.

Roof, Wade Clark. *Spiritual Marketplace: Babyboomers and the Remaking of American Religion*. Princeton: Princeton University Press, 1999.

Roth, Gabrielle. *Sweat Your Prayers: The Five Rhythms of the Soul*. New York: Tarcher/Putnam, 1998.

Ruse, Michael. *The Evolution/Creationism Struggle*. Cambridge: Harvard University Press, 2005.

Rush, Anne Kent. *Getting Clear: Body Work for Women*. New York: Random House, 1974.

Rush, Anne Kent. *Moon, Moon*. New York: Random House, 1976.

Sanders, Joshunda, and Diana Barnes-Browne. "Eat, Pray, Spend: Prive-Lit and the New, Enlightened American Dream." *Bitch: Feminist Response to Pop Culture* 47(2010):29–33.

Sanneh, Kelefa. "Powerlines: What's Behind Rhonda Byrne's Spiritual Empire?" *The New Yorker*, September 13, 2010, pp. 84–88.

Satir [Virginia] Collection. HPA Mss 45, Department of Special Collections, University Libraries, University of California, Santa Barbara, 1916–1993.

Satter, Beryl. *Each Mind a Kingdom: American Women, Sexual Purity, and the New Thought Movement, 1875–1920*. Berkeley: University of California Press, 2001.

Schutz, William. *Joy: Expanding Human Awareness*. New York: Grove Press, 1967.

Schutz, William. *Here Comes Everybody*. New York: Harper and Row, 1971.

Schwartz, Barry. *The Paradox of Choice: Why More Is Less*. New York: HarperCollins, 2004.

Schwartz, Tony. *What Really Matters: Searching for Wisdom in the World*. New York: Bantam, 1995.

Selver, Charlotte. *A Taste of Sensory Awareness*. Mill Valley, CA: Sensory Awareness Foundation, 1979.

Shapiro, Stewart B. *The Place of Confluent Education in the Human Potential Movement*. New York: University Press of America, 1998.

Shiao, Jiannbin Lee. *Identifying Talent, Institutionalizing Diversity: Race and Philanthropy in Post–Civil Rights America*. Durham: Duke University Press, 2005.

Slater, Philip. *The Pursuit of Loneliness: American Culture at the Breaking Point*. Boston: Beacon Press, 1970.

Spiegelberg, Frederic. *The Religion of No Religion*. Stanford, CA: James Ladd Delkin, 1948.

Stark, Rodney. *The Rise of Christianity: A Sociologist Reconsiders History*. Princeton: Princeton University Press, 1996a.

Stark, Rodney. "Why New Religious Movements Succeed or Fail: A Revised General Model." *Journal of Contemporary Religion* 11(1996b):133–46.

Stark, Rodney. *One True God: Historical Consequences of Monotheism*. Princeton: Princeton University Press, 2001.

Stark, Rodney. "Upper Class Asceticism: Social Origins of Ascetic Movements and Medieval Saints." *Review of Religious Research* 45(2003):5–19.

Stark, Rodney. *The Victory of Reason: How Christianity Led to Freedom, Capitalism, and Western Success*. New York: Random House, 2005.

Stark, Rodney, and William Sims Bainbridge. *A Theory of Religion*. New Brunswick: Rutgers University Press, 1996.

Stein, Stephen. *The Shaker Experience in America*. New Haven: Yale University Press, 1992.

Sutich, Anthony J. "The Founding of Humanistic and Transpersonal Psychology: A Personal Account." Ph.D. Dissertation, Program in Psychology, The Humanistic Psychology Institute, San Francisco, California, 1976.

Tarnas, Rick. "Esalen," [1978] 2007. www.esalen.org/air/essays/tarnas_1978.htm (retrieved March 28, 2011).

Temerlin, Maurice, and Jane W. Temerlin. "Psychotherapy Cults: An Iatrogenic Perversion." *Psychotherapy: Theory, Research, and Practice* 19(1980):131–39.

Thompson, William Irwin. *Coming into Being: Artifacts and Texts in the Evolution of Consciousness*. New York: St. Martin's Press, 1998.

Time. "'God Sir' at Esalen East." *Time*, January 16, 1978, p. 59.

Tipton, Steven M. *Getting Saved from the Sixties: The Transformation of Moral Meaning in American Culture*. Berkeley: University of California Press, 1982.

Tolle, Eckhardt. *A New Earth: Awakening Your Life's Purpose*. New York: Dutton Adult, 2005.

Tompkins, Calvin. "New Paradigms: A Profile of Michael Murphy." *The New Yorker*, January 5, 1976, pp. 30–51.

Trine, Ralph Waldo. *In Tune with the Infinite, or Fullness of Peace, Power, and Plenty*. New York: Crowell, 1897.

Tuan, Mia. *Forever Foreigners or Honorary Whites?: The Asian Ethnic Experience Today.* New Brunswick: Rutgers University Press, 1998.

Turner, Victor, and Edith Turner. *Image and Pilgrimage in Christian Culture: Anthropological Perspectives.* Oxford: Columbia University Press, 1978.

Ullman, Deborah, and Gordon Wheeler. *Co-Creating the Field: Intention and Practice in the Age of Complexity (Evolution of Gestalt).* New York: Routledge, 2009.

Verter, Bradford. "Spiritual Capital: Theorizing Religion with Bourdieu Against Bourdieu." *Sociological Theory* 21(2003):150–73.

Warner, R. Stephen. "Work in Progress: Toward a New Paradigm for the Sociological Study of Religion in the United States." *American Journal of Sociology* 98(1993):1044–93.

Watanabe, Teresa. "Esalen's Identity Crisis." *Los Angeles Times Magazine,* November 5, 2004, pp. 10–14.

Watts, Alan. *This Is IT and Other Essays in the Zen of Spiritual Experience.* New York: Vintage, 1973.

Weber, Max. *The Sociology of Religion.* Boston: Beacon, [1922] 1964.

Wellman, James. *Evangelical Versus Liberal: The Clash of Christian Cultures in the Pacific Northwest.* New York: Oxford University Press, 2008.

Whalen, Jack, and Richard Flacks. *Beyond the Barricades: The Sixties Generation Grows Up.* Philadelphia: Temple University Press, 1990.

Wheeler, Gordon. *Easy Come.* New York: Random House, 1974.

Wheeler, Gordon. "Gestalt Reconsidered: A Theoretical Critique and Revision of the Goodman/Perls Model of Contact Analysis." Ph.D. Dissertation, Department of Counseling Psychology. School of Education, Boston College, 1988.

Wheeler, Gordon. "Self and Shame: A New Paradigm for Psychotherapy." Pp. 23–58 in *The Voice of Shame: Silence and Connection in Psychotherapy,* edited by Robert G. Lee and Gordon Wheeler. San Francisco: Gestalt Institute of Cleveland Press/Jossey-Bass, 1996.

Wheeler, Gordon. *Beyond Individualism: Toward a New Understanding of Self, Relationship, and Experience.* Cambridge, MA: Gestalt Institute of Cleveland Press/ Analytic Press, Inc, 2000.

Wheeler, Gordon. "Man to Man with Esalen President and CEO Gordon Wheeler." January 6, 2010. www.goodmenproject/org/blog/tsg/gordon-wheeler/ (retrieved April 4, 2010).

Wheeler, Gordon, and Daniel E. Jones. "Finding Our Sons: A Male-Male Gestalt." Pp. 61–100 in *The Voice of Shame: Silence and Connection in Psychotherapy,* edited by Robert G. Lee and Gordon Wheeler. San Francisco: Gestalt Institute of Cleveland Press/Jossey-Bass, 1996.

Wheeler, Sue. *Habitat.* London, ON: Brick Books, 2005.

Winks, Robin W., and Bruce Babitt. *Laurance Rockefeller: Catalyst for Conservation.* Washington, DC: Island Press, 1997.

Wolfe, Tom. "The Me Decade and the Third Great Awakening." *New York* 23(August 1976):236–40.

Wong, Albert. "A Fine Young Athiest." Pp. 15–23 in *Radical Spirit: Spiritual Writings from the Voices of Tomorrow,* edited by Steven Dinan. Novato, CA: New World Library, 2002.

Wood, Linda Sargent. "Contact, Encounter, and Exchange at Esalen: A Window to Late Twentieth-Century American Spirituality." *Pacific Historical Review* 77 (2008):453–87.

Wood, Robert. *I and Thou: An Analysis of Martin Buber's Ontology*. Evanston, IL: Northwestern University Press, 1969.

Wright, Erik Olin. *Class Counts: Comparative Studies in Class Analysis*. New York: Cambridge University Press, 1997.

Wuthnow, Robert. *The Consciousness Revolution*. Berkeley: University of California Press, 1976.

Yontef, Gary. "Gestalt Reconsidered: A Review in Depth." *Gestalt Journal* 15(1/1992):95–118.

Yontef, Gary. "Response to Wheeler." *The Gestalt Journal* 15(2/1992):134-40.

Zuckerman, Phil. *Society without God: What the Least Religious Nations Can Tell Us about Contentment*. New York: New York University Press, 2008.

Index

1965 Immigration Act, 9, 56

Academy of Asian Studies, 28, 30, 149
Adams, Ansel, 54
affinities for spiritual experience. *See* religious/spiritual affinities
Alfassa, Mirra (Sweet Mother), 29–30
Allen, Woody, 143
Alpert, Richard (Ram Dass), 54
altered breathing, 173, 175–176
alternative masculinity, 136–138; and difference, 136; and equality, 138
alternative spirituality/religions, 10–11, 13, 56, 63, 79, 81, 83, 148, 159; at Esalen, 5, 6, 8, 16, 59, 162, 163; commitments to, 95; funding of, 141–147; outside the U.S., 9; and personal fulfillment, 158, 44; social networks, 18–19, 83; spread of, 1, 2, 86, 99
American Association for Humanistic Psychology, 6–7
American Psychological Association, and humanistic psychology, 153, 154–155
Anderson, Walter Truett, 19; and the Walter Truett Anderson Collection, 181–183
archetypes, 134–135
Arica, 64
Art Barn, 20
Asian religions/spiritualities, 13, 58, 118
Association for Humanistic Psychology, 6–7, 152, 157
Atman, 27
Aurobindo, Sri: and community, 28; evolutionary human potential, 29, 31–32, 98, 150; and group activities, 29; integral philosophy, 27–29, 33–34, 39, 43, 47,

147, 149, 175; and personal growth, 29, 31–32; and sparks of divinity, 103, 108; and spiritual diversity, 26; synthesis of Eastern and Western philosophy, 28
Aurobindo Ashram at Pondicherry, 22; doctrines, 29, 31–32
authenticity: emotional, 110, 112; personal, 26, 34, 35, 40, 115, 118; spiritual, 46, 112

baby boomers: and resources, 11; and spirituality, 11, 44, 52, 55, 60, 68, 89, 99
Baez, Joan, 140–142
Bagwan Shree Rajneesh, 64, 128
Baker-Roshi, Richard, 144–146, 147; and human potential, 146; and spiritual privilege, 145
Beats/Beatniks, 25, 123
behavioral psychotherapy/behaviorism, 57
Bergen, Candice, 129
Berzon, Betty, 124
Big House, 53, 61, 87; renovation, 87–88
Big Sur, 2, 48–49, 55, 71, 80, 85, 166, 174
Bob & Carol & Ted & Alice (motion picture), 129
bodywork/bodyworkers, 7, 14, 15, 49, 52, 57, 60, 61, 63, 64, 65, 66, 67, 68, 69, 71, 79, 81, 82, 86, 89, 105
bohemians, 49–51, 85, 123; and personal growth, 50; and resources, 50, 77
Bordieu, Pierre, 77
Brahmin, 27
Brandeis University, 37, 140, 156, 178
bricolage/bricoleur, 8, 10
Brown, George, 60
Brown, Jerry, 143, 146
Buddhism, 9, 35, 69, 73–74, 105, 148, 156

California Academy of Asian Studies, 149

California Institute of Integral Studies (CIIS), 143, 147–151, 154, 158, 162; and alternative spirituality, 150; and Esalen, 149–150; and evolving human potential, 150; funding, 147–150; and inclusive spirituality, 150

Campbell, Joseph, 134, 135; anti-Semitism, 134; archetypes, 134–135; gender relations, 134; spiritual privilege, 134

Cannon, Dyan, 13

Canyon Ranch Spa, 10

Center for Democratic Institutions in Santa Barbara, 140

Center for the Whole Person, 5

Center for Theory and Research at Esalen (CTR), 14, 17, 18, 20, 21, 38, 40, 42, 52, 69, 71, 81, 83, 92, 99, 105, 168; bohemian connections, 50; conferences, 33, 43, 44, 45, 86–88, 87, 106, 120, 145; contemporary changes, 43, 45, 50, 68; cultural capital, 89; emphasis on theory and research, 38, 79; and evolutionary human potential, 71, 79, 82; exclusivity, 89–90, 169; gender differentiation, 14–15, 83–84, 121, 122, 138; inner circle, 51; masculinity, 135; Psychology Council, 106; social networks, 85, 108, 167; spiritual privilege, 80–90

Chaudhuri, Harridas, 30, 149

Chinmayananda, Swami, 108

chocolate appreciation, 176

Chopra, Deepak, 46

class. *See* social class

Cleese, John, 13

Clinton, Hillary, 11–12

Columbia University, 65, 140

Confluent Education Program, the University of Santa Barbara, 6–7, 45, 60

conscious eating, 68, 176

continuing education units (CEUs), 65, 168; and social networks, 168

Cottle, Dulce Wilmott, 98

counterculture, 60, 94

Coyote, Peter, 146

creation narrative for Esalen, 51–56, 59, 121, 169–170

Crestone Mountain Zen Center, 146, 147

cultural capital/cultural resources, 23, 77, 79, 89, 90, 106, 131

Cultural Integration Fellowship, 149

Cunningham, Imogen, 54

Dalai Lama, His Holiness the, 46

dance, ecstatic, 39, 64, 116, 117, 167; and gender, 83; human potential, 84

death and the afterlife, 23, 42–44, 168

Didion, Joan, 17

diversification/religious commitment, 22

divine sparks, 3, 8, 11, 21, 23, 25, 32, 71, 93, 103, 113, 143, 148, 162, 167, 170, 175–176; accessibility, 3, 74, 79, 84, 155, 174; and the afterlife, 42, 44; in broad religious system, 31, 42; and class, 4, 81–82, differing explanations, 12; and the authentic self, 34, 47; and spiritual privilege, 8–9, 46; and Sri Aurobindo, 103, 108; and Swami Chinmayananda, 108; and Swami Muktananda, 103, 108

Dobermans, Night of the, 122–125, 130, 169

Donovan, Steven, 65–67; spiritual privilege, 66

Doyle, Jacqueline Larcombe, 156–158

Drawing on the Right Side of the Brain (Edwards), 159

driving awareness meditation, 174–175

drugs/psychedelic trips, 53, 55, 56, 70, 109, 117, 132; and Aldous Huxley, 74, 75–76; and Timothy Leary, 53–56

East West House, 52, 149

Eat, Pray, Love (Gilbert), 10

eclectic spirituality, 32, 47

economic resources, 23, 61, 79, 80–81, 83, 131, 164; and access to opportunities, 79

El Nino, 67, 86

Ellsberg, Daniel, 140–141

encounter groups, 7, 13, 34, 35, 39, 42, 45, 55, 161, 178; and Jacqueline Doyle, 157; and Carl Rogers, 128; and Will Schutz, 36–37, 90, 157

Esalen: achievements/impact, 5–8, 23, 45, 158, 161; and the afterlife, 42–44; and aging, 23, 168; boundaries, 121, 122–125; and celebrities, 13, 85, 95, 121, 125–130, 169; and CIIS, 149–150; clothing, 82; conflicts, 20, 46, 57, 107; contemporary, 23, 38, 39, 42, 43, 44, 45, 46, 66, 67, 125, 154, 165–166; contributions, 2–5, 23; counter-narratives, 169–170; cultural impact 52, 122, 126, 130, 161; and democratization of spiritual privilege, 82, 95, 118; discrimination, 122–125, 130–135; division of labor, 57, 60, 70, 83–84; doctrines, 21, 22, 23, 25–47, 59, 61, 68, 71, 72, 73, 83, 91, 92, 94, 97, 107, 113, 114, 119, 131, 133, 154, 158, 162, 167, 168, 170; eclectic spirituality, 31–32, 47; and education, 7, 8, 9, 21, 45, 140, 147–150; entitlement, 81; Esalen/Viking Book Series, 6; experiential approaches, 41–42, 54, 55, 152; and family life, 23, 84; and femininity, 121, 135; financial issues, 44, 62–63, 64, 65, 66, 85–86, 168; founding, 3–4, 12, 17, 22, 23, 49–56, 58, 59, 76, 80–81, 120, 121, 125, 130, 131, 138, 139, 161; and gender, 14, 21, 23, 46, 90, 120–138, 177–178; hierarchy, 60, 61, 70, 72, 90, 169; and humanistic psychology, 34–38, 42, 60, 154–155; inner circle, 72, 89, 90, 105, 116, 120, 122, 124, 130, 131, 134, 135, 144, 157, 159, 169, 178; innovations, 99; and the Internet, 8, 159–160, 163, 170; location, 2, 48–49, 55, 71, 80, 85, 166, 174; and mainstream faiths, 7, 8, 9, 45; marginalization, 130–138; and masculinity, 23, 101, 121, 123–124, 130–138, 169; and media, 5–6, 37, 55, 76, 134, 155; mission, 23, 55; naming, 55; and nature, 48–49, 170; organizational strategy, 64–65, 67, 85, 169; perceptions of, 2, 6; and personal heroism, 124; and politics, 156; and psycho-spirituality, 154; and race, 45–46, 63; redefining 63, 105–106, 107; and religious/spiritual diversity, 8–10, 22, 25, 26, 71, 73; resources, 19–20, 50, 51, 58, 59, 60, 72, 80–83, 86–90, 164; and rule-breaking, 121, 125–130; scholarship, 2, 21, 86–88; and sex, 55, 70, 84–85, 123–125, 131, 133; social context, 56–59; and the Soviet Union, 46; and spiritual emergencies, 154; spiritual practices, 23, 31, 57, 59, 71, 73, 92, 94, 95, 113, 119, 128, 167, 168; and spiritual privilege, 51, 56, 59, 60, 61, 70, 71, 72–91, 92–119, 122, 139, 140, 158; and sport, 29, 70, 84–85, 96, 97, 133, 138; spread of, 2, 7–8, 23, 56, 71, 74, 126, 130, 158; wildfires, 86; workshops/seminars, 2, 4, 30, 31, 33, 38–42, 44, 54, 60, 61, 65, 67, 70, 71, 76, 83, 84, 91, 98, 104, 106, 120, 125, 134, 137, 152, 154, 168, 169, 170, 173

Esalen Athletic Center, 98
Esalen Board of Trustees, 67, 68, 105, 157
Esalen Cookbook (Cascio), 68
Esalen Massage and Bodywork Association (EMBA), 15–16, 18, 20, 40, 44, 67, 69, 89, 90, 91, 92, 107, 168, 169; Esalen criticisms, 83; social networks, 167
Esalen Residential Fellows Program (psychonauts), 62–63, 131–132
Esalen San Francisco, 63, 64, 152
Esalen/Viking Book Series, 6, 84
Esselen Indians, 55
essence spirituality, 18, 32, 170
European Gymnastik Movement, 15, 16
evolutionary human potential, 32–34, 38, 71, 162
existential psychology, 34
extrasensory perception, 32, 46

Fassetts (family), 50
feminism, 46, 63, 83, 135, 136, 157
feminist spirituality: growth, 120–121; and human potential, 121; and spiritual privilege, 121
financial challenges, Esalen, 44
Fire in the Belly: On Being a Man (Keen), 136
Fonda, Jane, 13
Food for the Senses (Price), 68
Ford Foundation, 7, 60
Friends of Esalen, 86, 116
Freud, Sigmund, 57, 97

Fund for the Enhancement of Human Spirit, 143
Future Evolution of Men (Aurobindo), 27–28
Future of the Body, The (Murphy), 144

gays, lesbians, and transgenders at Esalen, 122–125
Gazebo Preschool, 64, 65, 69, 111–112, 131
gender differentiation at Esalen, 14, 21, 23, 46, 83–85, 90, 118, 120–138, 169, 177–178; and narratives, 120, 121–130, 169–170
generational gaps at Esalen, 18, 64, 68–71, 91, 125, 163;
Gestalt awareness practice, 35, 55, 63, 65, 102, 107, 108, 109–110, 112, 117, 154, 167, 168, 176–177
Gestalt Institute of Cleveland (GIC), 104, 106
Gestalt Model for Education, 112
Gestalt psychology, 7, 8, 22, 34–36, 40, 57, 67, 95, 99, 102, 103, 104, 105, 125–130, 134, 136, 140, 161; and Fritz Perls, 125–130, 131, 153, 174
Ginsberg, Allen, 25, 124; Allen Ginsberg Library, 148
Goffman, Erving, 93
Gold, David, 19
golf, 70, 84, 96, 97, 176
Golf in the Kingdom (Murphy), 30, 64, 70, 98; film, 98
Golden Door Spa, 120
Grant, Cary, 13
Grateful Dead, The, 145
Green Gulch Farm, 144–145
Greenhouse Growth Center: and progressive social change, 156; and social equality, 156
Greens Restaurant, 144–146, 147
groups, power of, 173, 174–175
Growing Up Absurd (Goodman), 104
Gunther, Bernie, 61
Gurumayi, 120
gurus, 73, 120, 125, 130

Harvard University, 37, 75, 89, 101, 104, 106, 140, 143, 144

Hayworth, Rita, 50
Heard, Gerald, 53, 54, 58
Hecksher, August, 60
Heider, John, 63
heroes, 130–135, 138, 170; and autobiographies, 133; and Joseph Campbell, 134; and personal journeys, 133; and spiritual wholeness, 133
Highway 1/Pacific Coast Highway, 48, 49, 55, 123
HIV, 46
holistic medicine, 53, 72, 148, 168, 174; and Rachel Naomi Remen, 120
Hollyhock, 5
Hopper, Dennis, 126
hot springs: as private property, 122–125, as spiritual retreat, 25, 48–49, 53, 54, 55, 61, 66, 67, 69, 76, 86, 109, 122–125, 167, 170
Houston, Jean, 11–12
Hubbard, Barbara Marx, 19
Hudson, Rock, 128
human potential, 1, 6, 8, 13, 14, 23, 43, 55–62, 74, 79, 84, 92, 95, 117, 118, 124, 139–141, 161–165; and dedication, 162; and education, 147–150; and integration of psychology and spirituality, 34; and rule-breaking, 125–130; and Morrie Schwartz, 155–156; and spiritual privilege, 125–130, 138
human potential movement, 4, 54, 152–157, 181; funding, 141–147; George Leonard, 57; and the media, 36, 158; and spirituality, 34–38; Will Schutz, 35–38
humanistic psychology, 1, 4, 6, 8, 13, 31, 44, 62, 72, 128, 142, 147, 148, 150, 157, 159, 166; demand, 162, 163; and Esalen, 34, 35, 152–155; Gestalt methods, 35–36; and Abraham Maslow, 34–38, 140; Fritz Perls, 35–38; and Carl Rogers, 128; seminars, 35; social networks, 18–19; Will Schutz, 35–38; and transpersonal psychology, 34, 151, 154–155, 157, 181
Humanistic Psychology Archives at the University of California at Santa Barbara, 18–19
Huxley, Aldous, 34, 52, 53, 54, 58, 74–76, 83, 85; and drugs, 74, 75–76; and mentoring, 74, 85

I and Thou (Wood), 115, 117
"The Impossible Dream," 90
In and Out of the Garbage Pail (Perls), 129
individualized spirituality, 1
inequality: class, 81–83, 164; sexual, 14, 23
Integral Transformative Practice (ITP),
  33–34, 39, 43, 175; temporary nature,
  33–34
Isherwood, Christopher, 58
iThou.org, 95, 159–160, 170

Jack Kerouac School of Disembodied Poet-
  ics, 148
James, William, 154
Jones, Jennifer, 126–130
Joplin, Janis, 145
Journal of Humanistic Psychology, 181
Jung, Carl, 52, 82, 154

Kairos, 5
Keen, Sam, 134–136; and diversity, 136; and
  interpersonal respect, 135; and social
  equality, 135, 136; and spiritual privilege,
  134
Kerouac, Jack, 50
Kesey, Ken, 54
Kimmel, Michael, 135
Kingdom of Shivas Irons, The (Murphy), 70
Kitchen Table Wisdom (Remen), 120
Knight, J. Z., 78
Kripal, Jeffrey, 21
Kripalu, 10

Leary, Timothy, 54; drugs and Huxley,
  75–76
Lederman, Janet, 64, 131, 164–165
Lenz, Frederick (Rama), 148
Leonard, George, 33, 34, 45, 57, 60, 61,
  63, 67, 73, 105, 126, 128, 157; cancer
  and death, 42–43, 168; and the human
  potential movement, 57; and ITP, 164,
  165; and the media, 76; and monogamy,
  124; and personal growth, 162; resources,
  61; and Saybrook University, 153; and
  social responsibility, 45; and Jeremy
  Tarcher, 159

liberal Protestant/mainline Protestant, 10,
  29, 37
Lifestyles of Health and Sustainability
  (LOHAS), 11
liminal space at Esalen, 48–49,174;
Lindisfarne Association, 143, 146–147; and
  the Fetzer Institute, 147; and the Lindis-
  farne Foundation Fellows, 147
Little House, 53, 61, 87
Litwak, Leo; 37, 39
Lucas, George, 134
Lunney-Wheeler, Nancy, 65, 67, 104–105,
  131; resources, 131; social networks, 131;
  and spiritual affinities, 131

Mack, John E., 144
magic, 31, 72–73, 169
masculine spirituality, 132–138
masculinity, 23, 101, 121, 123–124, 130–138,
  169; alternative, 136–138; masculine
  spirituality, 132–138; and the media, 132;
  and power, 136–137; revising, 135–138;
  and self-actualization, 132–138; as a set of
  relationships, 135–138; and social reform,
  137; and spiritual experience, 132–138
Maslow, Abraham, 35–36, 54, 140, 152–154;
  departure from Esalen, 37, 152–153; and
  the hierarchy of human needs, 37; and
  human potential, 34–38; privilege, 36;
  and self-actualization, 38
massage, Esalen, 2, 14–16, 38, 48, 61, 64,
  118, 140, 160, 167, 169; certification, 65,
  168; and gender, 83; and human potential, 84; and pets, 178, 179; and recognition, 131, 177; and Anne Kent Rush, 120
McGraw, Ali, 129
McLain, Shirley, 129
meditation; as Esalen practice, 31, 33, 38,
  52, 53, 56, 95, 96, 97, 102, 116, 118, 147,
  148, 158, 159, 163, 168
men's movements, 4, 5, 132–138; and emotional authenticity, 110; and the human
  potential movement, 132; and nurturing,
  110
Miller, Henry, 50
Monterey, California, 48, 70, 109

Moreno, Jacob Levy, 39
movement groups, 38
Muktananda, Swami (Baba), 99, 102–103, 106, 120; sparks of divinity, 103, 108
Murphy, Dennis, 98
Murphy, Gardner, 34
Murphy, Mac, 98
Murphy, Michael: affinity for spirituality, 94; and aging, 43, 69, 168; and the afterlife, 43–44; and Sri Aurobindo, 26–31, 47, 98; avoidance of confrontation, 96; biography, 12, 27, 95; and conscious eating, 68; and CIIS, 149; and the CTR, 68; cultural impact, 52, 143; dedication to Esalen, 93; education, 94, 97; and Esalen San Francisco, 63–64; and evolutionary human potential, 32–33, 35, 36, 85, 96, 98, 118, 165, 168; family, 92, 94, 95, 96, 98; and gender, 83–84; and golf, 70, 84, 96, 97, 176; and human potential, 14, 118, 152, 166; and ITP, 33–34, 164, 165; and George Leonard, 22, 33–34, 42, 57, 67, 97; management skills, 67, 91, 96, 105, 169; marriages, 98; and masculinity, 131, 134; and Abraham Maslow, 152–154; and media, 27, 38; and meditation, 98; and monogamy, 124; and the NCC, 7; networks, 46, 58, 95, 120, 123, 126, 144, 145, 146, 152; personality, 139; and Dick Price, 54, 55, 65, 98, 121, 122; Dick Price, road trip with, 53, 59, 121, 122, 169; resources, 19–20, 50, 56, 57, 74, 76–77, 79, 81, 85–90, 92, 94, 95, 96, 97, 98, 99, 139, 168; and Saybrook University, 153; and self-actualization, 94, 118; and sex, 97; and spiritual experience, 57, 96, 97, 162; and spiritual growth, 97, 98, 162; spiritual privilege, 61, 77, 92, 94, 96, 98, 106, 113, 139, 145, 162; and Jeremy Tarcher, 159; and writing, 97
Murphy family trusts, 66, 81, 87
muscular Christianity, 133
mysticism, 148

Naranjo, Claudio, 64
Naropa University, 148–149, 153

narratives, power of, 122–130, 169–170
National Council of Churches (NCC), 7
Nepenthe, 50, 108
New Left, 141–142
New School for Social Research, 15, 140
Nine, The, 65

Oasis, 5
Olatunji, Babatunde, 110, 11
"On the Edge of the Future" (Conference), 86–88
operations staff at Esalen, 14–16, 167, 168, 169; and Dick Price, 57, 66, 107; focus on practice, not theory, 40, 79, 89; and personal growth, 82; and spiritual privilege, 71, 79, 81; and suicides, 63; treatment of, 36, 60, 64, 68, 69
Oprah (Winfrey), 10, 158; and co-creating, 165; and spiritual privilege, 165
optimism and spirituality, 32

Pacific School of Religion, 141
paranormal research, 57, 58
past life connections, 4
peak experiences, 38
Perls, Frederic (Fritz), 35–36, 57, 63, 73, 125–130, 153; critiques of, 99, 153; and gender, 129–130, 134, 131; and human potential, 35–37, 153; and inner divinity, 130; privilege, 36, 60; and psychodrama, 39, 174; training, 36; use of physical force, 128–130
personal growth. See self-transformation
personal growth psychology: and Esalen, 2, 23, 34, 47, 51, 59, 63, 65, 98, 99, 109, 118
Pike, Bishop James, 63, 140
Price, Christine, 65, 68, 110
Price, David, 18, 67, 94, 98, 142; and acting, 112, 117; and Aleksander, 111–112 ; biography, 107–112; dedication to Esalen, 93; education, 109, 110; family, 92, 94, 95, 107–108, 111–112, 137; and Gestalt awareness practice, 107, 108, 109–110, 112; leadership, 107; and marginalization, 108–109; marriage, 107, 167; and music, 109, 110, 176; networks, 108; and Baba-

tunde Olatunji, 110, 111; and personal
growth psychology, 109; in Poland, 112;
resources, 92, 95, 108, 109, 112; and the
second generation, 94, 120; and self-actualization, 94, 107, 112, 118; and spiritual
experience, 108; and spiritual privilege,
92, 94, 107–112, 113; and yoga, 108, 109
Price, Richard (Dick): and Aurobindo,
31; childhood, 12; cultural impact, 52;
death, 19, 54, 57, 65, 105, 110; economic
privilege, 19–20, 50, 56, 74, 79; and gender, 14, 36, 83; and humanistic psychology, 35, 166; in the inner circle, 61, 61,
leadership, 64–66, 68; and masculinity,
131; and monogamy, 124; networks, 120,
123; opposition to mainstream psychiatry, 30, 47, 57; and Michael Murphy,
friendship with, 57, 98, 121, 122; Michael
Murphy, road trip with, 53, 59, 121, 122,
169; and David Price, 107, 109, 137; and
psychotherapy, 2, 30, 57; and spiritual
privilege, 31, 77, 107–112
psychodrama, 20, 39–42, 117, 148, 174; definition, 39; spiritual dimensions, 40
psychosynthesis, 157
psychotherapy, 2, 4, 5, 7, 8, 9, 155, 157, 160,
161, 166; and personal growth, 4
public service, 45–47; and spirituality, 67
Pursuit of Loneliness, The (Slater), 156

quests, ethical/mythical, 90 138, 170

race and ethnicity, 46, 114–115, 158
racial encounter initiative, 45–46, 63; and
social privilege, 46
Rajneesh, Bagwan Shree, 64, 128; and the
Shree Rajneesh Ashram, 61, 64
Rancho La Puerta, 53
re-fathering, 137–138
Reich, Robert 13
religion of no religion, 26, 40, 149, 155–156
religious pluralism, 2, 9
religious/spiritual affinities, 23, 31, 48, 61,
77–78, 108, 131, 160, 166
religious/spiritual capital, 23, 29, 77–78,
79, 103

religious/spiritual inclusivity at Esalen, 26,
47, 69, 95, 165
religious/spiritual marketplace, 21, 22,
23, 44, 58, 71, 86, 95, 120, 122, 161, 164;
throughout American history, 165–166
Remen, Rachel Naomi, 120
residential living program: financing,
62–63; and Will Schutz, 63
Revisioning Philosophy (Ogilvy), 116
Robards, Jason Jr., 126
Rockefeller, Laurance, 59, 80, 86–87,
143–147, 168; and CIIS, 147; and spiritual
privilege, 143
Rogers, Carl, 128
Rolf, Ida, 61, 131
Roth, Gabrielle, 39
Rush, Anne Kent, 120

San Francisco Bay Area/Bay Area, 49, 50,
52, 53, 56, 58, 59, 79, 110, 140, 144, 149;
Esalen San Francisco, 63–66, 152; and
the feminist movement, 120
San Francisco Zen Center, 46, 143, 144–146
Saybrook University of San Francisco, 157,
158; and The Humanistic Psychology
Institute, 153
Schutz, Will, 6, 54, 60, 63, 73, 157; and
encounter groups, 36–37, 90, 157; and
human potential, 35–37; and the media,
37; and psychodrama, 39; privilege, 36;
training, 36–37
Schwartz, Morrie, 155–158, 178
Second Great Awakening, 166
The Secret (Byrne), 164
The Self-Knowledge Symposium (SKS),
159–160
self-actualization, 2, 4, 6, 9, 13, 18, 27, 72,
92, 93, 94, 98, 99, 153, 162; and the U.S.
Constitution, 166
self-transformation/personal transforma-
tion/personal growth, 1, 4, 9, 11, 23, 27,
46, 55, 63, 86, 90, 91, 94, 98, 114, 155, 157,
158; access, 161–170; and Sri Aurobindo,
26, 29, 31–32; definition, 4; demand, 162,
163; at Esalen Institute, 48, 71, 72, 82,
106, 108, 125, 147, 154, 161, 162, 166,

self-transformation/personal transformation/
personal growth *(cont'd)*: 167, 168, 170, 178;
and health, 158; and Gerald Heard, 53; and
the hot springs, 123; and masculinity, 132–
138; and Abraham Maslow, 38; and politics,
140; present day, 44, 148; and sacrifices, 93,
129; through spirit, mind, body, psyche,
31–33, 42, 55, 111, 118, 141, 157, 158; spread of,
147–151, 157–158; and Gordon Wheeler, 99,
100, 101, 102, 106; and women, 120. *See also*
self-actualization
Selver, Charlotte, 15–16, 61, 131
Selznick, David O., 126
sensory awareness, 7, 15, 140
sensitivity training groups, 6, 156, 178
Sequoia Seminars, 58
sex and sexuality, 29, 47, 55, 70, 84–85,
124–125, 131–132, 167, 170
Shakti, 102
Shivas Irons Society, 70
Silverman, Julian, 64
Slater, Philip, 156–158; and CIIS, 157; *Pursuit
of Loneliness,* 156
snowball sampling, 17–18
social capital, 26, 58
social class/class, 4, 80–81, 96; elements of,
80; inequality, 82, 83; security, 81
social networks: at Esalen, 23, 54, 56, 58, 61,
76, 77, 78, 79, 85, 118, 126, 139–140, 144, 167,
181; and opinion leaders, 25; and Gordon
Wheeler, 101, 103, 106
social reform/social responsibility, 4–5, 6, 23,
45–47, 68, 91, 100, 101, 104, 118, 133, 136,
141, 158, 162, 170; and environmentalism,
45, 67, 68, 91; and peace, 45, 46, 67, 88,
90; and self-actualization, 5; and social
justice, 45, 67
socioeconomic resources, 23, 32, 40, 56
soul rush, 1, 10–12, 23, 34, 118, 170; and
access, 138; growth, 10–12, 147
Soviet Union, 46, 98, 114, 145
sparks of divinity. *See* divine sparks
Spiegelberg, Frederic, 27, 28, 29, 52, 149
spiritual affinities. *See* religious/spiritual
affinities
spiritual dimensions of awareness, 173, 176

spiritual experience, 22, 31, 56, 78, 162, 167;
rewards of, 173
spiritual growth, 1, 29, 31, 48. *See also*
self-transformation
spiritual inclusivity. *See* religious/spiritual
inclusivity at Esalen
spiritual marketplace. *See* religious/spiritual
marketplace
spiritual privilege, 1, 9, 21, 25, 28, 32, 47, 71,
109, 128, 143, 164, 170, 174; and affinities
for religious meaning, 48, 61, 77, 78; and
age, 14, 68; attributes, 3; critiques of, 164;
and cultural capital, 23, 61, 77, 78, 79, 109;
and divine sparks, 46; definition of, 1,
22, 77; demand for, 163; democratization
of, 73–77, 122, 162, 164; dynamics, 77–80,
92–119; and economic resources/class 9,
23, 56, 68, 73–74, 76–77, 78, 79, 80–82,
121, 166; and education, 155; enacting, 23,
179; and gender, 23, 83–85, 118, 120, 131,
138; and human potential, 79, 125–130; as
a human right, 2–3, 158, 162; and the Internet, 159–160; impact of, 23; and personal
transformation, 72–91; and psychotherapy,
155; and spiritual/religious affinities, 23,
77; and spiritual/religious capital, 23,
78, 79; and religious diversity/choice, 5,
8–10, 141; rewards of, 4, 70, 72, 79; and
rule-breaking, 135; and social networks,
23, 61, 77, 181; and social power, 74; and
socioeconomic resources, 32, 61, 77, 141;
and spiritual capital, 103; spread of, 2, 3,
21, 23, 103, 158, 161, 165; through equality,
136; through decency, 136
sport as spirituality, 29, 70, 84–85, 96, 97,
133, 138
springs, *See* hot springs
St. Martin's Press, 159
Stanford University, 27–28, 52, 56, 58, 79, 89,
96, 97, 140, 142, 144, 149
Stanford, Thomas Welton, 142, 144
Sufi mystery schools, 44
suicides at Esalen, 19, 20, 30, 43, 63
Sunday, Billy, 133
synchronicity, 52, 55, 56–59, 123, 179
Szekeley, Deborah, 120

Taoism, 35
Tarcher, Jeremy, 117, 158–159; and drugs, 117; and human potential, 117
Tarcher/Penguin, 159
Tassajara Zen Monastery and Retreat, 144–145
Templeton, John, 143
Thompson, William, 147
Tolle, Eckhart, 10
Toots Shor, 95–96
Toward a Psychology of Being (Maslow), 37
Toynbee, Arnold, 54
Trabuco College, 53
Transcendentalism, 3, 52
transpersonal psychology, 34, 151, 154–155, 157, 181
Trine, Ralph Waldo, 165
Tuesdays with Morrie (Albom), 23, 155–158; and evolutionary human potential, 156; and fulfillment, 155

University of California at Berkeley, 140
University of California at Santa Barbara, Esalen's influence, 45,
University of Pennsylvania, 143

Vedanta Society, 58–59, 158
vision quests, 4

Waters, Alice, 146
Watts, Alan, 52, 58, 83, 157
Welles, Orson, 50
Wheeler, Gordon, 18, 44, 89–90, 94; and alternative spiritualities, 99; biography, 99–107; critique of Fritz Perls, 99; and cultural capital, 106; dedication to Esalen, 93; education, 99, 101, 102; and emotional contact, 137; and encounter groups, 102; family, 92, 99, 102, 104, 106, 137; and gender, 90, 121, 135; and The Gestalt Institute of Cleveland, 104, 106; and Gestalt psychology, 99, 102, 103, 104, 105, 118, 136, 176; and inequality, 90–91; and interpersonal connection, 137; and leadership, 65–68,

105; and Nancy Kaye Lunney, 104–105; and masculinity, 101, 136–137; and meditation, 102; and Muktananda, 99, 102–103, 106; networks, 101, 103, 106; and racism, 135; redefining Esalen, 105–106, 107; and re-fathering, 137–138; resources of, 67, 92, 95, 99, 100, 101, 104, 106; revitalizing American psychology, 103; and the second generation, 120; and self-actualization, 94, 98, 99, 100, 101, 118; and social responsibility, 99, 100, 101, 104; and spiritual capital, 103; and spiritual privilege, 92, 94, 99–107, 113; and social reform, 136; and Vietnam War, 89–90, 102; work, 101, 102, 104, 105, 106; and workshops, 104, 106; and work study, 106; and yoga, 99, 102, 105, 106, 107, 118
Wong, Albert, 14, 18, 158, 159–160, 170; and acting and Gestalt, 94, 117; biography, 112–118; and Confucian ethics, 114–115; and the CTR, 113; and dance, 116, 117; dedication to Esalen, 93; education, 81, 94–95, 113, 114–116, 117–118, 176; and the EMBA, 113; and ethnicity, 114–115; family, 92, 94, 95, 112, 113–115, 116; and fundraising, 116; and Gestalt awareness practice, 113, 116, 117; intelligence of, 92; and meditation, 116–118; and Michael Murphy, 113; networks, 113, 118; and psychodrama, 117; resources of, 81, 92, 95, 113; and science, 112–113, 115–116; and the second generation, 120; and self-actualization, 94–95, 113, 118; and spiritual privilege, 94, 112–118; vocation, 117, 118
Wood, Natalie, 126–130
work study at Esalen, 66, 68, 70, 83, 86, 106, 107, 113, 116, 125, 164, 166, 167

yoga, 4, 10, 14, 22, 27, 28, 30, 32, 38, 39, 47, 52, 64, 95, 108, 158, 160, 161, 167; integral yoga, 175; and Gordon Wheeler, 99, 102, 105, 106, 107; Siddha Yoga, 120

Zen, 13, 25, 35, 52, 58, 109, 143, 148, 168, 177; and golf, 70
Zen Hospice, 145

About the Author

MARION GOLDMAN is Professor of Sociology and Religious Studies at the University of Oregon. Her many books include *Passionate Journeys: Why Successful Women Joined a Cult* and *Gold Diggers and Silver Miners: Prostitution and Social Life on the Comstock load.*